HEALING
ACROSS
BORDERS

HEALING ACROSS BORDERS

a memoir of trauma, travel, and transformation

MARIA WASSINK

Copyright © 2024 by Maria Wassink

All rights reserved. No part of this book may be reproduced or transmitted in any form or by any means without written permission from the author.

All Scripture quotations, unless otherwise indicated, are taken from the Holy Bible, New International Version®, NIV®. Copyright ©1973, 1978, 1984, 2011 by Biblica, Inc.™ Used by permission of Zondervan. All rights reserved worldwide. www.zondervan.com The "NIV" and "New International Version" are trademarks registered in the United States Patent and Trademark Office by Biblica, Inc.™

Scripture quotations marked HCSB are taken from the Holman Christian Standard Bible®, Used by Permission HCSB ©1999,2000,2002,2003,2009 Holman Bible Publishers. Holman Christian Standard Bible®, Holman CSB®, and HCSB® are federally registered trademarks of Holman Bible Publishers.

Scripture quotations marked (NLT) are taken from the Holy Bible, New Living Translation, copyright ©1996, 2004, 2015 by Tyndale House Foundation. Used by permission of Tyndale House Publishers, Carol Stream, Illinois 60188. All rights reserved.

Scripture taken from THE MESSAGE. Copyright © 1993, 1994, 1995, 1996, 2000, 2001, 2002. Used by permission of NavPress Publishing Group.

Scriptures marked KJV are taken from the KING JAMES VERSION (KJV): KING JAMES VERSION, public domain.

ISBN 978-1-7635468-0-6

This memoir is dedicated to:

God, the author of my life, who has shown me where I come from, why I exist, how to live, and has given me eternal life through faith in Jesus Christ. Without God, I cannot live; without faith in Him, I will waver on the waves of life.

My parents, who showed me the Way, the Truth, and the Life and stood by me through all my childhood challenges. Thank you, Mum, for being the anchor and showing me how to be a wife and mother. Thank you, Dad, for instilling in me the values of perseverance, love for the Scriptures, and holding onto faith.

My siblings, who have given me a sense of belonging and support throughout my life. Thank you for being there and opening your homes whenever I visited my country. My sister, who is my friend, even from a distance. My brother, who is always ready to lend a hand and share new insights into the ever-changing world of IT.

My husband, who has given me wings to fly and kept pushing me to get this book published. Thank you for your constant encouragement, love, and belief in me. You are my best friend, companion, travel buddy, sounding board, amazing father to our kids, and Godly husband. Together, forever, we will explore this world.

And to my early script readers, thank you for your invaluable insights and feedback that helped shape this memoir into the book it is today.

This book is dedicated to all those who have supported me throughout my life's journey, and to those who may find inspiration in my story.

CONTENTS

Introduction 1

Part 1: Childhood Years 5
1966/67: Beginnings—the Netherlands 7
Doorn, a Family Home 9
Life in the Orchard 11
At Home, Preschool Memories 14
1973: The Change 17
A Long Nightmare 20
Life on the Ward 24
God's Angels and
More Treatments 28

Part 2: School Years 33
International Search for Doctors 35
1975: Moving House 40
The Operation 43
Living with Pain 47
Bullied, Alienated, and Alone 49
Missionary Parents and a Brother 52
Miracles! 57

Part 3: Teenage Years 61
High School 63
1981: Driebergen, Province of Utrecht 65
The Adullam House 69
1983: Changing the Scenery 72
Future Visions 74
Coping with Life and Falling in Love 77

Part 4: Adulthood 81
A New Start 83
The World Opens Up 87
1987: New Zealand 91
Shattered Dreams and Nature's Respite 96
A Dying Relationship 100
Fleeing a Trap 103

Part 5: Married Life 105
1991: Curaçao, the Caribbean 107
Island Life 113
More Travel 117
Suriname 121
1994: Getting Married 126
The Cold, Unwelcome 132
A New Direction for Life 137
We Are Going! 142

Part 6: International Aid Workers 145
The African Continent 147
Crossing the Border 152
Compound Living 160
The People and Culture 166
Leprosy Colony 169
Planning Programs 173
1999: The Startup of Programs 180
Compound Boys 187
Team Changes Ahead 191

Part 7: Rural Sudan 193
In Search of Bush Schools 195
Life and Death 201
Women's Literacy Course 205
Stirring Encounters 213
Team Dynamics 219
In Dire Straits 223
The Cattle Camps 230
R&R and the Wet Season in Rural Sudan 235
Seed Distributions and Leaving Sudan 240

Part 8: Back to Europe 247
The Balkans: Kosovo and Its History 249
First Crisis Responders 252
Taking Over Leadership 258
A Positive Change 262
The Programs 266
Destruction Everywhere 270
Winter, Change, and Hope 275

Coming to the End of a Millennium 280

Part 9: Becoming Parents 285
The Year 2000 287
Back in Africa: Uganda 292
Ordeal in the Forest 296
Career Change: Adjusting to Motherhood 301
Changes Within Medair 305
A Growing Family 309
Life in an International Community 312
Local Experiences 319

Part 10: Immigration 323
Leaving Uganda 325
2005: Applying for an Entry Visa 329
Still, Another Will Write on His Hand: "I Belong to the Lord" 331
2006: Western Australia 335
Entering the Second Semester of Bible School 338
Southwestern Australia 341

Part 11: Dealing with the Past 343
The Dark Night of the Soul 345
The Slippery Slope 350
Broken 356
The Story of the *Doulos* 360
Seeking Support and Building Relationships 363
Hurts by Those in Authority 366

Part 12: The Healing Journey 371
God as Father 373
At Home in the Global Village 378
Four Universal Laws 382
Living Out the Healing 386
The Tool of Prayer Ministry 389

About the Author 395

Endnotes 397

Introduction

And we know that in all things God works for the good of those who love him, who have been called according to his purpose (Romans 8:28 NIV).

Some would say I was a compliant child. However, I often felt like a raging fire because larger-than-life questions consumed me. I was unaware of this early on, but I constantly analyzed my thoughts and searched for answers. I lived through circumstances for which I could not see a purpose, but they profoundly impacted my life. Traumatic events left a defined trace and influenced my choices; I questioned the meaning of my life and searched for my destiny. My parents wanted me, and they loved me. I felt called by God, and I knew I had a purpose, but circumstances made me wrestle with the core of my being: *Why do I exist?*

Consequences of a broken world were evident all around me— the sin in the world, the evil, and injustice— but these were burdens not meant for me to bear. Nothing in life is beyond God's sovereignty. I believe that more than ever. All of me—my past, upbringing, personality, and identity—were part of the blueprint He had created before the foundation of the world.

> *Even before he made the world, God loved us and chose us in Christ to be holy and without fault in his eyes. God decided in advance to adopt us into his own family by bringing us to himself through Jesus Christ. This is what he wanted to do, and it gave him great pleasure (Ephesians 1:4-5 NLT).*

Some years would flow by as if I had finally reached the shore without too many considerable waves to tackle. Other years were so hectic that it seemed I was forever in a hurricane, drowning and merely surviving.

During my teenage years, people encouraged me to write. (I love making up stories!) Some suggested writing stories from my life as they thought those were worth listening to. For years, it would enter my mind as something I could do, and I would write in my journal. Only when I turned fifty in 2017 was it time to put it all together, creating the memoir you have in your hands.

I lived life by chapters, mostly seven in a row before something new arose. And my thoughts went to the old Jewish cycle of seven years. The year 2017 was my year of jubilee:

> *Count off seven sabbath years—seven times seven years—so that the seven sabbath years amount to a period of forty-nine years. Then have the trumpet sounded everywhere on the tenth day of the seventh month; on the Day of Atonement sound the trumpet throughout your land. Consecrate the fiftieth year and proclaim liberty throughout the land to all its inhabitants. It shall be a jubilee for you; each of you is to return to your family property and your own clan. The fiftieth year shall be a jubilee for you (Leviticus 25:8-11 NIV).*

While writing this book, I asked my parents about their family history. Then one day, I got my father's detailed answer about my heritage. He quoted these verses to me, which I want to share with you:

> *Assemble the people—men, women and children, and the foreigners residing in your towns—so they can listen and learn to fear the LORD your God and follow carefully all the words of this law. ... Remember the days of old; consider the generations long past. Ask your father and he will tell you, your elders, and they will explain to you (Deuteronomy 31:12; 32:7).*

For me, it was essential to know more about my family's background and make it available to my children, as it is important to understand where one comes from. One day, my children and grandchildren will want to know where they came from and the foundations I laid for life. Knowing your family history can assist you in

Introduction

establishing your identity. If we listen carefully to the past, we might learn how to stop making the same mistakes and see what nourishment we took from the soil of our family's heritage. We might have formed bitter roots if the ground was spoiled. Then we produce bitter fruit that the next generation will eat later in life. So often, the pain of our parents becomes the platform from which we operate. Their hurts and reactions to life's experiences were modeled on us. It structured our thinking patterns and altered our behaviors. In the process, we subconsciously continue a cycle of family traits we pass on to our kids.

Or on the other hand, when the soil of our beginnings has been cared for and nurtured, fed with the knowledge of God's existence and Jesus's life modeled to us, we reap blessings. We break through destructive cycles from that safe and healthy ground, building solid foundations for the next generation. I have only included some details of my family background and their accounts that are significant to the general reader.

I want to share my story with you and take you on a trip, place you in another world where you can laugh and cry with me. We are designed to live; death is not the end. Life is worth living and obstacles only make you climb higher.

This book has twelve parts to it. In the first three parts, you will read about my recollection of my childhood and teenage years in which I share how an illness and traumatic experiences formed me and set the pace for much of my life. In these parts, I include my mother's account and her impressions of what happened. The chapters in Part Four through Part Ten tell you about my early adulthood, marriage, our adventures as international aid workers, motherhood, and immigration into Australia.

As you read the chapters, you will come across reflections pointing to a deeper understanding of how life changed, made, and shaped me. Other chapters, like in Part Six, *International Aid Workers*, mainly recount our incredible adventures overseas.

In Part Eleven, I will explain in more detail how I found healing from deep hurt and how God restored my soul and softened my heart. As I learn to surrender my all to Him, He is faithful and continues to refine and make me in His image. I pray you find solace and truths that will help and encourage you throughout life.

Part Twelve will have more details on applying prayer ministry tools, how these influenced my life, and how I used them to minister to others.

Finally, this book is a memoir based on my recollection and interpretations of events. I have strived to research the facts, seek confirmation, and obtain permission where possible, to share details, use names, and write about circumstances and my experiences within the event.

As you start to venture into the story of my life, I leave you with a quote from Dr. Charles Stanley that describes how my life's experiences formed me:

"We sow a thought and reap an action; we sow an action, and we reap a habit; we sow a habit, and we reap a character; we sow a character, and we reap a destiny."

"Unseen thoughts...produce visible consequences."[1]

Part 1

Childhood Years

1966/67: Beginnings– the Netherlands

When my parents married, medical specialists had been clear that they should prepare for adoption if they ever wanted to have a family. The young couple started their lives on the upper level of an old manor in Soest, a town in the Province of Utrecht. Life was all right if they both worked and stayed out of the way of the moody spinster who was their landlady.

The rental clause had specified that they could not have a baby in the house, and my parents didn't think that would be a problem as my mother could not get pregnant. Life and science do not care for well-educated doctors or their predictions because, within the first few months, my mother got pregnant with my sister, which meant moving house.

My parents built a wooden house on the land my mother's parents had bought after the war. It was a written-off orchard with a variety of fruit trees (and diseased apple trees that slowly died over time). The few acres were tucked away between meadows and farms. Fresh fruit and fresh milk were in abundance for all the family members who lived on this piece of land.

Mum had specific wishes for the house. It had to have lots and lots of windows. The sun should be able to enter through all the windows and overlook the meadows of the adjoining farmers. No building plans were ever submitted to the city council, as the shed-like house was no more than an oversized garage divided into livable spaces and wide passages.

Their first baby arrived too soon. For six long weeks, my tiny sister, Hannie, survived in an incubator. Mum cycled daily to the hospital to deliver her overflowing milk which fed more than only her daughter. Not that she had any deep connections to her own baby as she had not been allowed to cuddle or hold her, other than a slight touch through two armholes that were the entrance to the little surrogate womb.

Finally, after these long weeks, she could hold her daughter and bring her home. The first thing she did was to undress Hannie and lay her in the sunlit room. She looked closely at the little body for the first time: tiny ears, five perfect fingers, little purple nails, sprawling legs, and little feet. According to the doctors, this was her daughter that should not have been, and Mum felt unprepared for motherhood.

After having my sister home for a month, she became pregnant with me. Panic rose as she counted the children of her grandmother. Her mum (my grandmother) came from a family with twelve children: one child each year. What if that happened to her?

In her panic, my mother asked God what her future would look like. She and her husband desired to go on missions and serve God by helping the needy. How could she be a missionary with children? And in His wisdom, the answer was clear: "Your children are your mission field." So, Mum accepted the task of bringing us up according to God's Word, planting faith in her children as she lived her life day to day.

Doorn, a Family Home

The hospital doors were pushed open, and a man and woman stumbled across the threshold. Within seconds of passing through the corridors, the woman doubled over and moaned. The man looked around nervously and guided the woman toward the stairs. The woman leaned her weight upon the man every few steps.

On the next floor, a nurse hastened forward and asked the now sweating man if his wife would like a wheelchair. Oblivious to what was happening around her, the woman was shoved into a wheelchair while she cringed and bent over again. Then it dawned on her that the man pushing the chair had been called her husband. She started to snicker and tried to clarify and correct that this man was just her GP.

The wheelchair swirled toward the wall on her left, and she yelled to be careful. The doctor overcorrected, and the little front wheels swung to the right. The woman burst out in wild laughter, alternating with gasps of pain as the wheelchair swayed from left to right.

A new intense burning pain ended the laughter in an uncontrollable hiccup. She entered the final stage of labor. Three doors down the hall, the woman could finally be transferred to a ready-made bed in the delivery room. The birth was fast, and her husband soon appeared. She had given birth to her second daughter. Me!

My mother became my role model, and I established my worldview from her. She was the anchor in my life, explained life, guided me through dire circumstances. I observed how she programmed all kinds of activities into her day, and that shaped my day's program later in life.

When she cleaned the windows and aired curtains, she always ensured she treated herself to a nice cup of coffee. She would turn any mundane and tedious task into a challenge with an award afterward. I love the smell of freshly brewed coffee, and I still reward myself with this uplifting cup in the morning.

She brought balance into the life of a driven and purposeful husband by making it a point to sit down and read a book. She played word games and listened to classical music to broaden her mind. Secondhand clothes turned into unique creations for us to wear. Even our dolls and Barbie wore hand-sewn clothes from the scrap material of a new dress she would work on into the night.

She is a great listener, and I witnessed many telephone conversations in which distressed women shared their stories, and Mum gave her nuggets of wisdom.

Nowadays, I also find myself in a personalized place in our living room, surrounded by knitting needles and books. Instead of a large radio, I now listen to my small iPhone; although our bookcases are full, many books are now stored on a Kindle.

Still, I make sure coffee time and teatime are moments of peace and listening to each other's stories of the day. Mealtimes are for family discussions and studying the Bible together. When I have been busy and preoccupied with my chores, the children ask me to go to my corner and sit and just be.

And I see my mum being the core of the family, and like her, I am the hub from which all spokes turned and turned.

Life in the Orchard

Our wooden shed stood halfway on the main path through the orchard that my grandfather purchased just after WWII. The property was so extensive that multiple houses sat on it, and our entire extended family from my mother's side lived there.

My grandparents lived in a stone house at the entrance of the property. Close by, they built a small shack for American military couples who were stationed in this area, and two large glass greenhouses for tropical plants.

Following the main path, you would find a wooden cottage belonging to my auntie and her four children. There was also a small shack rented out to holidaymakers or single people who needed accommodation. Farther back was a small house occupied by my grandmother's single sister, and other extended family.

The single sister had a chicken business and kept noisy chickens in long barracks standing farther along the path. I remember this auntie in a canvas-type overcoat, pushing a wheelbarrow full of chicken poo which she emptied on an ever-growing pile just outside our house. She was unfriendly, often grumbling, and made me feel like I was always naughty.

My great-grandparents lived in a small, brightly painted white cottage at the very end of the path, close to the forest that bordered the orchard. Surrounding the cottage grew lots of little berry shrubs, fruit trees, a flower garden, a veggie patch. It had a neatly scrubbed porch, and a well-maintained, tiled sunspot where my great-grandmother would shell fresh peas, and my great-grandfather would suck a pipe. I will never forget that smell.

If I visited them, it would never be for leisure. I would be set to work either picking berries or beans, though there was usually a little treat. My great-grandparents were incredibly old in my eyes and extremely clean. Everything was black and white. White curtains and black clothes.

Their kitchen was the heart of the cottage. It had a gleaming, black stove in which coals were fed. On top, a kettle with boiling water stood, forever whistling. During winter, on either side of this steaming beast, a comfortable chair was placed where I would find Great-grandmother knitting black stockings and Great-grandfather still smoking his pipe. I always wondered where they came from and how they ended up in this picturesque cottage, wearing black layers of thick clothes and, of course, a starched apron for my great-grandmother.

During autumn storms, my grandmother would sit with us in our living room while the thunder rumbled through the sky. She described a world without electricity or motorized vehicles, and with harsh winters. In my imagination, my great-grandparents, her parents, were transformed from a wrinkled, bent-over couple into hard-working laborers who cared for a large family.

It looked like one happy community of family members. Underneath the surface were many unhealthy dynamics, mostly related to conservative and rigid religious mindsets.

One winter, a thick layer of snow covered the entire orchard. Shortly after, frost took hold, and each breath turned into a cloud of freezing air. Long icicles formed along the edges of the glass greenhouses. My sister and our nieces would knock them off, and the needle-sharp pinnacles would fall into the snow with a delightful tinkle. We picked up some of these and started licking them, squalling with fun as the icicles stuck to our tongues. However, these fun ice games were not without risk. The icicles contained harmful bacteria that flourished in my guts.

I got extremely sick when I was about two years of age and ended up in the hospital with paratyphoid for weeks. Out of fear of infecting other family members, I was isolated. Then my mother contracted the same infection, and for weeks, I could not see my mother at all. Only my dad and grandfather were able to visit me in the hospital. They recall

Reflection:

Much later, I understood that this was the moment where abandonment laid a foundation for developing my belief that I did not belong anywhere. Also, it started the feeling of betrayal that when you needed someone, those you wanted close would not be there for you. These two fundamental needs could not be fulfilled, leaving an inner wound that God would heal much later in my life.

me crying when visiting hours were finished, "Please do not leave me, do not leave me!"

After many weeks, Mum and I were able to go home. For months afterward, I could not let my mother out of sight; I was afraid she would abandon me again. It was tough for Mum, as I clung to her like a monkey.

The heavy course of antibiotics damaged the lining of my intestines, which later would bring more trouble than we ever anticipated.

At Home, Preschool Memories

Life felt mostly sunny as a preschooler, playing in the grassy backyard that stretched until the meadows started, which were planted with high corn in some years. In the backyard, Dad built a frame with swings and climbing bars. Our main playground was the orchard that started in the back of our garden and led us to our auntie's house. We would climb from tree to tree without touching the ground. We ate unripe apples until our bellies ached. Sometimes we would step into soggy rotten pears and get stung by wasps. We baked potatoes between hot stones and roasted chestnuts in the hot ashes of a campfire in the early dawn of an autumn afternoon.

Dad was a handyman and made our cubby houses. He organized great birthday parties at the height of the summer as my sister and I were a week apart in August. His single sister, Gieliena, would come, and we would be rolling in the grass, crawling under her legs, playing blindfolding games, and splashing around with the hose. Gieliena hated anything to do with God and religion, and the stay was often a little tense as Mum and Dad freely shared their security in God and the assuredness of eternal life. My parents faced opposition from Dad's sisters and parents, which greatly impacted our family relationships due to differences in their beliefs about Calvinistic theology.

Our garage was divided, and one half was turned into a sunny and cozy apartment with yellow tones in the interior design. Another room was added as a visitor sleep-out, which was freezing in winter but warmed up during summer to become a pleasant playground under the sun.

Dad's great-aunt from Scheveningen stayed with us for her annual holiday in that additional sleep-out. I looked forward to her visit with great anticipation, as she wore a traditional costume with many layers of clothes and glistering brooches and golden jewels on her starched white headdress. At the end of her stay she would call out: "Hannie! Marja! (my Dutch name) Look what I have here!" Then diving deep under the apron covering her attire, she dug up her purse full of shining Dutch guilders. She gave us one, which we diligently stored in our piggy banks.

Another of Dad's aunts and her husband moved into the cozy apartment, and I thought they behaved strangely. Mum and Dad had committed to caring for them in their old age as both had medical issues. Auntie "Wies," as we called her, murmured and talked under her breath to herself. She limped, and her left arm was paralyzed. She could not do her hair, and she shooed all kinds of devils away from her as she was shuffling up and down in her little apartment.

I was afraid of Uncle as he was strange and secretive. He would sneak around on soft-soled slippers. I would not hear him come as I played in the garden, and then suddenly, he was behind me, breathing in my ear. When he smiled, he would pull up his upper lip, revealing his big golden teeth, which made him look even more menacing.

Later, I discovered that my uncle accused my parents of wanting his money. In reality, he had stolen money from Mum and Dad. He would cut the roots deep in the pot of an indoor plant, and it would be many weeks before Mum figured out why her favorite tropical plant had died. This uncle was a kleptomaniac and schizophrenic.

To be out of the picture so the family could not blame my parents for being greedy by going after Uncle's money, we moved away for a while to the north of the country until the accusations were settled. We rented a caravan that was parked inside a farmer's barn. This was one of the pleasant memories as it looked like we were on an extended holiday.

Other members of the family arranged for Uncle and Aunt to go to a psychiatric hospital where we sometimes visited them. As a child, I always felt uncomfortable; most people behaved differently than I had ever seen before. The doors were locked, and a lot of screaming happened behind those doors. These childhood experiences caused me

Reflection:

I would learn much about how family traits could be passed on to next generations. I would go through personal experiences that would break open the ground to root systems in our family of origin that had the potential to bring destruction to my own thinking patterns. Rejection was one of the core traits I had to deal with in my life.

to feel unsafe and uncertain about whether the adult world was a safe place to live in.

All the underlying animosity in our family from Dad's side made me wonder what roots were hidden in their history. There was so much jealousy, backbiting, and rejection in Dad's family. Often Mum and Dad had heated discussions after we'd visited family gatherings, and I hoped they would cease to go to family gatherings, as it made me alert, expecting more trouble.

1973: The Change

Everything changed for me the year I turned six. Autumn came with flaming colors and thick carpets of leaves that you could kick and fall into. I remember the wonderful musky smell of the mushrooms we found and the hazelnuts and chestnuts which we would make into small puppets with matchsticks. Winter came with lots of storms and rain. We walked and splashed around in our new Wellington boots.

But something was different this year, and I remember it being so chilly deep inside. The rain, the mud, seeped through my clothes and settled into my bones, I had such cold feet all the time. Every day I felt sick, and soon I lost most of my energy.

I left the small preschool close to home to go to the primary school in town. Early in the mornings, when it was still dark, my sister and I would huddle in Dad's big blue Ford Transit on the way to school. Rattling over the cobblestone roads, we held on to each other until we finally hit the main road to the bigger town where the school was situated.

The unfriendly building was huge with a long wall of neatly stacked red bricks with high windows that were all the same. No trees, no green. It was next to a busy road, and a black iron fence at the front kept us in and the traffic out. Vents were built low into the walls, and I soon found out that warm air was blowing from these openings. I shivered all the time, so I would huddle in front of the metal bars of the vents during breaks. One day I burned my padded, green nylon jacket, and Mum sewed a big butterfly over the melted hole.

The teacher was old and wore her gray hair in a firmly tied-back bun. It was held in place by a hairnet and pins. In my mind, I called her "Mrs. Pin." She talked with a shrill voice and was never friendly or warm. As far as I was concerned, everything I remember was gray. Each day felt like torment. I often came home crying, "I don't want to go to school." All the experienced mothers encouraged

Mum by saying she should be tough and push through this adjustment period. "It will change, don't spoil the child, be firm and consequent." No one knew I was extremely ill and just couldn't cope with school.

I became a silent girl, and, since school had to happen, I resigned myself to the daily routine. Once at school, I crept into my shell. While at home, I played and momentarily forgot about the hours at school that would inescapably come the next day.

> **Reflection:**
> Years later, while living in Albany, Western Australia (WA), it was time to address the traumas that developed during my childhood years. On my psychiatrist's advice, my mother and I started to write out our experiences. In the following chapters, I include two perspectives: My mother's account and my story.

Maria

Every day I yearned to be at home instead of school so I could play outside in the orchard, or rest on the couch. Our house was cozy and comfortable. We had an old oil burner, and after our bath, we were toweled dry before the small grate that radiated heat. Mum bought us woolen under-singlets to keep us warm, they were itchy, and I fought the whole time as she pulled them over my head.

One afternoon I had to rush inside for the loo, and since the game was so good, I let Mum help me quickly get my pants back on to go back to play. With shock, Mum looked up at me as she saw the loo filled with blood. "How long have you been bleeding like this?"

I told her, "Mum! Just let me go. It's been like that forever; nothing new!" I hadn't taken the time to let her know. I just wanted to play.

Mother

One day she had to go quickly to the toilet. They were playing hide-and-seek. As a favor, I was allowed to quickly wipe her bottom as she was very prudish. I was shocked when I saw blood in the toilet. Without being conspicuous, I asked if this was more often like this.

"Oh, yes, Mum, already for ages!"

1973: The Change

The next day I visited the GP and took a sample of her stool. He sent me straight to the hospital in Zeist with the warning it could be that Maria would need to stay a few days for some research to get a prognosis. I was shaking and tried to bring this news as brightly as possible.

She was already such a serious child, and I was always trying to distract her and lighten her mood. Now I had to prepare her for what was going to happen.

Maria

November came, bringing rain and cold drizzle as we drove through the town. The streets shimmered like oil, and light from the lanterns reflected on the cobblestones. Mum talked continually to me, it sounded overexcited. "I need to drop you at a place where you can stay overnight. You will be cared for, and they will find out why you are bleeding." I was excited because we were going to buy a new nightdress and I got a long, soft one in a nice shade of purple. I was six years old when I entered the hospital.

Mother

"Come on, dear, we are going to buy you a pair of new slippers and a new nightie, the most beautiful one we can get." I talked with a silly grin on my face while my throat squeezed together from worry. I had seen enough during my years of nursing to know that this bleeding was not something minor.

When we arrived at the children's ward that afternoon, we were welcomed by a staff member who redirected us straight to the pediatrician. The GP had already informed her of our coming and seemed to listen to me with interest. Maria was immediately admitted, and the examinations began.

Visitors could come between the evening hours from 6 p.m. to 7 p.m. She lay fixed and glassy in her bed, timidly looking at the other children in the ward, very shy. She was not saying much. On questions, she only shook her head to say "yes" or "no." Period. We could not speak with the pediatrician, and the nurses were too busy and nowhere to be found.

A Long Nightmare

Maria

I was put into a bed with two rails on either side of me. If someone came to check on me, they had to lift it a bit and then it would slide down. When they had finished with me, they pulled it up until it snapped into place with a hard click. It had various levels—low, medium, and high. I didn't like my bed; it was hard and unyielding with only a thin cotton blanket.

I was in that bed for a long, long time. Early in the morning a nurse would come, and she had a thermometer which she pushed through a crunchy plastic cover, then a smear of Vaseline, and then in my bottom. It was incredibly painful. After she had done this to all the children on the ward, she would come back and yank it out again. For a long time afterward, my bottom hurt.

Mother

After one week, I was finally able to speak to the doctor. She said she would tentatively treat Maria and warned us that it might take a long time. They administered some medicine, but I did not get any details from her, and I did not hear what the treatment consisted of.

Maria became increasingly silent as the days went by. She asked if she was allowed to pray underneath the bed sheets because she was teased when she kneeled on her bed. We had never told her to pray on her knees, but she was always a very conscientious child.

Finally, I heard that the next day she would have a colonoscopy (a scope with an inflexible pipe), which would be done under anesthetic. I wanted to be there and hear the outcome of the examination when she woke up from the anesthetic. I was not allowed. "No, you will get a report from the doctor later," the nurses sharply point out. "At noon she will be back in the recovery room. And no, you are not allowed to be present or visit her at that time."

I shrank back at the nurse's vicious response, feeling out of control and frustrated that I could not take care of my daughter.

Maria
One day I had to undress and put on a short cotton dress with an open back. I felt a foreboding that was chilling. They pushed stuff in my bottom that made my tummy hurt, and I had to go to the loo all the time, so they sat me on a big aluminum bedpan. The rim was freezing. All the children in the ward could see me. I did not get my undies back; I felt such shame.

After a few hours, two nurses came back and, without saying a word, closed the rails up to the highest level. The bed had wheels, and they took the brakes off the wheels and carted me out of the ward and into the hallway. They had me sitting on the potty while my backside was bare. It was cold and still in the hall. They pushed me into a small side room where other silvery materials were stacked on all sides. There I was left alone for a long time.

Machinery hummed, and I could hear people walking in the hall beyond the closed doors. One nurse returned, took me off the bedpan, and told me to lie on one side. She pushed more stuff into my bottom. I could not hold what she was squirting inside, so she yelled at me. She told me to go on all fours, with my head between my hands, and raise my bottom. My head pounded as blood rushed to it, and I felt naked and ashamed with my bottom up in the air.

The nurse said, "If you can't keep the liquid inside, we will have to do it this way." Harshly she squeezed my butt cheeks together to keep the stuff inside, while I kept crying that I could not keep it in, the pain was excruciating. She kept yelling at me, I *had* to keep it in, and I was not allowed to cry. My bottom was so very sore, as if it was on fire. Finally, I was allowed to come down and sit on the bedpan again. The nurse was angry and threatened to hit me. She kept telling me to stop crying as crying wouldn't help me anyway. Nobody else, besides the nurse, was with me in that little, chilly side room.

She rolled me out of this narrow room full of equipment, into the wide hallway again. It was dark outside, and the hall had only a few frosty bulbs lighting the corridor. It seemed we went for a long time from one lane into another until we came to two wide swinging doors which the nurse pushed open with my bed. This room was something I had never seen before as all the clothes and linen were green. There were many large, wide tubes and silvery, shiny flat surfaces. To say I was scared would be an understatement; I was terrified. I was transferred to a cold table surface of a treatment trolley.

Another masked face came to me and asked, "Do you want the gas mask or the injection?" The girls from the ward had already warned me about the gas. It would make you sick and you would not be able to breathe normal air. I concluded that it was scary enough to get something over your nose, so you had to breathe the gas and then slowly fade out. I remembered that injections didn't hurt at all. So, I told them to give me an injection. Lost in a timeless world, practitioners did what they needed to do. This was the last time I was anesthetized as a child for this kind of procedure. When I woke up, I was in a lot of pain, but Mum was there.

Mother

All the nurses could not keep me away with their restrictions, and I decided that I would be there when my child woke up! At 11 a.m., I was sitting in the corner of the hallway, waiting until I saw her little bed pass by. I waited till the hallway was empty, then I slipped into the room where Maria was sleeping. I held her hand. She opened her eyes briefly and said, "Mama, ouch, everything hurts." She fell back into a deep sleep.

I wanted to ask someone what had happened and if they had found anything. I could not find a nurse, and nowhere in any office was a doctor present. The children in the ward finished their lunches and were in their rest time. At one o'clock, a passing nurse asked me what I was doing there. I ignored her angry tone and asked for the senior nurse or a doctor for their report. With an air of rigid authority, she told me, "Of course, you will get these in time, but not today. Just give the pediatrician a ring tomorrow. You will have to leave now."

The next day, I did get the doctor on the telephone. He told me, "You don't need to be worried about your daughter. Nothing is wrong, but she needs to stay in the hospital until the bleeding has ceased." After weeks, we finally got a report which only said it would take months for her to be released. I never saw another report or received an official diagnosis.

As time went by, we approached the Christmas holidays. When would she be able to come home? I kept talking to Maria to keep her spirits up, as she seemed distant and withdrawn. We started to mark each passing day with a pencil dash on the lid of a little wooden box in which she kept all her bits and pieces. Soon, we started to draw a dash per week because if we counted each day, there were an overwhelming number of dashes. It would take many dashes (weeks) before she came home again.

Reflection:

These specific events during the hospitalization confirmed to me what I had already experienced earlier on in my life when I was a two-year-old. A core belief had already formed that if you needed rescue, no one would be there. I would experience the feeling of abandonment on many more occasions in my early life.

Later, I understood that these were the initial traumatic incidents where I made a vow that, if possible, I would not cry or show pain to anyone. Being so very young, I didn't have the resources to regulate back into an inner calm and safety; I started to form defense mechanisms so I could survive. These promises were cemented into my unconscious, and it started what the Bible calls strongholds and negative thinking patterns. Calling out for help would not be heard, crying was forbidden, and sharing your pain would not be acknowledged.

I kept to these promises and started to isolate myself and built a wall around my heart. I became lonely and introverted. Maybe that wasn't my blueprint, but I had set up a strong protection around my heart to prevent any more emotional pain.

I also became burdened with shame. Shame does not come because you did something wrong; it is felt because others did something to you that was wrong. Because I was subjected to the wrong and had no choice, I resorted to saying to myself: "I am wrong." That burden would also be lifted in later adult years. I will write about this in Part Eleven of the book.

Life on the Ward

Maria

The ward was at full capacity with six children. Most of the children had complex medical issues and would be on long-term treatment. I was the youngest girl. Linda was the eldest and had the bed next to the window. Next to her lay Hester. I liked Hester and she was very pretty. I had the bed by the door. Opposite me was the new arrival. She had a foreign name: "Natja." She was Polish and so restless, she tossed and turned all the time, day and night. There were two other children whom I cannot remember.

We only saw the nurses in the morning when they came to measure our temperature. Then during lunch and dinner when they brought the meals, and finally in the evening to give us a tin basin to brush our teeth before we had to go to sleep.

When the lights went out, darkness took over. Linda was the boss. She would ask each of us to do something for her. You had to do what she demanded, otherwise you could not be part of the ward and she would tell the nurses the next day that you were not complying. When it was my turn, she conferred with Hester about what I had to do to belong to the ward. The outcome was that each night when the nurses turned off the lights, I had to follow a sequence of actions that I would now classify as being forced to engage in indecent exposure. I did not want to do it. I begged them to give me another assignment, but nothing would change their mind; I had to do it. They would think of another assignment later, but that never came, and I had to repeat the ceremony each night. To me, day and night ceased to be separate. I lived in my bed, and the surroundings were always colorless and dim. Seldom did I see grown-ups, besides the nurses, and my parents for one hour from 6 p.m. to 7 p.m. I started to dream about that one hour. Then I started to worry about that short moment in which visitors were allowed as it would be finished too soon and after everybody had gone, the torment would start all over again.

Days went by, then weeks. It snowed one night, and it looked so pretty outside. Natja had been taken outside the ward sometimes, and whenever she came back, she became even wilder. The nurses yelled at her and slapped her. She was put into a harness, a straitjacket. What did they do to her? When everything was dark, she called out to me, "Maria, please, can you loosen the tight straps, I can't breathe!" The straps were buckled, and it kept her immovable. I slipped out of my bed to loosen them so she could sleep on her side.

On the other side of our wall, divided by windows with curtains drawn, was another ward. Through a slit in the curtains, I could investigate the other ward. The bed on the other side of the wall was occupied by a small girl who was attached to many tubes. She screamed all the time. One day, I decided that I must go to her. Maybe if I told her a story, she would forget her pain. When Linda was not looking, I slipped from my bed, and, on my hands and knees, I crawled through the hall. There I backed up against the wall. Hiding my head from under the window, I slowly inched toward the next ward. Suddenly I stopped when a lady doctor doing her rounds saw me. My knees started to shake.

"What are you doing out here, you should be in your bed." Her stern voice resounded in the quiet hallway. "What are you planning to do?"

I explained that the girl next door was screaming nonstop and that I was going to tell her a story. The doctor stared hard at me and then quickly looked around and let me go.

I felt incredibly happy and light as I walked straight into the next ward and stood next to the screaming girl. She was naked from the bottom down. Tubes led into her urethra, and I could see yellow fluid drip into a bag. When she saw me, she stopped screaming and we talked for a while. Later I found out she had had a bladder operation and was in constant pain. I did not visit her again as she was moved away.

Finally, I was allowed to get up from my bed, as the nurses no longer wanted me to eat in bed from the swinging table that hung from the rails. I had to sit at the small table by the window. As the nurses prepared that table, I begged them to please let me stay in bed. It was safer in bed. Linda and Hester were eating at the table. In my mind, it was a dangerous place, and I would be at their mercy. I had no choice but to join them.

At lunch and dinner, nurses set down the trays of food and then disappeared again. I had to go to the table to get my food. I tried to sit on the edge of my chair, and Linda commanded me to lay my napkin out properly on the table and put the plate of food on top of it. Obediently I unfolded and laid out the napkin, taking as much time as I could. As I reached out for the food on the tray, she quickly grabbed the napkin and threw it across the ward. "Now get up and get your napkin, I want to see you walking through the whole room alone!" she ordered. This happened every day during the entire hospital stay before I could eat my food.

As a rule, you had to eat quickly before the nurses collected the dishes again. Mealtimes became a personal torture and had the same sequence every day. I would sit at my place, then the napkin was thrown numerous times around the ward which I had to get before I could eat. As I returned, Linda screwed her eyes up and demanded, "Every time you return you need to ask very nicely if you can sit." She continued, "And you have to say, 'please, Linda, can I now eat,' before you dare to start."

Often, I refused to eat because getting to my lunch or dinner had become a daily struggle. I decided food was not important in my life—I would never allow hunger to control me—and waited for the hunger pangs to pass. It was safer not to eat. I just denied being hungry and fought against the need for food. It was no wonder my parents were always trying to get food into me for years after my stay in the hospital.

Reflection:

Much later, I was confronted with this internal decision, or internal vow. I had made a promise to myself never to feel hungry or want food; it had become a mindset. Throughout my life, I have struggled with the notion that you require food to live. As I was very slim, I was often asked if I suffered from anorexia.

Only after it was exposed as an internal vow, through an inner healing course by Elijah House[12], was I able to break free from this unconscious, powerful, and harmful mindset.

Mother

Every day when I visited Maria, I looked into the nurses' office to see if they could update me on her progress. Seldom did I find a nurse on duty. During lunches, nobody was ever on the wards, so I found that to be the best time to slip in and give her a quick kiss. Then I quickly got out again.

After a few weeks, I ran into a doctor again. She assured me, "Yes, it is going very well with your daughter, you should not be thinking so negatively." Thinking negatively? When I was visiting her during the evening hour, I often needed to help her onto a potty. Sometimes this happened twice within the hour, and she always had diarrhea with blood! I didn't see any difference from the day she was admitted.

One day I slipped in again. I looked for a nurse in the office and found a report about Maria lying open on the table. Quickly, I started reading: "Her stool is normal, seldom has she had any visible blood in her stool...." Was I going crazy? They were lying here! I called the doctor and finally, I got an appointment. The pediatrician who had been so friendly during the admission was now a haughty woman. She did not look me in the eyes when she mumbled, "Don't you worry, she can go home soon." And off she went. I felt like a shriveled-up, young, silly little mother.

God's Angels and More Treatments

Maria

It was Christmas, although it did not make much difference for me. The nurses put a large record player on the bench next to the door and placed a shiny, black vinyl record on it. As it began to play, they disappeared again.

It was a narrative, a story that I didn't like or understand. It was called *Alice in Wonderland*. The story scared me because Alice ate some chocolate sprinkles and grew and grew so that she did not fit in the small house anymore. She grew so big that her head popped out of the chimney and her hands broke out of the windows. She also had to do funny things for the creatures in a funny country that was far from Alice's own home, just like me. And I feared eating food even more.

Mother

Christmas. It was a time of celebration. We were allowed to visit Maria twice a day for one hour! In the afternoon, her sister and her cousins, Gerrie and Margreet, were allowed to wave to her from outside the window. An hour of waving to a silent girl in the far-sided bed was not much fun, so they went off to play in the snow. It was beautiful outside in the forest, outside the window.

New Year's Eve was another celebration. Again, Maria's sister and cousins were allowed to play just outside the ward window. My sister, Maria's aunt Hannie, joined the fun and showed off the snowman they made. Uncle Ton brought a watch for Maria. It was too large for her tiny wrist.

Maria

The husband of my auntie (my mum's sister) visited me! He gave me a watch. Soon I had figured out the times, so I knew when it was time for Mum to come and see me. My uncle showed me how to wind the little knob at the side of the mechanical watch to keep it going. Every night I made sure it was wound up properly so I would always know when it was time for Mum to visit me.

Linda stopped me from winding it. She said she hated the noise. I tried to do it under the blanket, but it was a thin blanket. She yelled at me, "Stop it, Maria, I can still hear it!" I tried to do it slowly over a prolonged period. Suddenly I heard her loud voice again, "Whatever you are trying to do, I will always find out and hear what you do under the blanket, and I will stop you!" I felt incredibly sad; the watch would stop working if I did not wind it and then I would not know when Mum was coming.

I could not look at Linda. Whenever I so much as glanced at her, she yelled at me not to look at her with my big, ugly cat eyes. That refrain, "You! With your ugly cat eyes," stayed with me for years until a unique experience of instant healing occurred later in life while I lived in New Zealand. A story of healing is still to come up in Part Twelve.

The rest of the children's ward took up the names she had come up with for me. I was called a "witch with pointy ears," which was true as I was born with a wrinkled top ear. And of course, I was the one with "ugly cat eyes." Under my thin blanket, I softly cried, but Linda would hear it and ridicule me.

Life on the ward was a torment and as time went by, I learned another coping mechanism. I learned to dissociate. The only constant certain was that I knew God was with me.

Two women I had never seen before came to visit early on a sunny Sunday morning. "Would you care to come with us to chapel today?" they asked, standing at the end of my bed.

"Yes, please!" A surge of expectancy

Reflection:

Two internal vows were born in this hospital: "I will not cry anymore," and "I do not need food." I also started to believe that I was ugly. I was not liked by anyone. Nobody would come to the rescue when horrible things happened to me. The nurses would not care, and my parents were not there or were not able to comfort me when I needed them most. Letting others see when I cried was a no-go zone. The best thing to do was not be seen or heard. I became silent and glided into nonexistence. This all had to be healed one day because in adult life, it made me unapproachable, introverted, and on a constant alert for possible pain and rejection.

went through me, and my heart started pounding. I had never been to a chapel or church before. Nobody else was asked from the ward but me. They gently rolled my bed out into the corridor and kept asking me if I felt okay. They tucked me in my blanket because the hallways were breezy.

We entered a big chapel with stained-glass windows. The ceiling was angled and remarkably high. The sun played light patterns on the wooden panels of the walls. I was parked at the back from where I saw a sea of beds, all lined up neatly. In front of the chapel were wooden benches where other visitors sat. Next to me lay a woman with wonderful brown, short hair. She smiled at me and whispered, "Hello, dear girl, do you have a song that you want to have sung this morning?"

I nodded and whispered back my wish. She pushed herself up on the handle that hung from a frame above her head and waved her hand to the minister. She called out to him that next to her was a girl who would like to have a song sung. Soon the whole chapel was filled with my song:

> *Safe in the arms of Jesus, safe on His gentle breast,*
> *There by His love o'ershaded, sweetly my soul shall rest.*
> *Hark! 'tis the voice of angels, borne in a song to me.*
> *Over the fields of glory, over the jasper sea.*[2]

As I had not been to church before in my life, I did not know where the song came from. It was in my head. My parents might have played it on a vinyl record during the times I was playing in the living room when I was home. I still wondered if those ladies who took me to the chapel were angels in an answer to my many prayers for Jesus to come and help me. I never saw them again.

The weather had changed. It was sunny, and suddenly something else changed too. The children in the ward were getting better. Linda went home; soon after, the rest of us were invited to take a walk outside with a volunteer to visit a park with deer and ducks and rabbits. We took some bread and went to the fenced area and fed the animals. I did not feel cold at all. Soon I was able to go home too. I had been in the hospital for three months and the experience changed my life.

Mother

It was early March. Maria could come home with the conclusion that she was incurable; she would have to learn to live with it.

Where was Maria, my daughter? She was detached, aloof, and switched off, as if her spirit died. I got the feeling she was not home; her spirit was crushed. She did not let me out of her sight. She lived in fear that I would abandon her again. Fortunately, spring turned into summer, and she could play outside with her sister and cousins. These moments of joy and lightheartedness seemed to bring back the girl I knew, although she was never a happy girl again.

It was a shocking discovery to hear from a retired nurse from the hospital in Zeist that the children's department was closed shortly after Maria had left. There were reports of many unusual activities between the nurses. It was said that the nurses in charge were lesbians and were neglecting their duties to spend time together. Later, the whole hospital was demolished.

Reflection:

Later in life, I understood that these initial childhood traumas, through bullying and abusive behaviors in healthcare, shaped how I thought about myself and the world around me. The lie that nobody would be there for me when I needed it the most was a particularly strong lie, and a silent judgment formed in my heart: "Nobody can be trusted, nobody cares, nobody will listen." This would also influence my theology about God in years to come.

PART 2

School Years

International Search for Doctors

Although I was excited to go home, nothing was the same. It was not the sunny home I remembered; everything around me was strangely quiet, and mostly I felt silent inside. I did not go to school for the rest of the year. I spent most of the time in a folding bed next to a large window in the dining room from where I could see Mum puttering around.

When autumn came, my tummy got worse again. On my daybed, I would see the moon rise in the early darkened afternoons. The trees lost their leaves after the first frost, and the empty branches swayed in the autumn storms. Mum vacuumed the house, cleaned, and cooked in the kitchen. An old transistor radio played soft classical music. My sister played on the floor next to my bed when she came home from school. On dark winter evenings after dinner, Mum softly sang a psalm as she played a small manual pipe organ. Music soothed my soul.

We visited a lot of doctors. One doctor wanted to send me to a sanatorium in Switzerland. I pictured myself on a sunny porch, tucked into a comfortable armchair, staring at the majestic mountains. My parents never consented to send me away on my own.

Then there was another scary doctor. He only looked me in the eyes and kept mumbling, "You've got worms, deeply burrowed inside of you, you've got worms." He had a lot of posters of eyes in his rooms too, still, he explained that he was not an eye doctor. Later, during my adult years, I found out he practiced iridology.

Some doctors altered my diet drastically. I had to eat lots of various kinds of food, sometimes it consisted of only very dark rye bread, layered with homemade jam. Then it would change to solely eating old crumbly white bread and white rice with melted butter. One diet was more ridiculous than the other and none of them made me feel better.

Mother
We looked for and found a naturopath. Again, this doctor confirmed the inevitable conclusion that there was no cure, then she heard of an acupuncturist in London we could try. We planned to go by plane because a journey by car and boat would be too exhausting for Maria. After some acupressure point treatments in London, her condition worsened. With no improvement, we went back home.

As I cleaned the house and took care of the family, my heart cried out to God, "Will I lose this child?" We had already made provisions for her funeral several times over the last year.

The answer came suddenly and clearly, and I found it to be a verse from John 11:4: "This sickness will not end in death. No, it is for Gods' glory so that God's Son may be glorified through it" (NIV).

Maria
Friends of my parents heard about a miracle-working doctor in England who had cured people. In desperation, my parents decided to give this doctor a try. Since I felt too weak to walk much, we would go by plane! I had never been on a plane before. My sister was so jealous.

The airport was an exciting place. Proudly, I carried a little travel cot with a baby doll in it. When we arrived at the entrance of the jet bridge, a friendly stewardess asked, "Am I allowed to frisk your baby doll and maybe even you?"

A bit nervous, I let her unpack the travel cot. She felt the blanket, the doll, and then gentle hands swiftly frisked over my sides. Then we were allowed to go through the gates and walk over the concrete runway to airstairs attached to the plane.

Now came the best part. We entered the plane, and I flew high above the clouds. We were on our way to see a miracle doctor! I thought this was the most interesting thing I ever experienced.

Everyone around me spoke English. A lovely girl my age taught me to count to ten and the names of colors. She showed the colors of her felt pens in her pencil case and called out for me to repeat, "Red, green, blue!" She went to school in a uniform, and she even had a special school hat. It looked so uncomfortable and very formal. I would rather wear my normal clothes to school.

We traveled by a diesel locomotive to the doctor's practice. He lived in a massive mansion with beautiful, manicured gardens. I sat in the large formal waiting room and looked through a wide hallway, feeling very small. One of the doors opened, and a man walked through the hallway, with heaps of bouncing needles poking from his backside. He disappeared into another room. It looked so scary; I hoped I would not have to have all those needles in me to be healed. The doctor in England talked a lot, I did not understand anything he said. The only thing that went through my mind was that he poked needles into people.

The doctor himself didn't do much. After a few minutes, his wife came in and wanted to put her hands on my head. I heard her softly shuffling through the room as I lay facedown on a table. When I glanced at her hands, they shook and were angrily red. For some reason, I felt afraid. Suddenly, my mum's voice sounded strong and demanding. "What are you doing to my daughter?"

The doctor's wife startled and stuttered, and I heard her running away from the table where I lay. She went to the washbasin and scrubbed her hands over and over as if she were dirty. She explained to my mother, "I have special healing powers coming through my hands."

Later Mum told me she was not sure what was happening. She was struggling to put her hands together for prayer and found she could not, as if an unseen power stopped her from praying. By softly calling on the Name of Jesus, she suddenly could fold her hands and say a prayer of protection. The lady then had to leave my bedside and told Mum that her powers had left her. We later learned that this was called *Reiki* or *Magnetic Therapy*.

We left the stately house and stepped onto the train to travel to our guest quarters. It was

Reflection:

In the search for healing, my parents introduced me to occult practices. As they grew in their faith, they also learned how destructive these practices were and repented. We asked for cleansing by the Blood of Jesus and cut off any ties with the occult. I also had to do this later for myself when I was made aware that any agreement with the enemy, and being exposed to his tactics, could have opened doors in my spirit that needed to be closed again through personal repentance and renouncing any hold Satan might have tried to hold over me.

an amazing sight when the old locomotive pulled into the station. Clouds of steam escaped from the smokestack and a loud whistle made me jump. The sound of squeaking brakes scared me a bit. The trip only lasted a few stations before I doubled over with horrible cramps. We all got off and I ran into the bushes. I squatted for a long time, feeling nauseous, and spouted bright red blood into the leaves. I grew very weak.

As I looked around in the English thicket, I spotted a large banknote under the bush. I took it to Mum who started to cry. I didn't know yet that we were too early to get back to the house where we were invited to stay. Mum and Dad were trying to book a hotel for which they didn't have the money. The banknote covered one night's stay. Although the doctor did not do the miracle of healing me, we experienced a miracle of provision.

Early in the morning, we packed up again and left the hotel to travel to a large country manor with many chimneys on the roof. The people who lived there were acquaintances of church members back in the Netherlands. They warmly welcomed us into their home. Horrible headaches and weakness caused me to sleep the majority of our stay there.

We never went back to that doctor again during our time in London. We did visit the palace gardens, and I was allowed to stand between huge soldiers with high, black, hairy hats. Their shoes had large shiny noses that stuck up in a curl. I wondered about their toes getting all hot and deformed.

Then we went back home. I was not healed. I felt sick all the time and wondered if I was dying and asked Mum to say a prayer for me to ask Jesus to take me to heaven. I believed it would be much better there. She knelt before my bed and chokingly asked Jesus to come and help me. Sleep overtook me and I wondered whether Mum had even prayed for Jesus to take me home, because it never happened.

We kept searching for doctors who could help me. The next one was a German doctor who gave injections in my bottom. It worked for a few weeks, and then we returned for more. It was a four-hour trip in the car with Mum. I loved these trips. We drove through the Dutch countryside and then into Germany with its rolling hills and sunny forests. The steady hum of the car motor made me sleepy. I dreamed and fantasized that we would keep on driving and driving, going on forever into different countries, crossing many borders, gliding through vast plains with high blue skies and wide green scenery. If only we could drive forever, away from all the darkness, the cold, the pain, and the feeling of being pressed down all the time. After the injection, I would feel particularly good and have no pain for a day. Mum would even treat me to chocolate. Soon the injections had to be done every week and then every other day. One of Mum's friends was a nurse, and she administered them, either at home on Mum's double bed or at her place. She was not good at doing them, and my buttocks started to hurt a lot when she injected them. Mum said it was because there wasn't enough fat stored there to jab an injection into.

Mother

We heard from a specialist in Germany. Because we had followed the naturopath's advice with all the different diets, the growth of her digestive system and bowel flora had diminished. The doctor in Germany gave injections to stimulate flora growth again. He told her to eat what she liked, and her diarrhea stopped. Incredible! After two weeks, the bliss was over. We now needed to get the injection every two weeks, and it took a day's drive back and forth to Germany. Soon it was every week and finally, we got the medicine with us, so a nurse at home could administer the injection. After a few more weeks, the effect had worn off completely and we stopped administering the drug altogether.

1975: Moving House

The old school with bare brick walls had to be demolished, and my sister and I now went to a brand-new building somewhere else in that same town. This new school was so much better. It was built on pillars, and you could play underneath the classrooms. There were newly planted trees, and the sun had free rein through the windows. I liked the classroom. My teacher was lovely. She told wonderful stories of fairies and forest creatures. Then she drew colorful sceneries on the blackboard with screeching chalk. We went out for trips to the forest to collect leaves and mushrooms; I searched around for the places where fairies might have danced the night before.

Then I got sick again. The lovely teacher came to my house to give me some homework which I did in bed under the large window or at the dinner table. Sporadically I went to school, mostly I was at home.

Mother

The attacks continued and alternated from severe to mild. Then during one weekend, Maria started screaming from pain. Her stomach bloated until it looked like a balloon. We drove to another city for a doctor who was on duty. She got some painkillers, and they checked her hemoglobin. It was 4.0 g/dL which was too low as it should be around 11-14 g/dL. The medic was shocked and wrote out a prescription for an iron drink and asked why she had not been on this already.

She got some extra energy through the syrup and started to play again, although she did not go to school a lot. She was a bright kid; she didn't re-do any of her classes except Primary 1, due to those months in the hospital.

Maria

I turned eight that year. Mum and Dad had started attending church from time to time over the last few years, but my grandparents did not agree. As we piled into our car on a Sunday morning,

1975: Moving House

Grandmother stood at the entrance of her house shaking her head and wailing, "Now you take my grandchildren away from God" and she would cry.

My auntie, Mum's sister, also didn't agree with us or the Bible teachings my father was now giving to us and our cousins on a Sunday afternoon. We had less fun when we played with our cousins, although I didn't know what was wrong, it just started to feel different.

Much later I understood that my parents had left the denomination of my grandparents who followed the conservative theologian, Reverend Paauwe. This preacher fell out of fellowship with the Dutch Reformed Church back in 1913 and started home churches where his followers would read his sermons to each other on a Sunday morning. Both my parents had been brought up with Reverend Paauwe's teachings and were now exploring another spiritual direction.

My parents were sad and felt they were not welcome in the orchard anymore, so we moved from the orchard into a townhouse in Zeist in the Province of Utrecht. It was the same town as our school. This was much better because we were now able to go to school on our bicycles. Still, Mum often had to take me. She had to tie a pillow on the metal rack on the back of her bike, otherwise it would hurt my bony bottom too much.

We now visited a church instead of staying home on Sundays. Zeist was a nice town to live in. At the end of the street was a public park where we played with some neighborhood kids. The houses were built as four-in-a-row and then separated into small, roofed alleys where we played with marbles. We had adventures and climbed over the fence edges separating the neighbors' gardens and would aim half-eaten apple cores into the open toilet-room windows of people we didn't like. Once, it hit the head of someone in the bathroom and a face appeared in the frosted window yelling, "I know who you are, children of Beekhuizen (my maiden name). I will speak to your parents!"

For weeks on end, I had good times in which I could run and play outside, followed by weeks of bed rest. Mum made a bed in front of the French doors where I looked out over the backyard. I lived my own private life of books, paper crafts, and needle crafts like knitting and crocheting. Birds were my greatest interest, as I followed their flittering, chirping, building nests, and feeding their young outside the windows. They were so free and happy; I longed to be free like them.

Sometimes in the evening, Mum and Dad visited a Bible study group since they were exploring and searching out Christianity. One evening, the son of a friend came to look after us. He had to do homework downstairs. When Mum and Dad had gone, he came to my room, pulled back my blankets, and snuggled in with me. He said he was going to read me a story and that he had licorice if I was as good as my sister. He had just been with my sister, and she had been nice to him and listened to him. Furthermore, he told me I should not tell Mum and Dad about him sharing my bed.

I learned dissociation techniques while in the hospital. When dreadful things happen to your body, you can always fly away in your mind. I made up my own story in my head about a little bouncy ball that went on an adventure, jumping everywhere, throughout the entire world, free like a bird... I did not want his sweets. When Mum and Dad came home, we told them anyway what the boy had done. He never came back.

Reflection:

As I reflect on these childhood incidents, I can say that if not dealt with properly, these have the potential to settle in a child's mind and develop into an unhelpful victimhood mindset. By minimization—denying that it was improper or saying it was unimportant—we could set a pattern of not establishing personal boundaries. We might not be able to say "no" to unhealthy relationships later in life, or we might develop a conviction that we were powerless and did not have choices. Living with a victim mindset always carries disgrace and shame.

When boundaries have been crossed, they need to be re-established. The poison it leaves produces fruit in our minds and later influences our behavior. In this instance, a lie found its way into my mind, "I am powerless, I have no right to say "no" or put up personal boundaries or stand up for my values." I believed I could not stand up for myself, so later in life, I became a victim to those who sought to have power over my weaknesses. How I found freedom from this mindset is written about later in this book.

Of course, our parents instructed us later in life when we had our children never to leave them behind with young teenagers who were not properly screened.

The Operation

Mother

The attacks had become more severe as the years went by. We were referred to another hospital in Amersfoort. A kind, older pediatrician there thought he knew the diagnosis. Diverticulitis of Meckel. He assured us, "It's nothing serious. Only when the pain attacks come together with vomiting will she need to be admitted to hospital." Unfortunately, this doctor also diagnosed it wrongly.

Maria

One wintry and dark evening in November 1976, I started vomiting and could not stop. I did not care about anything anymore, I just tried to breathe between throwing up. *This is how I will finally die*, I thought.

Suddenly I felt Dad carrying me to the car. He kept one hand on the horn as we sped through the streets. It was my grandfather's birthday, and he had been called to meet us to look after my sister. I vomited during the brief stop when we met him halfway. The cold rain dripped through the open window as they talked, and dread came over me when I realized we were on our way to a hospital.

In the hospital, I was put in a bed behind a curtain. This time it was not so dark or scary. Just light and people talked all the time to me. They held my body as it contracted in dry retching. They explained everything while they placed the IV in my hand. It hurt. Then oblivion took over and I slept.

Mother

What the doctor had warned us about happened a week later. We now lived in a city called Zeist, and her grandparents needed to come in a hurry to look after Hannie as we rushed to the hospital. It was the night of the fifteenth of November, my father's birthday.

A scan was done and was inconclusive, and Maria was admitted that same night. After one day, another scan was made, and this time it was much clearer. The diagnosis of a septic appendix was given! She needed to be operated on fast! This time we were allowed to stay with her for the whole afternoon and the evening. What a dissimilar experience to all the other hospitals.

Maria stayed in a small room with a real children's toilet. After she recovered from her anesthesia, I stayed as long as I wanted. I looked at her incision and was shocked to see how huge the wound was on her stomach. It ran from her pubis to far above her belly button. It looked like they had opened my entire child. The nurses were very friendly. The surgeon told me that the operation had been a success. There was an extremely infected appendix that they removed, but they could not find any other abnormalities in the intestines! Surely, her troubles would be over. She was in a lot of pain. I assured her, "You will be better very soon!"

The next afternoon when I visited her, she needed to go to the bathroom. When I wiped her bottom, I found a lot of blood. I tried to pull her toward me, but she turned around and saw the blood too. "Mum, it has been all for nothing," she said as her face turned white. I tried to comfort her and told her to have patience. After a long silence, she told me that I didn't need to stay with her the whole afternoon. She was not afraid anymore, and she was allowed to go to the children's ward where she could play and watch TV. The atmosphere seemed relaxed.

Was everything truly okay in this hospital? One day, her father visited her after work. He came home with a strange story of a woman who had tried to get access to Maria and had to be removed by the nurses. A strange incident indeed and I was worried about her well-being.

Maria

The day after I was admitted, the doctor decided to operate on me. When I woke up, I was in a lovely room full of windows. Sunlight danced across my blankets, but my tummy hurt terribly. Mum was there, and my auntie and Dad as well. A nurse came in and said I was allowed to get out of bed as soon as I was able. I could not stand up straight. They had cut from above my belly button to my pelvic bone. It looked like a zipper that curved around my belly button.

The Operation

Nurses came in and out. I got many presents whenever visitors came in. This hospital didn't seem to be too bad.

Within days I walked around and was upgraded to a ward with only two patients. As I slowly recovered from the operation, I ventured out of the ward, into the hallway. I felt naughty as I peeped around the door. Would I be detected? I had been in this kind of situation before and that had been a scary experience. Nurses had been cruel and doctors disapproving. Up to this moment, the staff was great, although I did not trust it. Would it turn out all right this time?

As I stepped outside, I found the long hallway deserted. Suddenly a nurse appeared from the far side. She was disheveled and her hair stood out in wisps. She swayed from side to side as if drunk. I froze on the spot. When she saw me, she pointed her finger at me and shouted, "Yes, it is you, I know it's you!" She then spoke an incoherent language and charged toward me. As she passed the nurses' room, other nurses appeared in great haste and grabbed her by her arms. One nurse hurried toward me and ushered me back inside my ward.

This incident confused and disturbed me. Some nurses here were very strange. Would it be the same as the other hospital? I did not feel safe in this hospital either!

The next day, the kind nurse said to me, "You are getting so much better. Would you like to move to the children's ward and see if you like it there instead of staying on this side of the hall?" I thought they asked me this because of the scary nurse's behavior. Much later I learned that she had a drug addiction and would steal medicine from the hospital pharmacy.

The children's ward was lovely. I decided to give it a go and stay on this ward even if there were other children present who could potentially bully me. Time would tell if they were safe to be around. We watched TV and there were children's books to read. It was a large room on the top floor of the hospital with sunlight streaming through the windows. Only four children were in the room. I had the window bed and I looked out over the canopy of treetops of a Dutch national park.

After three weeks, I could go home. My time in this hospital was not a terrible experience. But because I had adopted the idea that life was not safe, I'd remained hyper-vigilant. I could go back to school, but my heart started racing the moment Mum dropped me off. Panic rose and a deep loneliness come over me straight away. I could not stand watching Mum go. Every time she left me behind at school, I was afraid. To help settle my anxiety, the teacher gave me a place at the window so I could see Mum go home and come back to pick me up. I looked out the window toward the sky and the streets below. I could see the trees and the birds. Just like at home where I was safe in my daybed. Inside I felt so sad, so very sad, I wanted to cry all the time for nothing. What was wrong with me?

Reflection:

Throughout my life, I fell in and out of depression. Much later, a psychiatrist diagnosed me with compounded post-traumatic stress disorder. When we talked about the early traumatic events, it mostly had to do with abuse, bullying, abandonment, rejection, neglect, betrayal, and mistrust. Sickness, injuries, accidents, and losses like death, divorce, moving house, or even countries were also on this list. Secondary to the primary trauma was the exposure to and witnessing of these events described above. This included witnessing any type of violence, war, human suffering, poverty, and destruction. I experienced all of these later in life.

Destructive thinking patterns had started early in my childhood. This had to do with the abandonment I experienced while in the hospital with paratyphoid when I was two, as well as later during those months in the hospital when I was six. I endured extreme bullying by my peers on the ward and suffered neglect in primary care by the nurses. Later you will read about my high school years which also contained elements of extreme bullying and ridicule by authorities like teachers and the principal.

These destructive thinking patterns led to feelings of betrayal, loneliness, insecurities, victimization, being overwhelmed, powerlessness, and an overall sense that I was unworthy of being. I developed coping mechanisms, developed facades, and used many masks. In some areas, I remained in denial of the severity of what had happened, then I wouldn't need to face the loss and pain I experienced. I will write more about this in my story because there is hope and healing. We can deal with the scars, develop an identity and even extend vital support to those who are going through similar traumatic events. We can glean benefits from having gone through suffering ourselves.

Living with Pain

Mother

After the operation, the doctor was confident that things would get better. After three weeks in the hospital, she was allowed to come home again. "Rest and good food" was his advice to get back her strength.

At home, she was in bed for two more weeks with a ghostly white face. She could not move because of severe pain in her tummy. When I checked on her at night, she only whispered, "Mama, pain." When we went for a check-up, the surgeon thought it to be a hernia which they would not do anything about. Throughout the following months, she grew a bit stronger, unfortunately, she didn't recover as we all had hoped.

Maria

Somehow after the operation, the worst of my tummy aches seemed to be over, although I was still very ill. I kept bleeding and was often at home. We visited other hospitals, and in one academic hospital, I was told I needed another colonoscopy. The nurses in this hospital were stern and unfriendly, and Mum was not allowed to be with me. Bad memories flooded my mind and raised my anxiety.

I was admitted into a chilly room with dimmed lights. I had to undress and slip into a short, shirt-length gown that did not cover my lower parts or back. This felt all too familiar. Half-naked, I walked through a door and into an eerie, gloomy dark space.

This time I was not given any anesthetics. I lay down on the metal top of a trolley covered with a white sheet. I looked around and saw a huge stick which they told me needed to be put inside of me. It was made of glass, I remember. More bad memories flooded me as I tried to fly away in my mind. Floating toward the ceiling, I kept telling myself that the half-naked girl on the table was not me! Then suddenly I was jerked back into my body—back to reality—when the doctor inserted the tube and started to pump my intestines full of air. The excruciating pain was all I could think about. I wished I were dead. Would this life of pain go on forever?

Mother

We were referred to a specialized children's hospital in the big city of Utrecht. A doctor there specialized in her kind of illness. She endured countless colonoscopies during her life. I was treated very coldly and was completely ignored by the staff as they interacted with Maria. I was not even allowed to enter the day surgery ward to be with her but had to wait in the hall. The staff pulled my child from me, and from behind several doors, I heard her screams.

Coolly my child was handed back to me a little while later. "Madam, you will be informed concerning the outcome of the examination," the nurse curtly said. After many fruitless telephone calls to the doctor who had referred her to the specialist, I finally saw her assistant who told me that everything was fine. Nothing was wrong with my child. "Just keep up the medication that she's been taking." That was the brief advice.

Whenever I administered those huge pills, I had to be forceful because Maria hated to swallow four to six of these pills, a couple of times a day. Maria became excellent at hiding them.

I wondered why I was treated so coldly and kept at a distance in this hospital. Years later, during Maria's teenage years and at the end of the whole saga of her illness, I got an answer to that question. It was unearthed when we moved to yet another town and had to find a local GP in the new area. During this transition, I collected all the medical reports from our last GP. All reports had been severely altered with subjective opinions of the doctors and specialists of whom none had been able to give a proper diagnosis.

Reflection:

Many years later, Mum and I sat opposite each other at the dining table in Albany, Australia. As we wrote down the story from our perspectives, I could see the pain in her eyes as she recalled these years. She had suffered as much as I had.

When I was in my forties, I started to share more freely with others about my life events, experiences, traumas, and the effects they had on my life. Wise and Godly counselors guided me through a long healing process that took numerous years. I allowed sadness to come back to the surface, and I learned to cry again. I had been repeatedly violated on so many levels. This had laid the first layers of strongholds (mindsets) and many foundational lies. Through the years, I became more introverted which was perceived as someone with a strong personality. In reality, I had built a solid, protective wall of independence. One day this wall had to come down, so I could trust others, and God, again. A deep-rooted pain had settled into my heart: The pain of rejection.

Bullied, Alienated, and Alone

I got good marks at school and the teachers were satisfied with my performance, but I never belonged to my peer group; I always felt like the odd one out and kept my distance. The hospital experiences made me incredibly cautious and on high alert. I did not venture out to make friends. I didn't know how to make friends and didn't know about the TV programs they watched, or the games they played. I had no idea why they were happy or what made them laugh, didn't pick up on jokes, and was afraid to join in the groups that milled around at the playground. Plagued by fear that they would notice me, only to reject me soon after.

However, I did one friend, who also seemed to be an outcast. She was the daughter of the town's fish salesman and often smelled of fish. That was why nobody wanted to be her friend. Her name was Petra, and we played a lot together. She was very bright, especially in math. Numbers eluded me, I was much better with words. As we sat on the top bunk bed in her room, she listened breathlessly to my made-up stories. I always got giggles when I looked at the mantelpiece and studied their wedding picture. He had to stand two steps higher on the stairs to the city council to match her height as she was much taller than him He was also a gifted church organ player. When he sat behind the layers of black and white keys, the music he produced made my skin prickle, and I would be swept away from the dancing notes that came from the outstretched flutes.

Year six was my final year at primary school. I had nearly made it through. That was when I got the principal as my class teacher. Heavyset, always in a gray suit, balding head, and beady eyes, he took it upon himself to severely ridicule me in front of the class. I kept my head high as I told myself, "You have nothing to lose, nobody will like you anyway." I had resolved that neither children nor adults might ever like me, and I could expect trouble from adults who were in charge and in authority. My distrust in others grew and solidified.

I seemed to have an invisible label saying, "Come and get me," and it became firmly stuck on my forehead for everyone to see and try out.

I testified freely about my faith in God which most children found strange and weird. It did not line up with the religious teachings they heard at home and kids just didn't share such things. This school was a strictly Dutch Reformed school and deeply religious and based on the theological system of John Calvin. The theology in the Reformed Church and the school taught that you cannot be sure of your salvation. Salvation was an issue of election and predestination. This implied that even if you believed in Jesus and thanked Him for His death on the cross where He carried away your sins, you could not be sure He did this for you. Who could know if they were predestined and chosen by God to be saved? Neither could you know for sure if heaven was your destiny, as that was something you only found out after you died. You had to be good and do good works to qualify for heaven.

In my mind, this did not make sense. Why would you want to believe in such a God who kept you in suspense regarding your entry into heaven? My confession of faith was not looked upon as a good thing. The principal ridiculed me in front of the class. He would say, "There are some of you who *think* they are saved by the cross of Christ. Those who believe that and apply this faith to themselves are especially deceived. They are proud and self-righteous, and God hates pride. This was Satan's first sin, and it is punishable. Such people end up in hell." As he spoke, his eyes would fix on me. During the break, the kids avoided me and whispered among themselves.

I did not understand it all. At home, my parents spoke about a different God than the principal talked about at school. At home God was good and Jesus loved me. I knew this because I had experienced it in the hospital. I knew God listened to me and He was eager to be heard by me. Many of the children in my class laughed and shied away from my decision to be water baptized at the age of twelve. I invited them all, although I knew this would alienate me even further. Some girls were told by their parents not to associate with me anymore and most playdate offers ceased.

Early one morning, as I arrived at the playground, my classmates formed a line on either side of me. I walked through it while they called out names, teased, and chanted, "Maria is converted! Maria is converted!" Behind the entrance glass doors, I saw the principal, his hands clasped behind his back, and he nodded his approval as the children ridiculed me.

Only Petra was steady next to me and never departed from my side. At school, loneliness and insecurities overwhelmed me.

Reflection:

Something about that early abandonment and bullying created so early in my developmental years, created an unsatiated hole of wanting to be accepted, acknowledged, and affirmed. Through the years, I tried to cover up the wound of rejection in many ways.

As I revisited some of these moments, I became aware of how important it is to forgive people. I had confirmed and believed the lie in my heart that I would always be the outsider. I realized I needed to ask God to forgive me for siding with voices that whispered lies into my mind. Living from defensiveness made me in control of my life instead of living from God's provision. I kept a tight rein on what and whom I accepted into my life. I banned those who mattered out of my heart as I doubted and continually judged people's motivations. As long as this wall of self-protection stood, I could not let others come near my heart. Loneliness became my companion.

Missionary Parents and a Brother

During the years of battling my sickness and hospitalization, Dad had become a faith missionary. This meant he gave up his full-time job so he could spend more time visiting the sick and elderly people in hospitals and nursing homes. He told nobody that he had quit his job or that he now had no regular income.

He started to distribute little flyers with the Gospel explained throughout our neighborhood. Piles of neatly packed flyers stood in the hallway, and on a Saturday morning we all sat around the table and repacked these in smaller stacks for easy distribution.

Soon we had a large Bible study group at home and some teachers from the Dutch Reformed school even attended. The consequences of attending our group were that they were asked to leave the school as they did not adhere anymore to the teaching of the Reformed Church denomination. Both these teachers became missionaries. One went to Belgium, and another served in Nepal.

Dad also started a youth group at home. He was a great organizer for so many activities! For hours on end, he bent over rows of slides, carefully choosing those he could use to tell Bible stories with. At the end of a school semester, he hired a hall where he told the story of John Bunyan's *Pilgrim's Progress* or other topics with a slide show with audio sound effects attached. He organized crafts and arts, and he always finished the school year and youth clubs with a treasure hunt.

On a warm July evening, we were blindfolded and dropped off at the gate of one of the national parks close to our hometown. Several young people helped Dad get us on the way. They ushered us in the right direction toward the entrance of the forest. The hunt was cleverly put together with riddles, clues, retelling, and the use of memory verses which we had covered throughout the year. Dad hid a tape recorder in the branches of a large tree that was activated by someone who sat behind the tree trunk. The moment we arrived at the spot, the helper pushed the recorder, and it played a story with instructions and off we went to the next post. We came to another part of the park which led into high sandy dunes. It was hard going in the soft sand; the moon had come up and cast light on the path. As we walked the trail, suddenly a dark structure appeared, half built into the dune.

Our instructions were to enter the old WWII bunker and wait for the next clue. Hesitantly we stepped into the dark entrance and walked right into a tripwire that spanned the opening. It triggered another tape recorder, and a hollow voice told us to find a puzzle hidden in the sand at the far end of the cave. After digging around, we found a yellowed piece of parchment with a treasure map and a puzzle that gave us instructions for the next destination. These activities were the highlights of our youth events, and I even used Dad's ideas when I became a youth leader many years later.

One teaching I never forgot was how God truly could speak personally to us. Dad shared the fact that God wanted to have a relationship with us. He wanted to speak to us and had a plan for each one of us. A tingling radiated in my whole being as I thought about how it would be if God made Himself known to me. I asked Him if He would. And as my twelfth birthday approached, I decided to take God at His Word: "I love them that love me; and those that seek me early shall find me" (Proverbs 8:17 KJV).

I took this literary and on an early morning on the sixth of August—my birthday—I woke up to an already warm day. I just wanted to be with God that morning and I knew the perfect place where I could find Him. It would be close to the old castle where we would gather blueberries in the autumn. A small creek with grassy sides was the place I wanted to go and read my Bible. I was so sure God would meet me there and let His voice be heard. I started to walk, and within half an hour I had reached this quiet spot. When I lay flat on my stomach, I saw my reflection in the still water. Floating lily pads partly covered the edges like a comforting blanket, and it served as a haven of safety for bees that got trapped during their drinking spree. Small spider-like insects skated over the water's surface. I marveled at their ability to move so smoothly and not sink.

I read my daily devotional and prayed, "God, please come to me and talk to me; I want to know Your voice and get to know You better." How would His voice sound? Although I loved that time at the side of the creek, I didn't hear His voice. Time went by and suddenly I realized that my parents would wonder why I did not come for breakfast. Walking back, I decided to open my Bible while I meandered through outstretched gardens that surrounded the old castle. My eyes roved over a beautiful passage.

> *Ascribe to the LORD, you heavenly beings, ascribe to the LORD glory and strength. Ascribe to the LORD the glory due his name; worship the LORD in the splendor of his holiness (Psalm 29:1-2 NIV).*

I looked up and told God that I believed in Him. As I looked down to read further, a loud thunderclap rolled through the air. There were no clouds; I had not seen any on the horizon, and the thunder rumbled through the air. Chills ran down my spine and the hair on my arms stood up…further on I read:

> *The voice of the LORD is over the waters; the God of glory thunders, the LORD thunders over the mighty waters. The voice of the LORD is powerful; the voice of the LORD is majestic.*
> *The voice of the LORD breaks the cedars; the LORD breaks in pieces the cedars of Lebanon. He makes Lebanon leap like a calf, Sirion like a young wild ox (Psalm 29:3-6 NIV).*

I searched the sky high above me and imagined calves skipping in endless green meadows. The lightning flashes came quicker and quicker, and the whole air filled with thunder. I had no fear and was overwhelmed with awe. God talked right now through the thunder! He is real. I had asked Him to talk so I could hear Him. And He was talking right now, and I heard Him! As the first thick raindrops fell, I began to run. My heart sang; He had made Himself known to me, He had listened, and He wanted me to hear Him speak.

With great inner peace, I came into the house as Dad was making breakfast. He was surprised that I had been out already and asked what happened. Giddy and light with happiness, I told him what I had done that morning and how God had made Himself known to me.

Not long after this experience, I woke up in the night as a rhythm of beats went through my head. Every time it repeated itself, a word was added to the beat. I lay very still and listened to the continuation of the beat as it grew to a complete sentence. I had never heard a sentence like this before and I wondered if it was important for me to know where it came from—or, *who* it came from. Early the next morning, I asked Dad if he had heard these words before: "The one who calls you is faithful, and he will do it."

Dad did not recognize it but thought it had something to do with God, maybe a verse from the Bible. At this point in my life, I had not read much of the Bible and was very curious to know if God spoke to me through it. We pulled a concordance from the bookshelf and looked up the main words from the sentence and found it in 1 Thessalonians 5:24. I still had no idea what it was about, only that God was calling me and would fulfill His purpose through me. I decided to start a diary and write these kinds of God experiences down. That way I would know that, although I was not loved by my peers or teachers, someone else wanted me and had plans for me: God!

These special moments with God gave me great comfort over the years to come. Even with the protective layers I'd placed around my heart, God still had access. I will never forget these moments and the weight they had as a personal experience of His Presence. From this moment onward, although I felt rejected by the world around me, I felt chosen and called upon by God. This awareness only grew over the years, even when life didn't become any easier. My faith had found a solid foundation.

For years, my sister and I wanted another sibling. We prayed specifically for a baby brother so when Mum told us the news that she was pregnant, we were sure it was because of our prayers. Repeatedly she had miscarried, and she asked us to stop praying because losing her babies was devastating. As young teenagers, we didn't see it that way…our prayers were heard; those miscarriages were proof that God listened, It just was not the right time yet.

I was twelve when Mum got pregnant with my brother. The pregnancy was not easy. She had to lie down most of the time. We helped her with housework as much as we could, and I learned to cook. I would make a nice salad and arrange the lettuce, cucumber, and tomatoes on a plate. It looked wonderful, and I carried it upstairs to my mother. With a weak voice she profusely thanked us for caring so for her and taking on the household tasks. When we came later to collect the plate, all the food seemed to still be there. Many years later, she explained that we'd never considered washing the lettuce and the salad was full of sand.

For the first time in my life, Mum was not available to me whenever I needed her assurance. During the months she had to lie down, I cycled to school with my sister. Suddenly, school didn't seem as daunting as it had been, and I didn't have time to feel too lost without Mum being around all the time. When the holidays came, we were sent to a girls' summer camp. It was there that I discovered I didn't feel homesick. It was like a taste of freedom. I found that I could be confident in a world without Mum at close range.

For a while, my bleeding seemed to dwindle, and I felt stronger. When my brother, Chris, was born, I was incredibly happy. He was so cute, the perfect baby. Hannie and I were such proud sisters. I felt lighter than I ever felt before, with no pain, no dark moods, or oppressive feelings of anxiety. The whole family focused on this new life. My brother was the light and love of our teenage lives and somehow, I was relieved. I could fade into the background and not take up any space or demand attention because of my sickness. I never enjoyed being in the limelight as it seemed connected to being "that sickly child." We could all focus on something good and positive in our lives.

Miracles!

Life did take on a different cadence after Dad gave up his full-time job. Although as children we didn't know the practical implications of not having a regular income, we did notice that spontaneous presents were not part of our lives anymore. Fun parks, a visit to the zoo, and other entertainment options ended. Mainly because it cost too much money. Dad would still go for bike rides with us or take us for walks in the forest. The exciting fairy tales and made-up stories dried up. He focused on the Bible, told Bible stories, and applied the Bible to life. In general, life became much more serious.

We now went to a lot of Bible conferences with Dad while Mum stayed home with our little brother. I did enjoy these outings, as I liked God and I must admit, I learned a lot from the Bible during those days. The basic Bible knowledge laid a foundation, and I still profit from the deeper layers of interpretations that were taught by theologians during these conferences. We joined youth programs and we socialized with our peers.

Sometimes we went away for a few days and camped in our grandparents' orchard. They had set up an old-fashioned canvas tent under the apple trees. We left the tent open during the night and would wake up with heavy dew on our sleeping bags. The sun rose low over the meadows, the first rays just reaching our tent. Lazy cows grazed noisily on the edge of the barbed-wire fence. It looked like they had lost their legs as they seemed to glide through the rising ground mists. It was here I read of the Father's love for me in the Bible, "For the Father himself loves you dearly because you love me and believe that I came from God" (John 16:27 NLT).

As Dad was leading the Sunday school and youth activities, we had unlimited access to art materials. Behind the couch were stacks of puzzles, Bible quizzes, and games. We were never without an array of craft projects and reading materials. All with Christian content, of course. We also had a steady flow of visitors and Bible studies at home, and Dad gave seminars at hired premises that could hold dozens of people.

From the start of his journey of faith, Dad had not informed the church, his extended family, or his social network. He hadn't told anyone that he'd withdrawn from all forms of government financial support. He had chosen the life of a faith missionary. This meant that he asked and trusted God to provide and care for us as a family. Many family members declared him insane after they discovered he had given up a secure life and his developing career as a mechanical engineer.

During this time in our family life, we learned together with Dad what living in faith meant. When there was a need for medicine, food, or petrol, Dad gathered us, and we knelt in front of the couch in the living room. There, he brought before the Lord any requests that we had.

Medical bills still came in at a steady pace in those early years of Dad being a missionary. There was no financial assistance from normal sources like medical insurance or government programs. Mum shared later that sometimes she felt as if her throat was squeezed shut because of the anxiety she felt.

After Mum gave birth to Chris, she never fully recovered physically. Or so it seemed. She seldom joined us on hikes or cycling trips and didn't come to Bible conferences. She stayed home. Sometimes, when she had energy, she engaged with us, told jokes, and even danced to music on the radio. Overall, she became more serious and somewhat withdrawn from the world outside her home. Unknown to me, she had suffered heartaches that she was not able to share with anyone. One of her major challenges was how to budget for the irregular income from the financial gifts of supporters.

One early morning in the middle of the week, Mum got a phone call from one of our regular Bible study participants. This lady had just been studying the topic of tithing and how you could best distribute money wisely. As she knelt to pray and ask God for direction, she kept hearing our family's name in her mind. She had not heard of my father's decision to quit his job, so she didn't know there were financial needs. As she inquired further in prayer, she also heard a specific amount in her head. Greatly confused, she rang my mum and asked her if anything was going on in our family that she didn't know about. She shared the unexplainable messages in her mind and added that she was convinced she had misunderstood God, as she knew my father had a well-paying job.

My mother started to cry as she shared her panic after she had opened the mail that morning and found another hospital bill. She then told the lady that Dad had no income and that the amount given in her mind would cover the bill up to the last cent. Both were astonished at how God took care of our family. Faith never disappoints.

It was a rainy Saturday morning when Dad got a phone call from his sister that she needed to be picked up from the airport. We had a small car but no money for petrol to cover an extra trip. During the weekend, no mail would be delivered, there was no chance to get a surprise check in an envelope.

Dad called a family gathering at the now-familiar place in front of our couch. He pleaded with God to show His might as this would be a testimony to his sister. She had no faith whatsoever at that time and considered it an insane decision that my father had quit a well-paying job and an established career.

Before we went to our knees Dad quickly checked the mailbox to see if anything had been delivered—maybe an anonymous envelope. But the letterbox was empty. The time to leave for the airport approached, so after a short prayer, Dad checked again. It was raining steadily, and it soaked his slippers, but still nothing.

Dad's prayers became more desperate, and suddenly we heard our mailbox slam. Dad got up and walked to the front of our garden, lifted the green plastic top, and this time he found an unmarked envelope. He came back into the living room and in total silence, he slit it open. There was no sender or address, just money, enough to fill up our tank and for Dad to pick up his sister from the airport.

As we were hosting many Bible studies at home, Mum always wanted to serve at least a fresh cup of coffee and some biscuits. Not having money to spare on such luxurious items, she could not always buy these. When the last of the coffee was used—when she needed it most—some guests would walk into our kitchen and leave a packet of ground coffee on the bench.

I do not know how often Mum must have gone to do the weekly shopping while asking God to replenish the money in her wallet so she could pay for the groceries. We were getting used to asking the

Lord to provide and the sequence of going to the couch, kneeling, and presenting our requests to God.

Sometimes we complained about the lack of something nice or simple treats like slices of ham on our sandwiches instead of cheap jam. Some nights we asked for the obvious, "Mum, I would really like a banana…or chocolate sprinkles on a slice of white bread, or the Dutch spiced biscuits…" She would always reply, "Ask God to provide." Safely tucked away in our beds, we forgot to pray about it and just accepted that it was not in the house, and complaining would not help.

Then one night, the front doorbell sounded loudly through the quiet evening. Mum opened the door, and on the slap of concrete was a large cardboard box. She put on the outside light and double-checked and although she looked around the corner, nobody could be seen. Dad had to come out and help her carry the box inside the house.

And just as we drifted off to sleep, Mum called from under the staircase. "Children, please come and check this out!" Sleepily we stumbled out of bed and staggered downstairs. We gathered around the overloaded box. On top lay a bunch of bananas, a packet of ground coffee, and a large piece of ham to be sliced off. Many other items like biscuits and chocolate sprinkles, and extras we would not have bought even if we were rich. Right there we experienced another miracle of God's provision. We all gathered in front of the couch to praise God. And with a very satisfied stomach, full of bananas, we went back to bed.

These experiences didn't stop throughout the time Dad lived by faith. Even now, present day, Mum and Dad share incredible stories of God's practical and faithful care in times of their needs. For me, those early days of living by faith set the pace of never doubting God and how I can ask Him for whatever we require. He is faithful. This does not mean I did not go through tough times or seemingly unanswered prayers, but it laid the firm foundation, that God's character is full of grace, full of tender mercies, and with no condemnation. He knows what we need, so we can rest in His care.

Part 3

Teenage Years

Teenagers

High School

August marked the beginning of a new school year, and I felt anxious about starting at a different school. Despite the warm weather and the fresh scent of cut grass in the gardens along my route, my heart raced as I cycled to school. This sudden change disrupted some sense of security I had found in primary school. Not that primary school was safe, rather a sense of security from knowing what to expect. Nothing was familiar about high school. As I parked my bike under the corrugated cover, I wondered how this new chapter would be different from the last.

I did not fit in. That much I got straight away as I flicked my long-braided hair over my shoulder and straightened my skirt. Most of the girls dressed in the latest fashion, wearing tight jeans with flared bottoms, bright-colored jerseys, and draped shawls. They had short hair styled with clips and hairbands that looked perfect even in the rain.

I tried to be "normal" by making a new friend, a friendly girl I met on my way to classes. Our high school was divided into several locations in the city, and we cycled between the classes just to arrive on time when the teacher started the lesson. My new friend even invited me once to hang out.

But as I opened up to her about my childhood illness and my dietary restrictions, she abruptly ended our friendship. It happened one late afternoon as we sat on the floor of her bedroom playing a board game. She said, "You know, I think that you are too intense for me, and I have found another cycling buddy to go to our lessons." Astonished, I looked up and could not say a word.

Intensely sad, I unchained my bike and hopped on. A quick wave to my late friend and I sped around the corner so she could not see my tears. After that, I would cycle to classes alone, and I felt so desperately lonely and vulnerable. Would life always be like this? Would I ever find the right way to relate to others? Petra had gone to another school, and starting new friendships was so hard and foreign to me.

Despite the bullying and rejection, I faced, I held fast to my belief in God. During class discussions, I shared my perspective on how faith influenced my life. My history teacher found it amusing to challenge me with tricky questions about evolution, which he believed was the correct worldview. I could not help but stare at his wildly outstanding ears as he walked back and forth in front of the blackboard. Looking at his ears, I wondered if these were the cause of his belief that humans came from apes. He treasured a few strands of thin hair that lay flattened on his nearly bald skull. He smeared some product into these few hairs, so it shone and kept them clumped together.

He drummed into us that evolution was the right belief, and I stubbornly didn't go along. Angered, he stomped toward my table, planted his hands on either side of it, and leaned over. As he lectured me on the stupidity of my faith, his garlic-laced breath wafted over me, and I felt disgusted. When my parents asked the school to add the biblical creation story to the curriculum, the teacher made it clear that he disagreed with this alternative viewpoint. He also made sure the whole class knew this added material to the lessons came from my parents. This only made me feel more like an outsider.

As I approached my fourteenth birthday, something unexpected happened. My health suddenly improved, and the intestinal bleeding stopped. It was a year of change, both physically and emotionally. We moved again to another town and despite the challenges I faced, I knew that I had to stay true to myself and my beliefs, even if it meant standing alone.

1981: Driebergen, Province of Utrecht

My father had worked as a full-time missionary for several years now in his own country. He visited the elderly, organized youth groups, and held many Bible studies which kept him busy enough. Then he purchased an old milk service bus and converted that into a Book and Bible Bus. He parked it at marketplaces and central parks, so people could just walk in and have a coffee and chat.

Through this ministry, more Bible studies were organized, and Dad got involved in pastoral care. Many people came for advice as they shared their problems. These were people with drug issues and other addictions or who had been in prison because of trouble with the law and needed a place to go and recover. Others suffered from burnout or were depressed. They all required a peaceful and safe place to be heard and receive positive input through counseling.

Our house in Zeist was sold, and a large house with many rooms was purchased Dad named the house *Adullam* and explained that this was the name of the cave David lived in during the time Saul persecuted him, and many outcasts or people with debts and difficulties would join him in the cave. The house didn't look like a cave, it was a mansion with eight bedrooms, two living rooms, a large kitchen, and an attached apartment.

Within two years, my mum got burnout herself as she was always helping others. She looked after my two-year-old little brother and was on call 24/7 to those staying at the house. When she experienced a severe breakdown, she had to leave us for an extended period. She went to stay with family in France and because Chris was still very small, he went with her. Anxiety rose in my heart because now she was not available for anyone, including me. She was the one who listened to my school stories.

I changed schools. I was not sad to leave the school where I was bullied so often and never felt safe. I asked my parents to send me to a neutral, non-religious public school where I could disappear into oblivion, and nobody would know me. It did not turn out as I wished. The special public school I went to prided itself on being tolerant of all faiths and had a mission statement to be inclusive of all religions, but that was not played out among my peer group.

One day I woke up with the familiar knot of anxiety in my stomach as I prepared to go to school. I looked out the window at another bleak winter morning. The sun was hidden behind a thick layer of gray clouds. I packed my bag with schoolbooks and jumped on my bike. As I pedaled against the wind, it started to drizzle. Cold and penetrating wetness seeped through my clothes. It matched my feelings deep inside: dark, cold, and full of dread.

That day we had subjects like French, music, English, and math. The knot in my stomach had to do with the French and music lessons that were given by an eccentric teacher who was not engaged with his students. The teacher had the habit of sitting cross-legged on top of his desk. Sometimes he took off his shoes to play with his toes, and I made sure I chose my seat as far away as possible. The teacher would be absentminded as he corrected assignment papers from a previous class that littered his desk. In those unguarded moments in class, the bullying was at an all-time high.

After the French lesson, he started straight away with the next subject which was music. A tall boy who had just had a massive growth spurt, got awkwardly out of his chair and stumbled to the teacher's desk. "Sir, could we bring our own music for the next lesson? We could analyze the piece during the hour." The teacher thought about this suggestion for a moment as he chewed on his fingernails. Then he said, "That is a clever idea, and we can incorporate it as an exercise and assessment for the contemporary part of our curriculum. We would have to discuss the music, and I will critique it with my expert opinion." The boy grinned as he turned around and gave a thumbs up to his friends who were snickering away.

A week later, a tape recorder was put on the front desk and music was inserted. At first soft romantic music filled the classroom, then, as the piece progressed, it suddenly swelled to an instrumental impression of a full-on sexual encounter between a man and a woman.

The teacher never looked up from his desk while the crescendo vibrated through the room. The whole class had turned their chairs and shuffled into angles to have a better look at my face and check my reaction. As the color rose to my cheeks, I wished I could dis-

1981: Driebergen, Province of Utrecht

appear under the table. They knew I was a Christian, and one day during a break I'd shared my thoughts about sex. My stand was that sex should be within the marriage covenant and confirmation of a commitment to each other. When I had expressed my moral views on sex, I had no idea how much leverage I gave the group to ridicule me at a later stage.

I started trembling deep inside as my stomach churned. I looked at their smirking faces and for a moment I was paralyzed. Once again, I was the center of attention, and their laughing clouded my mind. I packed my bag and pushed myself through the tightly packed chairs toward the exit.

Later that night, I gathered all my courage and called the school principal and told him the story. I added that I didn't want to return to school. Unfortunately, I was not old enough according to the law to leave school or drop out. I still had months to go until I was legally old enough to quit formal education.

The next day during the morning break, when most of my classmates puffed away on cigarettes, they formed a tight circle around me. The largest boy was given the task to embarrass me publicly. He pressed himself close to my back and started to imitate the sound of the music of the previous day, all the while thrusting himself against my back. I ditched school for the day.

The physical education teacher took it upon himself to help me try to fit in. He oversaw the organizing of outdoor activities and school camps. Every year he planned a sailing camp at the lakes in the northern parts of the Netherlands. One day, as a watery sun pushed itself through the clouds, he came to invite me, "Please, Maria, at least try to be part of it and join our sailing camp. This really will help to loosen you up and you will make some friends!" I refused to go and told him that I was not interested in the upcoming event. He could not understand my reluctance and even promised me a room for myself if I would only join. Still, I made excuses. I had listened to the girls talk as they huddled together during the breaks and whispered that on the sailing camp, everyone would lose their virginity. After that piece of information, I certainly did not want to join!

School was my personal, daily torment. I started to doubt if life had anything in store for me other than being rejected by my peers. What made people feel uncomfortable around me? Did I have an imprint on my forehead, telling others that I was not like them which gave them the right to pick on me?

There was a girl in another class who asked me to come over to her place and do some homework together. I wondered why she had asked me, especially as she was not in the same year group as I was. We would only ever greet each other occasionally as we walked through the hallway. I found out that she was adopted, and she thought I must have been too as she observed we were both treated awfully by our classmates. She confided in me that during the breaks the kids were talking about me. Lowering her voice, she said, "You are so different from the rest; I heard the girls say they even feared you! You come across as an extraordinarily strong personality and you seem to be far above them and act like you do not need anybody! They decided to see how they could break you."

This made me analyze myself. There seemed to be a discrepancy between the girl I thought I was, and the girl others saw. I felt the opposite, I felt vulnerable and insecure. What made me so unapproachable to others? I wondered if I ever would be liked or accepted for who I was. I was like all of them, I just wanted friends to talk and walk with.

The Adullam House

I had fallen in love. Oh, those crippling feelings that seared through me when he looked at me. Mum and Dad would never agree to me having a boyfriend at just sixteen. It made this feeling even more hopeless. Soon, I found out the boy liked me, and he wanted to be my boyfriend! I couldn't believe it—someone liked me!

Mum had talked many times about boyfriends and such. She warned both my sister and me not to start kissing and cross physical boundaries within a starting friendship. She explained it this way, "Dear girls, when you start with physical touch early in your friendship, it will bind you in a way that can cause lots of heartaches if the relationship breaks off. Start with a friendship and get to know each other a bit better. Eighteen is old enough to start kissing and have a steady boyfriend. You only date with the serious perspective of a commitment to marry each other." It sounded so serious and so elusive.

To me being in love was more about having a mental time out from the horrible drag of school. Everything had been so dim. And up to that point, my head was full of dark thoughts. I started to write poetry, dark, wild, and hopeless. It expressed my need to have someone reach out to me and brush through my messy thoughts, giving me direction. I started to dream about the times I could see the boy again. Of course, my parents held those visits off which crushed and upset me. It was about having a goal to look forward to.

The days and weeks dragged on; everything was like a dark tunnel with no light at the end. I got terrible headaches and stayed home from school. The enormous amount of homework lay in piles in front of me, and a rising panic threatened to choke me. I tried to learn chapter after chapter only to completely forget everything I had read by the next day.

There was a safe place where I wanted to hide the moment I came home from school. Under my bed. It was cave-like, familiar, dark, and quiet. It looked like the inside of my soul. I learned to play the guitar, and I liked all the minor chords. I would make sad songs and I wrote sad stories. Really, from what I had seen thus far, life was not worth living. Old feelings of abandonment returned as Mum was going through burnout herself and was not available to me. I just wanted her home while I rested on a daybed in front of the window, watching her doing daily household chores, like when I was a child.

So here we were as a family in this huge house with many rooms, occupied by people who had problems larger than life and Mum was away in France to catch her breath. Whenever I returned home from school, the residents came to me and told their sad stories. Some were on heavy medication, others just cried a lot, and some were so upset that they vomited all over the wallpaper in their rooms. One young lady who was only a few years older than me shared her intense sadness and regret after she had an abortion. Another girl my age had been kidnapped and raped. To deal with her trauma, she would cut herself and crush burning cigarettes out on her arm.

I just listened, my face straight, my heart pounding. Some stories made my skin crawl, and my spirit screamed on top of its unheard voice. By the time I had lived my sixteen years, I felt nobody had any reason to live. I hid under the bed often. One day I just stayed home and vowed never to go to school again. We were in this house for two years.

My mother wrote in her diary which she shared with me many years later:

> Maria experienced a breakdown when she was sixteen. She demanded perfection from herself and couldn't bear to make any mistakes. I had to forbid her from coming home with high marks since nobody expected that from her. She lived her life so tightly! We kept her at home for a while until she started sleeping better and learned to relax. We then visited one of the small Dutch islands, Texel, where she rode horses through the dunes and galloped through the breaking waves of the sea. She thoroughly enjoyed this time. However, back at school, things went downhill again. She couldn't sleep, was always worrying, and never satisfied with herself.

Finally, I received permission to drop out of school. After gathering all my books, I returned them to the school library, grateful to leave behind those hated surroundings. Astonished students watched me, and I happily left them behind and stepped away from that place of torment. I had just turned sixteen and still had to complete my secondary schooling to obtain my diploma. This meant that I had to take an alternative pathway and start evening classes later in the year.

1983: Changing the Scenery

We moved again. To a beautiful town called Bennekom, in the eastern part of Holland. It was close to forests and on the edge of the Veluwe National Park, in the province of Gelderland. Gentle slopes with tall pine trees or low shrubs of heather covered this part of the land. In summer the smell of pine needles was intoxicating, and in winter, snow transformed the scenery into a Christmas postcard.

It was as if I had gotten a fresh start and I tried hard to be a person without a past. I convinced myself that this move would give me time to become visible in another form, like coming out of a pupa and taking off into the world like a butterfly. We changed churches and we attended youth groups. I played my guitar during youth weekends and enjoyed the organized youth activities. Nobody seemed to, *not* like me...

I walked for hours in the forest behind our suburb and explored the vast heather plains of the national park. Getting up early, I took my camera and stalked deer; I climbed tall trees to see squirrel nests. I loved identifying the different trails animals made and started to recognize when a fox or deer had laid down in the undergrowth. Sometimes I got up before dawn to hear the first birds singing, and I followed birds like the chiffchaffs, blackbirds, and robins. Nature became my world; this was my home. Here I wanted to stay and never enter the real world where humans could hurt me.

I dreamed of traveling and living in the nowhere, making a treehouse as described in the book *The Swiss Family Robinson* by Johann David Wyss. Or live in a tree trunk far away in the hinterlands of America like in the book *My Side of the Mountain* by Jean George.

As spring brought wildflowers to the forest, I knew the secret spots where different flowers would draw in forest animals. Some places looked like they were created for the animals and the fairy world, I was only briefly allowed to peek into their world and breathe in the perfume of the forest. My heart felt free, and I yearned to dance. I made up dances, twirling among the wildflowers. How I wished my parents would allow me to go to art, dance, music, and performing classes.

Since my parents had moved away from their conservative religious upbringing, they had found personal spiritual freedom. They also left behind extreme restrictions like staying at home or buying anything on a Sunday. We now drove to church on Sundays and purchased petrol if needed. We visited different youth groups and joined activities or went to Christian camps that were not part of a specific denomination. I went to a gym and got a membership from a library. In earlier years, memberships of any kind were frowned upon as we were only true members of Christ's body. Yet they still held on to restrictions on what they perceived to be worldly activities. Life on stage and going to the movies and theaters were regarded as worldly entertainment, exposing young people to the wrong crowd. Dad still had strong views on what was accepted within the Christian faith.

I had to wait quite a few months before I was old enough to go to evening classes with mostly adult students. To my astonishment, they included me in their conversation during the lessons. Learning became fun and I started to crave knowledge somehow, I was even able to remember what I had learned. I got the headspace, and I loved the freedom to move around in a school environment without feeling watched, ridiculed, or criticized.

I was also introduced to a different, more mature peer group. My parents had transformed our garage and built several rooms that could be rented out to university students. In the late afternoon, as rain patted on the roof, we sat on cushions in their room and listened to classical music on tape recorders. One student played the electric piano, and I played my guitar, and we sang till our voices were raw. We got into serious discussions about morality, destiny, and different worldviews. We shared our future visions and what we expected of life. I finally felt alive and accepted.

Future Visions

One night I had a dream, a different kind of dream than impressions of your own bustle of life. This dream seemed more like a vision for the future:

I stood in a large area with trees, and a huge grassy patch extended before me. Between the trees, a podium with loudspeakers was set up. Someone asked me to speak to a large crowd that had gathered. Standing in front of the microphone, I started to speak with great conviction and urgency. I spoke with an authority that was unknown to me, and people looked up and listened intently. I knew I was talking about God and His plans for each person, the Gospel, and biblical principles.

After waking up, I could not repeat what I spoke about as I had spoken in a foreign language. I decided to record this dream. Was it part of what I was supposed to do in the future? Would I be speaking publicly and sharing my life stories with others? I did not know, it just made me happy as I seemed to be walking in my destiny. Maybe I did have a purpose, although my life didn't look even closely related to a dream like this. In the denomination I grew up in, women were not allowed to speak in church. I had no clue where else I would be able to realize a vision like this.

Many years later, when I lived in Uganda, Africa, I was again confronted with this dream, and it confirmed God's purposes. Yes, God speaks through dreams and visions, and if from Him, they will never contradict His Word and will fulfill His purposes, for His Glory.

For a few years, I was happy. I jogged through the forest, joined a choir, rode horses at a riding school, and took up photography. Unfortunately, the disease from my childhood didn't give up on me. In my seventeenth year, it once again interrupted my life. I had just graduated and worked in a retail shop to earn some money. It seemed my sickness was determined to shape my life without my consent. Would I ever be free from pain, be without restraints, and not live in

Future Visions

fear that when it popped its head up, I would be punished for wanting to start living? At least that was how I felt about it.

Since we now lived in Bennekom, we had to register with another GP clinic for our normal ongoing medical care and to start my treatments again. This also meant handing over all the documentation that had accumulated over the years from the previous clinics. My file was the largest of the family and contained correspondence between the GP and the specialists...these had a profound impact on each doctor that read the binder. I asked my mother to reflect on what happened next as she visited the new GP in the area.

Mother

Maria was seventeen and a half when she went to evening classes to finish high school. This was a much better solution, and within a brief period, she finished high school.

She wanted to become a nurse, but she was rejected by the Nursing Institute because of her history of poor health. She looked for work and found a job as a retail saleswoman.

At seventeen she started to get stomach pains again, complained of severe diarrhea, and started to bleed. We had moved to Bennekom, and I had to gather all her past files and documents from the former GP and specialists. It had to be done quickly so the new GP could start treating Maria again. So instead of a request to send the files by mail to the new clinic, I collected the files from our previous GP. Before I drove back to the appointment with the new doctor, I decided to read through the reports as I was curious about the results from her last hospital visit in Utrecht where we had been treated so coldly.

To my utter amazement, I found a referral letter from the specialist in Amersfoort where she had been treated years before, after her operation. It read:

> Dear John, herewith I refer to you a child with bowel complaints. The mother tells with obvious and immense pleasure all kinds of bloody stories about the child over the last few years. The pale child with huge blue eyes cunningly knows how to manipulate her mother...

This document had entered the files of different doctors throughout the years. It ended up on desks in different hospitals, and traveled with us as we relocated cities several times. This document came into the possession of another GP in Bennekom where we only lived for two years, and he had added another memo to this file: "She lives in a sickening religious environment, which makes the girl ill."

After reading these condemning papers, I sat in the car and cried out to the Lord, "If this is so, and we are the ones to blame for all the suffering of my child, Lord, be merciful to us. I cannot bear this burden."

I decided to take these files to our new GP with the words that he better lock me up in a psychiatric ward if I was able to sicken my family in such a destructive way. When the new doctor read through the files, he was very angry. After a short silence, he asked, "Do I have permission to destroy these papers? These reports are biased in my opinion and have subjectively influenced all previous doctors. These reports have nothing to do with medical science." Of course, I gave permission and before my eyes, these papers were torn to pieces.

All the examinations had to start again from point zero. She was admitted to the local hospital and this time there was a genuine diagnosis: ulcerative colitis. As the doctor came in to talk to me, he asked me why I did not fill in the admission papers with this diagnosis. He could see from the scar tissue in her intestines that Maria had been suffering from this for years! No one had ever given us a diagnosis before. We never had insight into the medical files and did not know what she was suffering from.

The treatment was kind compared with other hospitals where she had been examined before. I was even allowed to stay until midnight. Every quarter of an hour, her blood pressure was measured. It kept dropping and she became weaker each moment. A nurse came in and sedated her to keep her quiet. She had to lay as still as possible, so the internal bleeding would stop. She was in the hospital for several months and it took years to overcome this bout of colitis. Maria was an adult when it finally left her once again for a few years.

Maria

This is the last account of my mother that I incorporate in this memoir to show the reader what impact it had on her and how she experienced and had to deal with years of my illness.

Coping with Life and Falling in Love

For weeks on end, I was sedated to give my body the rest it needed to heal. Slowly the colitis was brought under control, and I gained more energy. One day a doctor asked me if I would be okay to have a psychologist help me make sense of life ahead. As of this moment, it responded to the treatment and the colitis could go dormant. I would have to learn to live with a disease that could be activated without warning.

I sat in a chair by the window and stared at the shorn grass of the hospital grounds. I felt rejected by life itself and put aside in most areas of society. By now I had lost friends, had no job and no future goals. I felt empty and dejected. After this last bout of colitis, I concluded that being a nurse, which had been my dream, was the last thing I wanted to be. I had forgotten how much I hated hospitals.

It was now early January, and winter had Europe in its grip. I left the hospital and needed some time alone to reflect and decide what to do with my life. I decided to go to friends of my parents in Luxembourg, a small country in Europe. Here I could recuperate and regain some strength.

I spent most days walking in the forest, breathing in clean, fresh air. I followed small streams that meandered through gently rolling hills, took pictures of half-frozen waterfalls, and walked through lingering mists between the evergreen trees. Late at night, I walked the family dog through the mostly silent village where the steep streets were dimly lit. Smoke lazily floated from chimneys and the smell of wood fires hung in the still air. During these few months of recovery, I became fluent in German. Finally, I felt strong enough and decided to go back to the Netherlands.

I explored what I could do with my life from now onward. A psychological test showed I had good insight into technical matters and so I tried to enroll in a technical college for fine mechanical design and engineering. As I walked through the buildings of the college and studied the different subjects, I got excited. Maybe I would get a trade and flourish.

I entered a large office where the dean of the school held enrollment interviews. He offered me a glass of water and asked me to sit down while he went through my application. Shuffling the papers in front of him, he nodded and finally looked up. "It is wonderful you have applied, and I am sure you can get a placement as the college board wants more females to enter the trade. However, I will need to further investigate your references and admit them to the board for the next meeting." Standing up, he extended his hand and said enthusiastically, "Keep it up, I would like to welcome you soon to our school."

Each day I looked in the mailbox, expecting the acceptance papers. A few weeks later a large envelope made my heartbeat go faster. I tore off the top and whipped out one page with the verdict in the letter. To my utter dread, I read that the board had rejected my application considering my medical history. Deflated, I walked into my bedroom and cried. All options and chosen directions for my own life seemed to be taken away. I concluded that I might only be good enough for an office job. I should stop having any ambitions.

Within a short time, I got diplomas in shorthand, word processing, and administration. The office jobs I was offered bored me stiff and since I sorted the mail and archived applications, I daydreamed throughout the day. If the weather was good enough, I used lunch breaks to sleep under bushes of the well-maintained gardens of the large complexes, so the day would go faster. During winter months, I read every magazine that came through the mail, especially the articles on travel.

Soon I saved up enough money to get my driver's license and buy a car. Life seemed to be just a little more attractive, as I now had the freedom to go wherever I wanted. And then I fell in love again.

I was seventeen going on eighteen. Sitting at the kitchen table, I saw the shadow of a man passing by the windows. With long steps, he strode through the backyard and entered the kitchen door. As I looked up at him, I was speechless. He was tall, muscled, and the image of my dreams. He wore a leather cowboy hat; long legs were dressed in faded tight jeans, and a wide leather belt decorated with a large nickel buckle circled his waist. He walked a little bent over as if he carried the weight of the world. A mustache made him look like the Marlboro Man on the cigarette posters displayed on the highway. During his stay with us, he did not want a bed, he just slept in his sleeping bag on the soft grass in our garden. His lifestyle was a total novelty to me. He represented freedom and seemed led by an adventurous spirit that I wanted to embrace.

The nights were balmy and warm in the weeks after summer. He came from New Zealand, and he introduced a life of travel to me as he recalled how he backpacked through Europe. While he was with us, we took him to the touristy places of the Netherlands. In the evening, we walked our dog and talked, talked, talked. He laid out his plans to visit his many extended family members during his stay in Europe. I could not help it; I was rapidly falling in love. I could not eat and looked forward to when he would come and visit us again before going back home. On our last walk through the forest, he kissed me and promised to write to me.

I embraced it all, the image of travel, a man who wanted me, and a possible promise of life overseas! To me it was obvious I could not be part of life in the Netherlands. The endless push for more academic papers and the rat race for higher-paying jobs depressed me. None of the jobs I did held any interest to me; administration proved to be so boring. My mind looked for expansion, and this society didn't offer it without higher education. And that was not an option in my mind since my health closed doors. Not to mention the struggle to belong.

Although I had made up my mind to leave the Netherlands as soon as I could, I was too young to marry and wasn't ready to leave my parents. But I had a goal in life: I would work hard and earn money for a ticket and would immigrate to New Zealand.

I wrote letter after letter to the one who promised to write to me. Occasionally he would write back, which made me wonder if he was still interested in me. Much later when we talked about this, he admitted that he had severe dyslexia and was not confident in writing and reading. I didn't know that when he promised to write, and the disappointment of not working toward a committed relationship was, in my mind, a failed attempt to get out of life in the Netherlands. It created despair in my heart.

A dark cloud of hopelessness descended, and depression settled in. How could I get out of this rut of a boring life? Was I destined for this ever-dreary lifestyle of going to work each morning, doing work I didn't even like, and coming back home after dark?

Over the next years, I had short-lived romantic relationships, just for the sake of falling in love. Life just came alive with color when you had adrenaline pumping through the body. Still, depression deepened as I slipped into a dark and deep pit. My colitis kept coming and then receding again. It never left me so I could get on with life. I was always on medication, always in pain of some sort.

Eventually, I got so depressed that I could not work and entered the horrifying treadmill of the unemployment dole. To get these government payments I had to visit psychologists and doctors who only wanted to push me back into the workforce again, while I felt unready to embrace that path. Only nineteen and dependent on government pay, I felt like an outcast and a failure.

Part 4

Adulthood

A New Start

One summer we went on holiday to the very north of the country, to the Province of Friesland. A small village lay tucked away between large lakes and outstretched meadows. We got to know a family who dedicated their lives to counseling and assisting youth who had run aground. Soon I moved to this small town, and I became part of a large family.

The young people around me seemed full of energy and with an incredible zeal for life, although they'd all had their fair share of difficulties. In summer we went fishing on the lakes or boating along the channels. The boys would rock the dinghy until I fell into the murky waters that stunk of sewage. I walked against the fierce winds that whistled through the tall reeds that hugged the edge of the lake. High waves pounded over the dikes when autumn storms scourged the water. I worked for weeks on end on an old farmhouse that needed restoration. I painted window frames and dug up weeds that had overtaken the gardens.

I told nobody how old I was; I felt like a young teenager and wanted to just play and exist, catch up on what I'd missed out on. For a moment in time, I felt happy as the change from a dull administration job to engaging surroundings lightened my spirits.

The nights though were bad. I had horrible nightmares and sometimes hallucinated. I got so scared that I had to wake the house parents in the dead of the night to calm me down. They gave me herbal pills that made me sleep throughout the day and soothed the crippling anxiety. It helped me not to think, not to worry about the future, and not to be so depressed.

Every few months, I had to get check-ups done for my colitis and the medication I was taking. During one of these visits, I finally got my hands on a printed *Consumer's Medical Information* leaflet. I read about how this type of medication had been in its final trial stages, and it informed me that one of the side effects was hallucinations. After I read this, I adjusted the medication to a level that allowed the colitis to stay under control and free my mind of destructive thinking patterns and horrible dreams during the night.

After the restoration job on the old farmhouse, I was asked to help with all kinds of little jobs around the house and assisted the elderly in the church and other extended family members. Most of them had lived in this small town for generations. It felt solid and secure; somehow, the old people made me feel as if I also lived fifty years behind the rest of the world.

One late summer evening, the news came that one of the elders of the little church I attended had died. His wife didn't cope very well with life as a widow. The couple had been together for over sixty years, and her husband had overseen most of their daily activities. I was asked to be her chaperone, while she adjusted to life on her own.

Her house was full of antiquities that old people gathered throughout their lives. Nicely polished copperware decorated the windowsill of the living room. On the kitchen bench stood a ceramic teapot with its knitted warmer. The boiling water on the stove misted the windows and was ready to be poured on tea leaves or ground coffee. The sink was made from baked earthen stones with only a cold-water tap. My bedroom was in the attic where there were no washing facilities or a toilet. On the wooden bench, under the slanting beams, an old-fashioned washbasin with a water jug had been placed. Just above it was a small window that you could open and secure with a wooden slat so it would not slam closed on the sloping roof. The lady of the house filled the water jug every day, so I could wash upstairs in my tiny loft room. The bathroom was in the outhouse, next to the garden at the back of the house. Somehow all of this felt right. Full of memories and hints of having lived a past life.

Then one morning as I chauffeured people to their activities, which was one of my daily duties, I felt this increasing pressure to finish it all. The skies were gray, the asphalt roads to the city were gray, the ancient houses in the village were colorless, and the insistent drizzle made the cobblestones a dull silver. Everything looked dim, and certainly, I had the right to die. The old fellow we had recently buried was more at peace than his now abandoned wife and me as her young—but at the same time, old—attendant.

As clouds gathered and the sun disappeared behind more gray patches, I decided to visit the graveyard. I just wanted to experience the feeling of lying on a patch of freshly uprooted grass. For years

A New Start

I had tried to live; there was not much point in trying to do much more of this. I sat for a long time next to the grave, burying my fingers in the dug-up earth. I stared out over the drenched, glistering meadows as it drizzled from the heavy clouds and obscured the horizon. Cows grazed close by, and swallows swooped around the small chapel. I decided to talk out loud to God. Nobody was there to hear me, and I didn't care if anyone was there to listen to my lament:

"God, I never doubted Your existence, but life doesn't seem worth living. I long to either live with purpose or just die. Please, God, show me if You are still interested in my life. God! Show me Your intent! I do not know how to live. If this is all You have to offer, I am tempted to start living the way I like. I could even end up being a so-called loose woman if that means it will make me feel alive. I want to go places; do things before I die. I want at least a taste of what life might have been like. God! Are You there?"

As I gazed around me, the shining shape of a Man appeared a distance away in the meadows. I could not see a face; it was just an outline of a Man. In front of Him, a young woman knelt, crying. He lifted His hand and laid it on her bowed head. As I watched, I felt the hand resting on my head! I realized I was looking at myself, kneeling in front of what must be Jesus. Then He spoke, "Maria, would you just like to sit down at my feet as Mary did, choosing the good part, which will not be taken away?"

I lost track of time; I lifted my face and the soft rain mingled with the tears I should have cried years earlier. As I cried my heart out, incredible joy flooded my soul. I didn't know what came over me, and as I stood before the lowering sun, I said again "Yes" to Jesus. If I needed to sit at His feet instead of living a life that I thought would bring me joy, I wanted to choose that life. It felt so good, His hand on my head, I would never forget the moment of penetrating love. Slowly, I rose from the gravesite and stood up. The last rays of the sun for the day peeked from under the clouds and cast a low light over the meadows as I made my way to the cemetery's parking lot.

That evening in the small attic, I fell asleep with a lightness that I could not remember having had for a long time. The next morning, I began to read my Bible from a totally different perspective. Not just taking in what it said and adding knowledge about the Bible and God. All at once, my heart received the living Word. Whatever I read made sense, it fell into place and came alive.

Whenever I went to church, the preacher seemed to speak to my situation, and I felt inspired. Every morning I woke up and read eagerly, chapter after chapter. I walked for hours while I read my Bible and found so much depth in it, so much understanding, so much to take in. The Old Testament came alive, verses sprung up as if highlighted and they gave me the impression the Word was alive.

I suddenly understood with much more clarity the reasoning of Apostle Paul which previously had just been long, heavy sentences to me. It filled me and guided me, it renewed my thinking, and a desire to live consumed me! I wanted to know how I could live a life at Jesus's feet, listening to Him, with His hand upon my head. This was the place where my soul had truly found rest. Slowly I crept out of the dark tunnel of depression and investigated life again. I started to make plans to maybe travel, study, and live!

I rented a place for myself and got several jobs, working at the checkout counter in the supermarket and even in administration again. I had become part of the small community I lived in, and I liked the stability. At the end of two years, I told God I was ready to break out and start somewhere else, whatever He had in mind.

An elder at church invited me to a Sunday lunch. I explained to him that the next day I had to visit a specialist for another check-up on my ulcerative colitis and discuss potentially an operation for a colostomy or stoma. Looking intently at me and sensing my worry, he offered to pray for me. We sat under his pergola; the white tablecloth rippled in the breeze. Some birds flew through the leaves of an old oak tree planted in the garden. As he prayed over me, he suddenly looked up and said, "Maria, stop your worrying as I believe you are healed."

I went for the check-up the next day, and, as the doctor bent over the emerging images of intestinal lining, he finally broke the silence and said, "I cannot find any activity of the colitis. I can see a lot of scar tissue which you will have to have checked out every two years to exclude wild growth or cancer. Young lady, your ulcerative colitis has gone dormant."

The World Opens Up

I felt fully alive! Like a flower blooming brightly, I was ready to be picked. Several young men asked me out. I received love letters and invitations to start a relationship. I basked in the feeling of being wanted, but none of them captured my heart as I had experienced when I was seventeen. To me, most of them lived boring lives and I wanted adventure, travel, expansion, and growth. I wanted to live with someone who would be as intentional as I was in life. Someone with passion, with the power to get things done in life, someone who could lead and be led, someone who would love me and challenge me to be the woman I was supposed to become.

I dreamed of travel and adventure, wild countries, exploring and being part of creation in all aspects. I longed to climb a high mountain, swim in crystal clear streams, sweat through jungle pathways, and see plains that teemed with wildlife. I was so ready to live life to the full! Without knowing it then, I would experience all of the above.

And then the man that had captured my heart at seventeen came back into my life for a second time. I was older now and we went for long walks. We connected on so many levels; we had so much to tell each other. I allowed myself to be captivated all over again as he described his life of adventure, setting up a business, flying a plane, and traveling all over the world.

It was easy to envision myself in that lifestyle. This time it would be serious. We told my parents of our intent to date which seemed to be fine by them. Much later I understood how much they prayed and worried over this choice of mine.

On the last day of his stay, early in the morning, he quietly woke me up. Later that day, he would leave for New Zealand. As not to disturb my mum who shared my room because we had guests, he softly kissed me long and hard and whispered that I should come to New Zealand and marry him. He gave me a thin gold necklace and promised to prepare his place for me so I had a house to live in.

What more could I ask for? It looked like he had everything to be able to care for a wife. It looked like the right time, as our family was on the brink of a new beginning. My sister was married and pregnant with her first child, and my parents were in the process of moving to the Caribbean to become missionaries on a small island called Curaçao. It was the perfect time for me to leave the Netherlands for good.

I did, however, have a huge question on my mind about God's perspective on my choice. How would I know I made the right commitment? I had promised God that I would only go where He guided me. Did He have anything to say about whom I should marry? I was also afraid that any of my children might end up with my colitis. I asked my doctors about this hereditary disease, and they assured me there was only a small chance that my children would inherit it.

I struggled through the questions, nonetheless. I was fearful of making a wrong decision. I asked God to speak to me about my children and possible diseases that ran in the family. On one of my many walks through the forest, I opened the chapter in Isaiah that spoke to me personally:

> *Woe to those who quarrel with their Maker, those who are nothing but potsherds among the potsherds on the ground. Does the clay say to the potter, "What you are making?" Does your work say, "The potter has no hands"? Woe to the one who says to a father, "What have you begotten?" or to a mother, "What have you brought to birth?" This is what the* LORD *says—the Holy One of Israel, and its Maker: Concerning things to come, do you question me about my children, or give me orders about the work of my hands? (Isaiah 45:9-11 NIV)*

It was quite easy to apply those words to my situation, regardless of the context or intention of the prophet Isaiah. I concluded that it was okay for me to marry, God would take care of my children, and I should not question God about it.

Once I saved enough money, I stepped confidently into a travel agent's office and booked a ticket. My heart fluttered as I handed over the money and got back a slab of thin paper with the travel details pressed into several carbon copies. Now I only focused on the immediate future. I was going to travel; I was going to live the life I had dreamed about. I packed my personal belongings in boxes and sold all my furniture. I thought it to be a pleasant surprise for my husband-to-be that I would arrive unannounced on a flight in late November 1987. I boldly stepped onto the rollercoaster of life.

> Reflection:
> I had to learn so much about God and how to apply Bible verses. He gives freedom to make life choices and keeps prompting along the way to include Him in the process. God's work through us is done best when we are in total surrender to His guidance. This means listening to Him carefully and obeying what He tells or shows us, one step at a time. We need to be careful how we fill in the direction.
> I do not think that the events that followed were the consequence of my choices alone; both of us were required to take responsibility and follow His principles. Both of us were accountable to Him for this relationship we chose to pursue. Despite the choices I made, He would accomplish what He had planned for me. It was going to be a painful journey.

I locked the door of my rented house for the last time. The weather had turned cold, and the first frost covered the winter grass. I made a last walk through the forest as if I knew this would become a long good-bye to my homeland. The leaves on the oak trees had turned into the autumn colors of orange and soft hues of brown, and it reflected my mood. Nature was preparing for the long winter months ahead. And I was preparing to go away from a life of pain and frustration, away from a country I felt did not want me.

The day of departure finally arrived. As we climbed up from the runway, the sun cast a long shadow of our plane on the gray clouds beneath me. Pale, blue skies stretched endlessly above me as I looked out from the small aircraft window. I would not be returning for many years.

A song from our church hymn book entered my mind and I hummed it softly. Suddenly, I became conscious of the words. It startled me and quickly I pushed it away. The song that played over and over in my mind said, "Your Name alone should be written into the depths of my soul."³ I didn't want to reflect on the gentle reminder of God to keep my focus on Him. I only thought of the years ahead with an expectation that I was starting life all over in a new country with the man of my dreams—traveling, living, and of course, as an afterthought, serving God.

Reflection:

Years later I would be reminded of these words when I had just done the opposite and had given my heart away without any reserve. I expected a human to soothe my soul, and—at that moment in time—I didn't turn to God to fulfill me. I was still searching for my own identity and wanted to fill the hole that the trauma of my youth had given me. I had fallen in love with the image and representation of travel and freedom, not the person who had introduced this to me through his stories.

1987: New Zealand

New Zealand's sloping hills appeared beneath me while the plane banked toward the landing strip. After more than thirty-four hours of travel, I appreciated the fresh breeze cooling my face when the aircraft doors opened. I could see far into the horizon as I stood high in the door of the plane. Hesitating briefly to step out into the bright sunlight, I inhaled deeply; there was a pureness in the air that intoxicated my spirit. Strange smells excited me. What else would be offered to my senses? I expected this new life to captivate me and sweep me off my feet and plant me firmly into my destiny.

Subtropical plants were in bloom as it was springtime at this end of the world. Butterflies danced in front of me as I walked over the tarmacked walkways to the domestic departure lounge. Auckland was a busy city, and the buzz of people around me made me feel lighthearted. As I dragged my suitcase behind me, I walked tall and with confidence. I lifted my face to the sun, and the rays felt different on my skin, more penetrating than I had ever felt in Europe.

A smaller plane carried me to my destination, the city of Wellington. This time as we descended, I could not see anything through the small window as rain enveloped the plane. High winds that channeled through the Cook Strait rocked the aircraft while landing. This was how the next years of my life would look like, sometimes breathtakingly beautiful, the next moment destructively ugly.

I had phoned ahead to break the news that I was flying into Wellington that day. With a pounding heart, I walked through the arrival hall, scanning the faces waiting for their loved ones. The tall handsome man that asked me to come over and marry him, stood at a distance from the crowd. Dread filled me as I looked at his unsmiling face, he certainly did not look happy to see me. Silently he loaded my suitcase into his car. The wind flapped through the canvas of his soft-top jeep, and water dripped through the partly zipped-up, plastic windows. He negotiated the traffic, and the gears of his car crunched as we entered the hills around Lower Hutt. He stated that he had never expected me to pack up my things and come to him that soon.

My head spun from jetlag, and I tried to keep the conversation going. Gone was the entertaining man with exciting stories of his travel and the jolly personality that would have a whole room dancing while he played the mouth organ. I was confused as he seemed a different person than the one I had fallen in love with during his visits to Holland.

He did arrange for me to stay with an older Christian couple for the first few weeks until I had found my feet. Springtime in Wellington was so much colder than I expected, and in the evening, they lit the fire in the hearth. The couple had emigrated from Austria years ago and spoke German at home, which I found easier to speak than the school English that I had not practiced much. The woman baked wonderful Austrian cookies and made elaborate meals. During dinnertime, they gently told me what they knew about my boyfriend's past. With carefully chosen words, they told me about his troubled childhood. They described the background he had grown up in and how early trauma could influence people. He had been in their lives for quite a few years since he had left high school and had become a competent tradesman and businessman. I got the impression that they were preparing me for some disappointment in my expectations of him. Were they warning me that this relationship could be a difficult one?

Whenever I was in turmoil, I went into nature and would find peace. I needed to be alone, and because I had not found a job yet, I looked for nature trails all around Petone. I walked for hours through the stunningly beautiful hills. I followed a small stream next to a track that led to the top of a hill on the edge of town. Clear water tumbled down from little waterfalls as I followed it upward. Peace entered my soul once again. The water was cold on my feet when I skipped the rocks that emerged after the receding spring floods. The sun pierced through the canopy of large trees of which the root systems kept the banks from washing out. Rays of light danced on the unique palm trees which looked to me as if they were dwarfed fern bushes. Later, I learned they were silver ferns.

As I explored the beautiful surroundings, I tried to come to grips with the man that I thought I loved and cared for. I concluded things would get better and I could change him back into the person I had known while he was traveling through the Netherlands.

After a few weeks, I discovered that he wasn't even thinking of getting married. Making money and working as hard as he could was more interesting to him. Sometimes he worked up to twenty hours a day (he slept only four hours at night) and did all kinds of handyman jobs, including house painting contracts and licensed tree felling. I often accompanied him on his jobs simply because I wanted to be with him.

One day, I found myself perched high on a ladder, sanding and polishing the windowsills of an old country manor. The next day, I would accompany my boyfriend on a tree felling job. Down in the hills, there were sprawling estates where owners wanted trees felled for firewood to last through the winters. My boyfriend climbed up the trunk with spikes on his boots and hauled up a chainsaw. The sound echoed through the treetops, and sawdust rained down on me as I gazed up in awe, watching him balance in the swaying canopy. Once the heavy branches hit the ground, I would use a smaller chainsaw to cut them into smaller pieces and then drag the leafy branches to one side and stack the wooden blocks to be split at a later stage.

He also imported small, high-quality power tools from Europe and other items from Japan. Sometimes, he imported secondhand cars from Japan and sold them to car dealers around the country for a good profit. His business was his top priority in life, but I was interested in a relationship, not money. In the following months, I had to adapt to his demanding schedule, which was unlike anything I had experienced before.

During a brief break from work to drink some water, he talked about his dad with a determined voice, saying, "My father, family, and teachers all told me that I would count for nothing. I will prove to everyone that they were wrong in their assumptions!" Was he working so hard just to prove himself to his family and society?

His house was built on stilts and stood on a barren hill of low shrubs and black granite rock. It caught the sea breeze that would have been lovely on hot days. It turned out, however, that a constant chilly draft played underneath the house. The house was surrounded by steep grassy lawns that were kept short by a grazing goat on a chain. When storms roved through the harbor, they thundered upward toward the house which got the full brunt of strong gusts of wind. The windows clattered, and the temperature dropped inside the house. The howling sounds gave me chills, and I longed for a warm place to relax. This fell far short of my dreams.

One night, after an exhausting day of arduous work, he asked me to assist him with his accounts and fill out ledgers for the GST (tax) return. Busily he went about gathering a pile of books and stacks of loose receipts. "When you finish the work, I'll take you out for dinner," he promised.

As the evening rolled on, and hunger pangs rumbled through my stomach, I thought of his promise that we would go out for dinner. I worked on the floor because the table was full of other equipment. My legs got pins and needles and my feet turned numb, and I shivered as the time slipped by. Night settled in, and I wondered if he ever planned to take me out for dinner. I got up and asked him if he had some food in the house because it was now too late to go to a restaurant. He responded that we could only go out after we finish the tax return.

My insides churned and I felt like exploding, *"Going out where?"* Did he have any sense of time? It was far past midnight! What was I doing in this bone-chilling house, with a workaholic who apparently did not even seem to have the normal desire to eat or feel hungry? I stomped out of the living room and slammed the door as I left the house. After taking a few steps, I turned to peek through the window from the outside. He was bent over the ledger I had left open, continuing to enter receipts, messing up my neatly written row of numbers. He had not even noticed I'd left. Slowly I walked up the steep hill, back to where I was staying. My throat constricted, and a strong, sharp pain sliced through my heart. I started to sob and pulled hard at my hair until I had a clump of it in my hand. It counteracted the heartache I felt.

It dawned on me—life would never be as I had dreamed it would be. That night, my heart broke, and the pain was severe and physical. It was only one example of how slowly my dreams faded into oblivion. I was too young, too innocent, and he wasn't ready for the commitment and responsibility of starting a family of his own. I didn't have the insight yet that much of his reluctance came from his family background and upbringing. I just thought it was because he didn't want us to get married.

1987: New Zealand

At one point, he showed me another property with a shack built on a very steep piece of the land. The shack clung dangerously against a cliff, braced by steel columns driven into the hillside. It was even more exposed to the fierce winds blowing from the Cook Strait than his other house. As we walked through the near empty building, he mentioned that if we ever marry, he could make this shack livable for us. How could he talk about this, while none of his actions pointed to such commitment? As I stood looking over the valley beneath me, my heart filled with sadness.

Suddenly, a clear picture formed in my mind of what my life would be like. I pictured the wooden workbench where he proposed to make the kitchen, where I could cook on a camping gas stove. I saw myself slipping on the way to the outdoor toilet that could only be reached by narrow steps into the bushes. It dawned on me that I might not want to get married.

Shattered Dreams and Nature's Respite

I had to move places several times and ended up living in a garage with a mattress on the floor. I believed that sex should wait until marriage, so we didn't live together. That's why I moved from family to family several times and finally rented the garage where I thought I could stay until we married.

I started to work as a waitress in various restaurants to earn money for some groceries and other necessities. Sometimes I cleaned cars for money, and when he went overseas, I would tend to his business.

I was drawn to him because of his exciting stories about traveling. I had dreamed about accompanying him on these trips. He repeatedly booked business trips, never inviting me to join him. I took care of his business from his drafty stilted house, where the wind squealed underneath. I never saw any pay as he would say when he left, "You do this to show me you love me." And I would do it, feeling trapped and unsure of my options.

Later he moved the business to a shopfront in the industrial area of town. Seldom did clients come in to buy something, and I was alone for days on end. Most equipment was sold through advertising by wholesale companies. I loved the high-quality tools he imported from Europe—hardware tools, engraving and wood-carving machines—and I started to experiment with the tools myself. I especially got the hang of glass engraving.

New Zealand had several expos throughout the country: the stonemason expo, a farm expo, and country fairs on showgrounds where rides were set up and cattle paraded. Working with these tools was a great asset during these shows, where we rented a booth to exhibit the wares. It helped to sell whenever clients saw what you could do with them. And it helped me through the dull pain that I experienced in the relationship.

During the daytime, I would work in the business, and in the evening, I worked as a waitress. After waitressing, I returned to work for my boyfriend till deep into the night. Whenever I could, I also went to a gym to work out and it stilled any physical and emotional hunger.

At times, one of the assistants at the gym would gently advise me to take days off to avoid damaging my body. I didn't listen to their advice and added more weights to the exercise machines. As music pounded, sirens blared, and motivational cues encouraged everyone to keep pushing themselves, I strained myself to the utmost of my limits. Suddenly my shoulder gave way, sending searing pain down my arm. Ignoring the pain and potential injury, I refused to give up exercising. I continued living from job to job, gym day to gym day, and surviving on biscuits and coffee.

I was unaware of the harm I was doing to my body. By the time I left New Zealand after three years in 1991, I weighed only 45 kilograms. Years later, I had to undergo shoulder surgery to repair the damage I had caused due to neglect.

Life became a strange experience. I lived a double life, together with someone, still always alone.

I went to church and was part of children's ministries and set up a Bible club in the area. A group of enthusiastic young people designed flyers and distributed them throughout the neighborhood to advertise our end-of-the-year show. I wrote a play where the children acted out several Bible stories. To make the play even more professional, I asked an artist to paint a backdrop for each scene. It became an immense success, and, as the last curtain dropped, I was surprised by the loud applause that exploded in the room. Afterward, we celebrated with some coffee and cake, and people asked me when I would create another show like that! My boyfriend was not part of it.

One of the youth pastors in the church who worked with troubled youth asked me to assist him on a three-day kayaking trip on the wild rivers of the North Island. Enthusiastically I booked the trip and expected my boyfriend to join me at least in this adventure. Then he pulled out at the last minute and headed back to the office. With tears in my eyes, I packed a duffel bag and drove to the place where we would start the trip. As I pushed off my kayak into the quiet water of the Waitangi River, I felt so lonely.

But as always, nature is a healer. As I floated on the water, my soul quieted down. The rugged beauty captivated me as we paddled through silent gorges and fought the white water of the rapids afterward. It lifted my spirit, and I pushed all my heartaches aside. The sun made the water sparkle, and fish jumped out ahead of my kayak. As the sun sank behind the riverbanks, we dragged the kayaks out of the water on a narrow strip. Some boys dug our campsite out of the embankment, and we laid our sleeping bags under the tightly roped tarp for the night.

From a watertight container, I grabbed some crackers and spread layers of peanut butter on them. Water boiled in a billypot hung over a small fire. I took my tin mug and prepared a rich, black tea. I leaned back against a tree trunk; thousands of stars appeared above the dark, moving river. The moon peeked over the rocky cleft on the opposite side and the soft light played on the water's edge. It turned the white pebbles on the small beach into glistering diamonds. If I half closed my eyes, it danced like fairy lights.

When we got back To Lower Hutt I decided that I would do more of these outings. I joined a nature group that organized trips into the bush. On one such trip, we bought truck tire inner tubes so we could float down a stream that meandered through the forests of Lower Hutt. I hiked local mountain trails of the hill country beyond Wellington as well as climbed waterfalls in a nearby reserve.

I changed jobs; instead of working at night in restaurants, I took an office manager's job with one of the car dealers in town. This also made me less available to work in my boyfriend's import business, but at least I felt less dependent on him. On this salary, I was able to buy a car and pay for rent and other expenses.

My new boss had a partner dealership in the South Island and sometimes imported cars needing to be transported there. Once, he asked me to drive a car to the West Coast, which turned out to be a few wonderful days of sheer beauty as I drove through the most stunning places on earth. Here I got a taste of New Zealand's beauty.

I drove the car onto the ferry from Wellington to Picton. As we slowly entered the inlet of the Picton Harbour, after three hours of rolling seas, I inhaled the pure, crisp air of the South Island for the first time. White-painted slat houses dotted the soft rolling hills at the foot of the Marlborough Sounds.

Early the next morning, I drove into the sounds and sheer cliffs rising left and right of the winding roads. It was winter, and the sun would disappear behind the rocky outcrops, leaving the roads in gloomy shadows. Suddenly I entered a breathtaking valley where country-style roadhouses offered hot meals and a bed for little money. The early morning frost over the meadows had dusted the grasslands into a crisp white blanket of crunchy blades that broke the moment you walked on them. It reflected my experiences in life. As the temperature rose, wisps of mist crept over the shallow inlets around Nelson.

After hours of travel, I looked up and took in the majestic peaks of the Southern Alps, where Mount Cook proudly topped the highest point of the South Island. I decided to take an extra day and climb the Franz Josef Glacier. With sharp spikes bound underneath my hiking boots, I braved the slippery slopes and gazed at the enormous mass of slow-moving ice. As I took some time to take pictures, an incredible peace filled me. Here I felt close to God and His creation.

When I returned from this trip, I decided to move farther north for a while and work in the orchards of the Fruit Bowl of New Zealand. I rented a small caravan in the backyard of friends and slowly built a different life than I thought I would ever live while in a relationship.

Whenever we did visit each other, we had long and hard discussions which often ended up in the exchange of harsh words that pierced through my already hurting heart. I didn't want to give up yet, even when I saw the rift widening between us.

A Dying Relationship

At my suggestion of taking some time apart or breaking off our relationship, he threatened to throw himself off a bridge. This confused me because from the first day of my arrival he seemed uncomfortable with my presence in his life. My mind became muddled. How did I end up feeling that I was responsible for preventing him from jumping off a bridge? I didn't see a way out of the situation— not enough money to go back home, no hope for a future together, always moving around, constantly entertaining a false hope that things would change. I finally stopped envisioning a marriage.

After a trip to Australia to promote his business, he came late to yet another place where I was staying. I was house-sitting this time, and he banged on the door. Yawning, I opened it and then offered him a drink. Instead of sitting down, he took my hand and pushed a large golden ring onto my finger, and announced this was my engagement ring. Stunned and still sleepy, I looked at the huge ring with a row of diamonds set in gold. It felt heavy and cold; I had to clench my hand into a fist as otherwise, the ring would slip off. I wondered what had gotten into him by doing it this way. Was he suddenly afraid he was losing me? Had he decided to get married, or did someone speak into his life, and he had a miraculous change of heart?

The next morning when I woke up, I had to look for the ring as I had lost it between the sheets. It was several sizes too big. I wrapped some tape around it to keep it on my finger. Later that day, I asked him what had gotten into him. I always had envisioned a romantic visit downtown to choose a ring that would fit me and would be something I liked. What did I have to conclude: that I now was engaged? He argued that it was a good ring and that he had traded it for tools with a business partner back in Australia. It also would have another benefit; this ring was an investment. It would be worth a lot more in a few years. "We will sell the ring if the business isn't doing

A Dying Relationship

well. We can put the money back into the losses," he said. I felt like an investment, not a partner for life.

I had taken on a second job and stocked shelves in a department store at night. I had cut my knee and ended up in bed with a nasty infection and on heavy antibiotics. With my leg high up on a pile of pillows, I got time to think and come to my senses. The friend I stayed with, and who looked after me, came into my room and sank beside me on the bed. With great care, she placed a tray with afternoon tea on my blanket. Looking out the bedroom window, she tentatively asked if this was the life I had dreamed about. She continued, "If you could envision your life now, does it look like what you thought it would be? Would these two pictures line up, and are you certain you want to continue this relationship?" She had overheard us on the phone and saw the pain I went through and knew this was not a healthy relationship.

I cupped the hot mug of tea in my hands and slowly sipped the brew, trying to formulate an answer. "Strangely enough, although I had suggested it to him a while ago, I didn't dare to act upon it. The last time I spoke about breaking it off, he reacted so strongly by saying he would throw himself of a bridge, that I decided it best never to mention it again." It was silent for a while. The wind rustled through the leaves of a tree outside the window, incessantly the branches scratched the awning of the house. I shook my head as if to stop the niggling truth from coming to the surface and I added, "I burned all bridges when I left the Netherlands and feel ashamed about the failure of our relationship." I had not stayed connected with friends in the Netherlands, and I had withheld the truth from those with whom I exchanged some letters. Deep down, I thought that maybe I was not entitled to a better life.

My friend nodded and laid her hand on my hand and briefly squeezed it. With her soft voice, she said, "You have the power to stop this painful relationship, you have the right to break up. You are not yet married, and you have no obligations. You can still walk away from this."

When she left, I contemplated the idea of walking out of this hopeless situation. I feared that there would be nothing on the other side, only an empty page. Wouldn't it be easier to just continue as I was, in a familiar setting, and learn to live with it? My childhood experiences taught me that when things went bad, you just bow your head and take it. Others were in charge of your life and had authority over you, so you submitted to it. Because of these ingrained feelings of powerlessness, I didn't feel like I could make a final decision.

Still, the thought of ending the relationship kept creeping back into my mind. I considered the three years of heartache and a total loss of a sense of what I was doing with my life. I began to face how far I was from a fulfilled life with the man of my dreams. The struggles during these years made me realize I had compromised my core values regarding family, finances, and faith.

I had come here with faith in God and the conviction that He would guide me. I had lost confidence in my relationship with God and ceased to invite Him to be involved and direct my life. I longed for those intimate moments with God when I freely talked to Him in prayer, and He graciously answered. I wanted to be free from guilt, shame, and inner condemnation.

I still believed that even if I had lost sight of the purpose of life at this moment, God might have a destiny and get me where I really should be.

As the truth dawned on me, I was utterly amazed by how blind I was. Why did I not see what was happening? I should have known this was not a healthy relationship. I had good models from my parents as I grew up. I had experienced God's faithfulness throughout my life; now I felt unworthy of His intervention. What made me choose to continue to live in a dysfunctional relationship? How come I made these choices that caused so much hurt? I had to find the answers to these questions to avoid losing myself or despising myself later.

I started to read my Bible more frequently to hear from God. And one of the first verses that jumped out to me was, "Free yourself, like a gazelle from the hand of the hunter, like a bird from the snare of the fowler" (Proverbs 6:5 NIV).

I laughed aloud; this was precisely how I felt, like a bird caught in a net. The reality was that I was free, not married, and had no attachments and no reason to stay. A sudden excitement soared through my whole body, the realization that I could make a choice and fly away! It was as if I had woken up from a long sleep. Once I decided, I didn't want to stick around too long or allow anything to change my mind.

Fleeing a Trap

Practically speaking, I had no money to buy a ticket, so I prayed for a miracle. Within the month, a lady approached me and asked if I could keep an eye on her property which she had just put on the market. She had booked a ticket to see her family overseas and could not be present if the house was sold. She promised to give me the commission fee if I sold the house. This would be a substantial amount—if I sold it for the price she had listed it for. I agreed to look after the sale while she was away and left it at that. I did not expect anyone to come forward to buy the house.

After a day's work, I walked back to the house where I was staying. Here I didn't even have a bedroom, just a camping mattress on the floor in the sunroom of my hosts. The moment I entered the house, the phone rang, and the caller asked if he could see the house the next day. After showing him around, he put in an offer. My hands started shaking, and I asked if I could think about it and call him back. I had no real estate experience and no clue if the proposed price was within a normal range or if I needed to negotiate further.

I asked a friend who said, "You do not sell a house for the price they offer. You put a percentage on top of the offer, and keep in mind the actual price you want to sell it for." I made a bold decision, and instead of negotiating the amount they had offered, I added ten percent on top of the amount the owner okayed. Miraculously I sold the house within a week. The commission I received from it was more than enough to pay for a ticket out of New Zealand.

I knew I could not yet tell my fiancé that I planned to leave New Zealand for good. I would only break off our engagement once I was somewhere else in the world so he could not convince me to stay or return to him. Three days before my flight I told him I was going to visit my family. By then I had booked a ticket to my parents, who still lived in the Caribbean. I didn't tell anyone, not even my parents, that I was going and leaving New Zealand for good.

As the plane lifted off and I entered the vast cloudless sky, a surge of freedom ran through me. The world was big; I was twenty-four years old, and I felt accountable to only God and myself. I ended this part of my life with the realization that there were no limits to what I could do with my life. I felt like a bird leaving the nest to start the long trek to wherever it was directed to by the seasons. It was the path of the sun, on the power of the wind under my wings.

It was also the first time I embraced the fact that I was an individual who could say "no" to people or situations, with the power to choose and the strength to fight for what I wanted in life. I had been in New Zealand for over three years, and it did leave its mark.

Reflection:

As I write about this chapter in my life, I have no intention of passing judgment or having the reader judge. God gently showed me how to deal with pain, sin, and injustice. I learned what forgiveness meant, forgiving myself and forgiving others. Years later, I would see how this chapter in my life worked out for good, how God restored and gave me a life with my husband who fully allowed me to pursue all the dreams I had as a young girl.

I counsel women and hear many stories of how young people entered relationships, expecting their partner would heal the gaping wound of rejection in their souls. Or how they expect their partner to change into the person they want. Through my own experiences, I quickly recognize when a situation is unhealthy. If any of my readers find themselves in such circumstances and want to escape the trap of losing self-worth or even fear for their safety, you need to reach out to someone you trust and contact Godly counsel. It is never too late to change direction in life.

I had to be healed of the deep wounds that this time had inflicted. I had to learn that I had made some of the life choices because of a root cause that grew from past traumatic experiences. God continued His work in me, and I am being restored to the person He had in mind even before I was born.

Living by the Power of God and receiving His wisdom and understanding can only be accomplished when the heart is open to be renewed and changed into God's image. It requires the surrender of self and acknowledging the sin of wanting to be independent of God.

It also means forgiving others and becoming free from exercising the right to be vindicated. Holding onto our hurt can quickly turn into anger, resentment, bitterness, and revenge.

Part 5

Married Life

1991: Curaçao, the Caribbean

On a hot and steamy tropical Sunday afternoon, after church, Mum and Dad went for a nice picnic on one of the sandy beaches of Curaçao. Curaçao is a long, arid, and primarily flat island, stretching some 64 kilometers from southeast to northwest and, at its narrowest just 15 kilometers wide.

Mum and Dad settled under the shade of a little shack with a thatched palm frond roof. As they enjoyed the beautiful deep blue water and a spectacular sunset, Mum saw the daily scheduled plane coming low over the sea water on its descent to the runway. As she looked up, a surge of emotion overcame her, and a strange thought occurred to her. She said to Dad, "I have the feeling that our daughter is on that plane." I was on that plane. The bond between a mother and daughter can be powerful.

The humid air caught my breath as I stepped off the plane onto the tarmac. The sun had set, and fairy lights illuminated the few booths for rental cars in the arrival hall. Snorkeling tours and diving schools were advertised on colorful posters. A display with business cards for hotels was placed close to a money exchange booth which was unoccupied.

After collecting my luggage, I was unsure of what to do. After the first hubbub of disembarking, the hall returned to a quiet space where ceiling fans buzzed and moved the humid air. I realized I was stuck at the airport, had no local currency yet and didn't know anyone. I got some change from the information desk and called my parents. Nobody answered.

I tried to remember any names of friends my parents might have mentioned in their letters, so I could call them as all taxis had been taken.

I went over to the phone book and started looking for familiar names, hoping to jog my memory. It was only a small island, so there couldn't be too many pages in the book... Then my eye caught a familiar name: a name that my parents had mentioned. Unfortunately, half of the island seemed to have that name. I just picked one, thinking they might know my parents, and asked the information desk for more change to dial the number. It was a miracle; I had called close friends of my parents who also visited the home church at my parents' place.

With a broad smile and very white teeth, a tall Islander came to greet me. He enthusiastically pumped my hand, which disappeared in his firm grip. With a booming voice, he said, "What an honor to meet the daughter of our pastor of the church!" They took me into their home, where I enjoyed a hot cup of sweetened mint tea. After several unsuccessful attempts, my mother finally answered the phone, "Maria, how exciting to hear your voice. I was right! You were on that plane! We will be there soon!"

Later, I had the privilege of meeting this kind man again. He turned out to be the CEO of the Center of Correction and Detention "Koraal Specht." He provided me with the clearance to visit the women's prison and give Bible studies. But that's a story you will read about in a later chapter.

I settled in quickly and was amazed at how my little brother had grown into a young teenager while I was away. They had a gorgeous little dog that often followed me around. I loved the house with the cacti spread throughout the garden and aloe vera growing in the shadows. A large frangipani stood in the sandy soil, and its white and yellow flowers covered the ground. Mum did her laundry outside in the open carport, and the gray water from the washing machine fed the banana trees, which gave abundant fruit.

After three years of living under high tension, I could finally let my guard down and relax. I grieved that I was not successful in having a relationship and getting married. I sought solitude and spent most of my days swimming and snorkeling in the warm Caribbean waters. Questions filled my mind, and I felt lonely and wondered if I would heal deep inside. At the same time, I felt relief from having been able to get out of a relationship that proved destructive for me. As I cried myself to sleep at night, my parents' little dog would crawl under my sheets, as if it knew I needed comfort.

The sun, healthy food, and the beauty of the underwater world had their effects; I began to think about a different future. I wanted to travel more and become part of a mission organization that went around the world, aiding less fortunate people groups. I might also want to pursue a different career; I thought about becoming a teacher this time.

There was a small church at my parents' place. Each Sunday, a group of people met, and my mother thought it was a good idea to do some activities with the young people. Chris had turned fourteen and had a seventeen-year-old friend named Nelson. These were the only young people in the church at that time.

A few weeks later, another young man turned up during the Sunday services. He was the son of another missionary couple from the Netherlands, and his parents worked in Suriname, a country in the northern parts of South America. He was twenty, named Bart, and had come to the island to study.

In the following weeks, life became sunny, lighthearted, and joyful. I rented a four-by-four and crisscrossed the island with these three young ones. We explored mysterious rock caves on the northern coast and raced over the barren coastal plateau. Every day, we snorkeled and swam around colorful corals and tropical fish. On one of our tours, we discovered an underwater cave and as we dove into the water, large schools of fish scattered only to return to swim with us. Breathless, we emerged within the cave to take gulps of air before we swam back into the shimmering ocean. Sun rays filtered through the blue water and surrounded me with the silence of healing peace.

In February, the island celebrated the carnival. Schools and universities closed for a long weekend of endless partying. Downtown was filled with the sound of drums, brass bands, and pageants. Show cars blocked the roads into the city center. The streets brimmed with dancing crowds wearing colorful costumes. Bart's boardinghouse was in the city center, and it was not safe to hang around during the weekend. Drunken people and "Chollers" (the homeless and drug addicts) would roam the streets, and this led to thieving and violence. He decided to spend the weekend with my parents as the celebrations would go on day and night.

For an outsider or tourist, it was an exhilarating experience. However, the cheap distribution of drugs killed many youngsters, and domestic violence exploded because of the binge drinking over several days. Every year a baby boom occurred nine months later for teenagers who had no idea who the father was.

Bart had to get some schoolbooks and clothes, and I drove him into the city before the festivities began. Partying had already started, and throngs of stoned and drunk people milled through the streets. I parked as far away as possible away from the commotion to safeguard the rented car. We still had to cross the crowded streets, and the uncontrolled mob scared me. Suddenly Bart firmly gripped my hand and guided us through the horde. The care that I felt and the gesture to reach out to calm my anxiety made me feel safe. There was more to this young man than I thought, and I started to like him.

Soon everybody had to go back to work and studies. Once again I explored the beaches alone. As I pondered my future, I asked myself, *What will you do with your life?* As I soaked up the tropical sun, I talked quietly and seriously to God about this question. How did I know if I was good enough for a life partner, had I learned from my mistakes? I wanted some assurance so that I would not end up as a lonely missionary in some forgotten place on earth. I came up with some suggestions for God that became a prayer: "Please, God, heal my broken heart, help me find the right man. Or open a way and direct me to the right study. If it is Your will for me to become a missionary, please provide clear guidance on how to pursue this path. And please clarify where that would be."

I gave Him plenty of choices. I started to write to schools and mission organizations; I didn't want to sulk away my time. By being proactive, I hoped it would fill the space inside sooner rather than later.

Out of the blue, I became sick. My whole body ached, and my eyes were so swollen, it felt like they wanted to pop out of their sockets. Each ray of light pierced through my head, which pounded as if ready to explode. The fever raked through my body, and the violent chills afterward exhausted me. Soon a local GP diagnosed me with dengue fever. A few days later, Bart showed the same symptoms, and as my parents had committed themselves to looking after him while he was on the island, they placed his stretcher bed next to mine in their bedroom so that my mum could nurse us day and night.

One late afternoon as we slowly recovered, a shadow fell across my bed. I looked up through the window, and a shock jolted through my body; outside stood my ex-fiancé! How could this be? I had written to him soon after I arrived in Curaçao, telling him that our relationship was over and that I would not return to New Zealand. I had been clear that the engagement was broken off. Seeing him now paralyzed me, and a knot formed in my stomach. He had spent a lot

1991: Curaçao, the Caribbean

of money to fly halfway around the world to see me again. I feared he might have revengeful intentions or would try to talk me into going back.

It suddenly dawned on me that Bart lay next to me, weak with fever. My mum rushed into the room and told Bart to get out through the back door. A wrong conclusion could be drawn, leaving Bart in an awkward position. My father intercepted my ex-fiancé and kept him in the office while Bart found his way to a friend's place.

Hours later, a very emotionally charged ex-fiancé sat next to my bed. As I expected, he pleaded for me to come back with him to New Zealand. He promised to be a much better man and would marry me this time for sure. He went on about his riches and how he would get me everything I wanted. I perfectly fit into his life and was an advantage when I accompanied him to all the woodworking shows. I could present my crafts and show potential customers how to use the imported tools. It would sell more products. He also mentioned that he had informed his clients and business partners that I had stopped working for him. Apparently they were eager to hire me as I would be a valuable asset to any business. I guess that could be taken as a compliment!

The night settled in, and the crickets began their evening concert. Their noise amplified the tumult in my head as I listened to him. I had wanted him but realized he would never make a good husband for me. The crickets were drowned out by a barking contest among stray dogs on the street. A warm breeze fluttered the curtains in the bedroom, and I shivered as the fever returned. I struggled to control my breathing and prayed for my pounding heart to slow down.

As the commotion outside died down, a lone owl hooted in the branches of the frangipani tree. Somehow, its sound reassured me, as if it were the guardian of the night. A peace entered my heart as I became aware of another thought: Physical attraction is a force to be reckoned with, but it is not a foundation on which to build a long-lasting relationship. I understood that I had projected an ideal image onto this man and never truly accepted him for who he was.

In the brief time I had enjoyed the carefree friendship with Bart, I came to realize that there were many other aspects to consider before entering a meaningful relationship. Commitment to God, common ground, friendship, and shared experiences, even growing up with a similar background was a much stronger, more convincing reason for a lasting relationship.

As I listened to his reasoning, it became a distant babble. I refused any of his offers and asked him to leave, as I felt weak from dengue. I thought this to be the closure and definite end to this chapter of my life. However, months later, I would find out he had not yet accepted the fact that I was gone from his life.

Island Life

Every weekend, Chris, Nelson, Bart, and I went on adventures like hiking, exploring the island, and swimming. Sometimes we went into the city and roamed the markets that sold mostly souvenirs to tourists. We enjoyed the views from the floating bridge in the middle of town and absorbed the Caribbean lifestyle. Steelband music filled the narrow streets, and we bought freshly squeezed orange juice from a small stall on the corner. An old fort wall that surrounded the harbor was a great spot to fish from.

When Chris and Nelson couldn't come, Bart and I met up on the beach and went swimming from bay to bay. We tucked away some money in our swimsuits for ice cream at the next bay. We enjoyed afternoons of swimming and sitting under the palm trees. We chatted for hours and discovered that we had so much in common.

Both our parents were faith missionaries, and we exchanged the unbelievable miracles that had happened in our families. Both our parents had experienced how God, in His faithfulness, always provided for all our needs. We both had grown in our faith as we watched our parents live out their Christian commitment to God. This confirmed to me that God was aware of our situations, and He had been shaping each of our futures as both of us searched for guidance toward our destinies.

The sun filtered through the swaying palm fronds, casting playful shadows on the sandy beach. We bought some hot chips from a vendor on the bustling beach and sipped an ice-cold Coca-Cola.

As Bart shared his future vision, I was struck by how mature he was. He understood the essence of life without any arrogance. After applying more sunscreen, he said something that further piqued my interest, "I would like to work in civil engineering and build roads to improve infrastructure for the impoverished. Work is only a priority if it allows me to make a living. I do not want to live for work, become a workaholic, or acquire riches. My motto is simple: I work to live, not live to work." His approach sounded so relaxed and balanced! This intelligent young man had a mission.

Growing up with a work-driven father who served as a missionary, the priority was always on serving people or supporting projects. Bart had noticed this trend in his own family and observed it in the lives of other missionaries. As missionary children, we often lamented the absence of our fathers due to their engagement in ministry activities and commitments.

Another major concern for us was the way our parents were supported financially. Since they were independent missionaries and not affiliated with any organization, there were not many long-term support groups organized for them for a retirement. Their finances mostly came from donations by immediate close contacts and subscribers to their newsletter. I saw the impact of this uncertainty on many occasions during my childhood, particularly on my mother as she dealt with a fluctuating income.

As independent missionaries, they had no access to cross-cultural training and simply followed their calling, packing up and leaving their home country. At the age of fourteen, Bart underwent a massive culture shock when his whole family was uprooted from an ordinary life in the Netherlands and relocated to a foreign culture without adequate preparation.

At the time, there was little written about the experiences of Third Culture Kids, who often found themselves moving frequently across the globe and experiencing long-term impacts on their development. There were also few resources to prepare families for the challenges of adapting to new cultures with unfamiliar customs.

Bart shared how he felt as he grew up in a multicultural setting. "I knew that I was Dutch, we spoke the language at home and ate Dutch food. Suriname is an ex-colony of the Netherlands, and their primary language is Dutch too, but that didn't mean they lived like the Dutch. My friends and I spoke another language on the streets and in school: 'Sranan Tongo.' At school, I heard Hindi, English, and other dialects that were spoken throughout the country. Suriname is home to many cultures and has a diverse socioeconomic background. I learned to adjust to several diverse cultures within my circle of friends. When I visited my schoolmates, I ate food that my mum would never cook. I was exposed to a different standard of life. None of my friends came from a privileged background."

Island Life

After spending many days and weekends together, we developed a comfortable friendship. I started to look forward to our times together. We formed a deep connection without even realizing it. At the same time, I felt pressure to move on and start my own life again. I needed to make some important decisions and did not want to burden my parents. Finally, I booked a ticket back to the Netherlands after the wonderful months of recovery from my heartache. I had to start somewhere, and I thought I should give my own country a second chance.

Early one morning I heard rustling at my bedroom door. Sleepy, I got up and found a folded piece of paper under the door of the small outdoor annex of the house where I slept. As I started to read the letter, all my fears and doubts about the future rose in me again. Bart had written a long letter to me. A tribute to our times together and that he would like to pursue a deeper friendship. Bluntly, he asked if I wanted to correspond with him when I left the Caribbean, with the intent of starting a committed relationship.

I spent most of the last days on the island alone on the beach. I frantically searched my heart to see if I had it in me to start another relationship so soon after breaking off my engagement. Could I give him what he deserved? I had already lived a life, messed up a relationship, and had no clue if I wanted to try again. I felt uncertain and shaken, my heart still so vulnerable.

He deserved a proper, honest answer. On one of these last evenings, I asked Mum what she thought to be the best type of man to marry. She repeated the answer we had discussed so many years ago while she would come and sit at my bedside. I was fourteen then, and already worried that I wouldn't marry the right man. She soothed the upheaval in a teenage girl's mind and counseled, "Maria, marry your best friend."

I realized that Bart had become a friend, maybe even a best friend. The next day, I would tell him I'd like to correspond with him and see if it would last, not yet entertaining the idea of a long-term commitment.

After an idyllic snorkel trip to the now well-known underwater cave, we climbed the rocky coastline and gazed over the impossibly blue waters of the sea. Bart stood next to me, and, as he sought my hand, he asked, "Please, would you consider not just an informal friendship; would you want to become my official girlfriend?" Then he leaned over, looked me in the eyes, and gently kissed me. Far below us, my brother and Nelson started to cheer, making faces, and giving us thumbs up. Embarrassed, I drew back from Bart, still unsure.

A few days later, he asked my dad for permission to court me. It seemed this young man had values and respect for older generations, which made me feel secure. We had a last dinner together, and the next day I flew back to the Netherlands, leaving a small waving figure standing on the runway by the setting of the Caribbean sun.

I didn't know what the future would hold, but I did find some answers to my questions to God I had asked only a few weeks earlier. He had already healed so much of my broken heart by just allowing Bart to come into my life. Still, I was careful not to give my heart away without checking with God first. I was determined that I would make decisions with full dependence on God. I wanted to listen very carefully as He guided me through the upcoming choices of life.

More Travel

As the plane slowly descended through a thick layer of clouds, the Netherlands appeared below me. Although I loved traveling, I wasn't looking forward to the gray, cloudy, and gloomy weather of the Netherlands. The wintry climate reflected my mood, and my anticipation for new opportunities plummeted as the temperature dropped. I immediately longed for the warmth and light of the sun.

I searched for a job to earn some money and tried to settle in while exploring the possible study directions available. Luckily, I was offered an administrative position at a company where I had worked before going to New Zealand. I rented a room with a family from the local church I visited and loved the friendship that developed with the lady of the house.

After a while, I established a daily routine and decided to put my search for universities and courses on hold. Bart and I corresponded every week, and I relished communicating with him in this manner. Whenever I returned from work, I eagerly checked the hall table for an envelope from Bart. We relied on snail mail, and to keep the weight down, we used special thin airmail paper. As time went on, our letters grew thicker as we shared more stories, daily activities, and thoughts. Waiting for answers to our questions required patience, but it was well worth it. Our correspondence allowed us to get to know each other in a profound way.

If I had thought all ties had been severed with my ex-fiancé after he visited the island, I was proven wrong. Unknown to me, he had found out that I had returned to the Netherlands, where I lived, and found the telephone number where I stayed. He started to call me again. Although I said repeatedly that I had no interest in restoring our relationship, he still wanted to come over and visit me. He wanted to hear it from my mouth without my parents present.

Uncomfortable and suspecting he would go to any extent to see me again; I thought it best to move places and only tell my destination to my immediate family. All I wanted was to be left in peace and simply get to know Bart better through our correspondence.

I rented a mobile caravan on a remote farmhouse in the north. It was not an official address, and the farmers did not need to inform anybody that they rented their caravan on their private property to a single lady. It was a peaceful place, and the large caravan stood at the end of a well-maintained garden. Beyond the pruned roses and other perennials, the open wide space of the meadow gave me a sense of freedom. The caravan had a small kitchen, a bedroom, and a lovely small living space. I felt safe in this secluded and quiet spot. I just drove to work, and, on my return in the afternoon, I enjoyed a cup of tea in the early spring sun. This was how I wanted to live for now.

One evening as I cooked a simple meal, a knock sounded at the door. Excited, I opened it as I expected the farmer to bring the mail. Instead, my ex-fiancé stood in the doorway. He somehow had figured out where I lived. To my surprise, this time I was not shocked and paralyzed by his appearance, like I was when he came to see me in Curaçao.

Silently I let him in and offered him a cup of tea. Then I sat down and asked him, "What are your intentions and why have you come to the Netherlands?" Of course, he said that he wanted to see me, but I knew it would not be just to see me; it involved spending money, so I suspected he was here because of business. He acknowledged that he was combining the visit with a trip to the tool factories which he imported tools from.

This freed me up to share that I had a boyfriend and had been writing to him for some months now. I told him there was no possibility that I would come back into a relationship with him and that he needed to accept that. It came as a shock to him, and, after a long silence, he asked, "Do you have any proof that you have been writing to someone?" I quietly got up and showed him a picture of Bart in Curaçao and a small postcard on which Bart had written that he loved me. It dawned on him that I had meant it by breaking off the relationship and accepted that I would not return to either the relationship or New Zealand. After this encounter, I didn't feel the need to hide or live in a remote place and I rented a room closer to my workplace.

After his visit, I settled into a quiet rhythm of work and life. I enjoyed the beauty of the spring flowers and absorbed the warmth of the summer days. The meadows turned deep green and were dotted with dandelions. I inhaled the harvested hay, and the smell reminded me of the late summer evenings of my childhood. I cycled for hours through the countryside. Still, I knew I would never be at home in the Netherlands or have the desire to live here long-term. The office job was dull, but inwardly I felt renewed and awaited the coming life seasons.

During these months, I received two proposals to marry. One man danced upon my desk, singing his longings for me. On the same day, another colleague knelt next to my office desk and asked me to marry him instead of the man who had declared his love earlier that day by dancing on my desk. I had a strong urge to giggle at the strangeness of the situation, and for a moment I was flattered. I saw the sincerity in both young men, but by just looking at their lifestyles, I knew they could not offer anything sustainable. The entire world lay before me, and setting up life in this small country town did not appeal to me.

Back in Curaçao, Bart entered his final years of study and had to find a temporary workplace for his six-month-long practical assignment in civil engineering outside the island where he studied. This was mostly because there weren't many civil engineering companies in Curaçao, with just one main road to maintain. An opportunity popped up in Suriname, and he decided to move back to South America for this workplace experience. While he packed and prepared, he wrote to me and asked if I wanted to join him, saying that he would like to introduce me to his parents.

I was somewhat hesitant because I had already left my country before to join a man somewhere else in the world. To safeguard

Reflection:

Years later, I would meet my ex-fiancé again. Time had healed some wounds, and we were able to express forgiveness to each other during a brief visit to New Zealand. It would take another twenty years to have a prolonged telephone call, in which we would be able to share some specific moments when so much pain had been caused. We acknowledged that we both had such different expectations while we dated and had lots of baggage from our pasts. After this conversation, he sincerely apologized for the deep hurt he had caused. We were able to conclude that God had worked through heartaches and shaped our characters. I can now thank God for the painful experiences of the past.

myself, I agreed to go only if there was a job for me and I would live separately from him and not be his responsibility. Soon enough, I received an invitation to work in an orphanage and manage the facility with another couple as the house parents went on long service leave.

Suriname

Suriname is sometimes referred to as the "Caribbean of South America." Indeed, although I came to the continent of South America, Suriname did not have the Latin influence like the other countries on this continent. It is part of the "Guyanas," tucked between French Guiana, where French is spoken, and English Guyana, where English is the main language. In 1975, Suriname became independent of the Netherlands and kept Dutch as the formal language. The vast tropical Amazon rainforest stretches from the Atlantic Ocean in the north to deep into the interior. All three countries share their southern border with Brazil.

The original inhabitants of Suriname are the indigenous Amerindians, nomadic groups that did not adhere to the drawn-up borders in the region during colonial times. Throughout the dark history of slavery, they played a significant role in liberating black slaves who were offloaded into the Port of Paramaribo to be sold in markets. The Amerindians staged raids on plantations and led the slaves into the interior, where traditional West African villages emerged deep in the jungle. Their language is still closely related to West African tribes.

Slavery was booming, and many slaves were put to work in the sugar industry. After the abolition of slavery in 1863, the country invited low-cost indentured laborers from India, Java, and Indonesia. Soon, the Chinese followed and operated small grocery shops scattered throughout the main city. Poor Dutch white farmers moved over in the nineteenth century, and Brazilian Amerindians, Jews, former Africans, Asians, and Indians became the main population of the Republic of Suriname.

The country is physically divided by multiple rivers that run from south to north, offering the colonial powers the opportunity to "divide and rule." This created natural borders between districts and segregated culturally diverse groups, allowing the country to be governed without too many uprisings due to the diverse cultural and religious expressions. When you travel through the districts from east to west, it feels like you have entered Africa, then Java, and finally India. When you drive through the Saramacca District, you will encounter vast, outstretched wetlands with waving rice fields, where the last sun rays color the sky red. Upon crossing the bridge over the Coppename River, you enter the Coronie District. The wetlands give way to dry, white sandy areas where high coconut palms sway in the breeze. Small boys climb these trees with a rope tied around their waists, and they clamber to the top to gather the coconuts. Once there, they throw the harvested fruit down to the ground, where another boy collects them in a wooden wheelbarrow and takes them to the markets.

On the roadsides, goats tied up with long ropes keep the lush grass low on the verges. White herons sit on the broad backs of zebu cattle that lie lazily ruminating between low scrub. Closer to the city, Malaysian people groups have settled in the suburbs, offering an exciting array of culinary opportunities. I loved the diversity of Suriname.

During the early 1980s, a military coup disrupted the relative peace of the country, and a military government came into power. The government soon turned bloody with the assassination of political opponents. In 1986, an interior civil war erupted around control of the drug trade, plunging the country into a time of great unrest and uncertainty. It was during this tumultuous period that Bart and his parents emigrated from the Netherlands to become missionaries here. Interestingly, it was the year 1987, the same year I had left for New Zealand.

Bart would often share with me the terrifying stories of military roadblocks and sudden raids by soldiers on buses. With their rifles ready, they demanded to see the passengers' identification papers. He described how large, armored vehicles rattled through the streets of the frightened city, and how the terror of the military was pervasive. People couldn't freely discuss politics or express their personal opinions without fear of being overheard and picked up at night, never returning home. Intimidation was rampant, and a second coup in 1989 led to a curfew being imposed at night.

When I entered the country in 1992, it was still not safe to visit the interior, and the palpable tension from unresolved political issues hung in the air. Food, especially milk powder and flour, was scarce due to strict import regulations. To obtain these items, we needed to collect ration coupons which allocated food items based on a family's needs. We would stand for hours in queues just to get extra bread buns for the orphanage. These buns would turn into bricks after a day as it was compromised dough—sometimes cassava flour and water were used instead of milk and wheat flour.

Bart's missionary parents worked primarily among the Arawak and Carib tribes. They also had a small home church where people from diverse cultures came to worship. Despite the passage of time, many cultural practices remained unchanged. On occasion this presented a challenge to their missionary work because the congregations came from diverse ethnic groups and religious backgrounds. Worshipping a Deity was expressed in many ways and Suriname is the only country where you will find a mosque, church, an Indian temple, and synagogue built next to each other without massacres among the main religious groups.

People groups in Suriname don't mix easily, and intermarriage between ethnic groups is still discouraged. Bart jokingly referred to the children of mixed marriages as the most beautiful girls who ever lived on earth. Perhaps he saw a glimpse of the original Eve, who would have possessed features of all people groups.

Noisy traffic, dirty streets, and smelly marketplaces were all part of this diverse country. Monkeys played in high palm trees in the governmental gardens as we sipped cold drinks from street vendors. Bart and I spent weekends exploring various places of historical significance or cycling to the next district to visit missionary friends.

I reveled in the beauty of the wild nature and lush jungle. We canoed along small waterways through the jungle, watching as dark clouds gathered on the horizon, announcing the start of the rainy season. I felt a thrill from the tension building up in the air. The sky was a churning cauldron of heavy clouds, all vying to be the first to dump their accumulating raindrops. Then, the storm would burst with peals of thunder and lightning, and the rain rattled onto the roofs like a freight train. Caught unprepared, we ran for a roadside shelter. As rain filled the muddy streets and turned them into rivers, we cuddled up and talked, talked, talked.

Bart's time as an engineering apprentice came to an end, and he had to return to Curaçao to start his next and last semester of study. However, my contract with the orphanage was not yet finished, so

I stayed on for another couple of weeks. The children in the house were as diverse as the country's population, and their stories were heartbreaking. When I arrived, the orphanage had only ten children living there. Halfway through my stay, a baby with HIV/AIDS was given into our care, and we were instructed to always wear gloves when handling his sores and scabs that covered his emaciated body. I bathed him in sea salt and let the wounds dry in the sun, feeling such compassion for him and wanting to give him all the love he needed. I donned latex gloves and prayed for protection, making sure I didn't have any cuts while I nurtured him. What could be more important than giving this young child all the cuddles he could handle and pouring love into him to enjoy life as it was presented to him? Unfortunately, a few years later, I heard that he had passed away; he had just turned five.

To surprise the children, we organized a trip to a small village a few hours from the capital. We navigated dirt roads and broken-down bridges until we reached a cluster of wooden huts in the jungle. A large, empty stilted house was built for visiting groups or local families looking to escape the bustling city life. A small creek called "Coca-Cola Creek" ran on the edge of the village. It got its name from the color of the water, which resembled the popular drink due to the tannins from dropped leaves. We enjoyed the cool water that silently flowed under the thick canopy of leafy trees and dangling vines.

I slept on the open veranda that faced the jungle. Shortly after dinner, I unfolded my thin mattress and prepared to read by candlelight. I had brought along the book, *This Present Darkness* by Frank Peretti, and the story became strangely alive as I heard the first village drums echo through the forest. This marked the beginning of a "winti" session, a local version of voodoo accepted as a natural healing practice in Suriname. Other drums joined in, and their unceasing bass throbbed throughout the moonless night.

The kids quieted down as they settled in their rooms, and most people in the village retired to their huts. The last flickering lights were dimmed, and I was alone with the sounds of the night. While the drums rumbled through the darkness, the jungle came to life. Howler monkeys called out to each other, and their howls made my hair stand up. Smaller monkeys swayed from tree to tree on their way to their sleeping quarters. Night animals rustled in the undergrowth, and I breathed in the musty scent of decomposing leaves.

A small wooden church had been built years ago, and it stood ghostlike on an overgrown patch that used to be clear from the jungle. It stood askew, and the white paint had taken on black spots of fungus. As I visited it the next morning, the door fell off its hinges, and a cloud of disturbed bats fluttered from the wooden bell tower. Looking up, I could see the broken ribs from which the heavy copper bell had fallen and killed a curious visitor some years ago, as a passerby told me. No one in the village would come and enter this place because they reckoned it was haunted by the dead. Church pews still stood in a row, some of them half-eaten by termites.

I chose a seemingly solid bench to sit on and prepared a story for the children to be told by the campfire that night. For years, the rotten walls had not seen an open Bible or heard the rustle of pages being turned. As I prepared, I sensed someone watching me. I looked up and gazed around. A small movement caught my eye, and just above the entrance door, I faced the largest, hairiest spider I had ever seen in my life! It was the size of my hand, and it just hung there, quietly staring at me. Slowly, I moved away and, with a pounding heart, exited through a side entrance. I entered the blazing sunlight outside, leaving the once-white building standing there in its silent shadows, slowly being overtaken by the jungle.

The story that night was good, and the children loved it as I took them on the Old Testament journey of Nehemiah, who rebuilt the walls of Jerusalem. As the embers died from the campfire, the drums deep in the village started to pound again. It sounded eerie, and I remembered it as the hollow heartbeat of a village that had turned its back on God.

The country was in upheaval again, and newspapers announced that the airport would soon be closed off. Once more, the country would be cut off from the outside world, and Bart's parents urged me to leave now while it was still possible. Hurriedly, I left Suriname and returned to my parents on the island of Curaçao.

1994: Getting Married

I surprised Bart by picking him up from his lectures, and on our way back to my parents' house in my borrowed car, he asked me to stop before we got there. He had been thinking while we were apart, and without much hesitation, he said, "Maria, I'd like to get married. Would you please think about it?" My heart leaped with joy as I realized he would be the best husband I could wish for. Our lives would never be dull or purposeless, and many adventures awaited us.

Later, as we swam in the blue ocean again, we climbed onto a small sandy beach in front of the opening of a cave hidden in the steep embankment of the rocky coastline. Here, he properly proposed to me and asked if I would marry him. A wave of expectations swept over me, and we began organizing our wedding day. Bart designed our wedding invitations, and we calculated our budget for living on the island.

Island living would have its peculiarities. In Curaçao, white people were not looked on favorably. The history of slavery was kept actively alive, and the overall attitude of the people was still hostile toward their former colonists. We encountered several incidents in which we were treated unfairly or even harshly because we were Dutch and white. It gave me a glimpse of how it felt to be discriminated against because of your ethnicity.

On one occasion, as I was traveling from Bart's apartment back to my parents' place, I turned into a shortcut and was surprised by a strange scene unfolding right in front of me. Around the corner, a small car appeared. It skidded sideways, blocking the road, and the doors flew open. Two young men jumped out and ran toward an oncoming car, forcing it to stop. One masked man pulled the driver's door open, and a frail older lady was thrown onto the tarmac. The youths jumped into her car, and the motor revved up and sped toward me. The moment they saw me blocking their way to escape, they pulled the handbrake and spun a hundred and eighty degrees back toward the trembling old lady. At this point, I started to shake with anger and pushed the accelerator to cut them off from the side road from where I had come.

We both skidded to a halt as I blocked their escape route. I looked at the flushed and contorted face of the driver while his companion tried to pull a hood over his face so I wouldn't be able to identify him. In his anger at being blocked, the driver opened the window and pulled out a gun. I looked down at the barrel and my mind went into overdrive. I hit the accelerator again, to get out of the way and came to a stop just in time to avoid driving into a house in front of me. The other car sped past with screeching tires and disappeared around the corner.

Immediately, I looked around to see if anyone had come to the rescue of the lady. The doors and windows of the surrounding houses were all closed, and some had even pulled the curtains shut. Nobody wanted to be involved in a robbery. Nobody came out to help. I got out of my car and guided the old lady off the road. A little later, I heard police sirens approaching.

Suddenly, the street became alive again. People rushed out of their houses and gathered around the lady to make their statements to the police. Nobody acknowledged me or asked me any questions. I saw that the lady was being taken care of, and I quietly left the scene and walked back to my car.

At home, I told my mum and called Bart to tell him the story. But I never thought about telling my side of the incident to the police. I knew that my statement would not be taken seriously. From their perspective, I, a white woman, had just interfered in a local incident.

Not long after the incident, Bart and I took a walk in the neighborhood when an old lady rushed out of her yard to greet us. She introduced herself as the woman whose car was stolen, and I had helped after the robbery. She expressed her gratitude and wondered what had happened to me after everyone else had surrounded her to tell their version of the story to the police. She had hoped that I would give my account of the incident to the authorities as no one else had witnessed the robbery. "People just wanted to be seen as heroes after the fact," she said.

As it turned out, we lived just around the corner from her, and when she learned that we were getting married, she promised to visit us on that day. She followed through on her promise and attended our wedding with her entire family, bringing gifts as well. They thanked us and God for the favorable outcome of what could have been a fatal experience for their mother.

Time flew by as we planned and prepared for the big day. My mother, who was both a seamstress and florist, offered to sew my dress and make the flower arrangements. I chose silk flowers for my bouquet so that it would last a lifetime, as the heat of the day would have destroyed fresh flowers within an hour. I also baked cakes, cookies, and treats for the guests. We decided not to serve alcohol and opted for sparkling apple cider for our toast. As we didn't have many overseas visitors, we invited mostly people from our local home church and Bart's university friends.

I didn't have many contacts left after years of traveling and living overseas. Two people from our church would act as witnesses and sign the marriage certificate: a Dutch friend who had married an Islander, and a young man who had just finished his prison sentence and had become a close friend. He had become a Christian during the prison ministry that my dad was involved in, and he faithfully attended our church.

Early in the morning of August 1, 1994, I crawled out of my bed in the little apartment attached to my parents' house. As I opened the door, tropical sunlight greeted me, and the garden was still cool. Colorful birds played in the trees, and my heart sang. It was just another tropical day full of warmth and sunshine, but to me, it would be one of the best days of my life.

A hairdresser arrived, and, for a couple of hours, she washed, dried, combed, and plucked my hair until I had a headache. The beautician lamented my darkened skin as she tried to apply a layer of makeup. Most Islanders wanted their skin to be as light as possible, they could not understand our fascination with sunbathing and getting a tan. I just felt happy and lighthearted and loved my sunburned skin nonetheless as I stepped into my wedding dress.

Around midday, Bart arrived with his parents and siblings in his beat-up Nissan. We had spent the day before cleaning the car, as we thought we would drive it to the city council the next day. As we all gathered for the last photo before we left for the official ceremony, suddenly a long, sleek limousine drove up in front of the house. It was a wedding gift from one of the ladies in the church. She had

1994: Getting Married

decided that Bart's old Nissan would not look good in the bridal procession. With a wide grin, she opened the doors to let us in.

The ceremony was nice and short. We signed the papers, and, as the doors of the council building opened, I stepped into the world as a married woman!

While the guests went for afternoon tea, Bart and I asked the photographer to take us on a tour to our favorite spots to capture our time on this island. He drove us to our hidden beaches where there were not many tourists and took stunning photos as we stood on a jetty surrounded by some pelicans. The blue ocean waters glittered, and rocky coasts decorated the background of our wedding photos. Who knew if we would ever return to this little island? We suspected that soon our lives would take a turn and send us on a worldwide journey.

I attempted to obtain a work permit, but the Immigration Department asked me to apply for a missionary permit instead, as they needed missionaries more than overseas workers who could take away local jobs. At twenty-six, I became a missionary without ever having attended Bible school or being sent out by an organization.

My parents had to wrap up their activities as my mother got sick and needed to move back to a cooler climate to recover. They were involved in many projects that changed people's lives. My dad made radio programs, and my parents visited the prison to minister to the inmates. They had a church at their house and led many Bible studies, including one with university students. However, their time here was coming to an end. They asked me to take over some of their ministries, so I assumed responsibility for the radio programs and continued to visit the women in prison.

It was then that I met the kind man once more, who had welcomed me when I first arrived on Curaçao unexpectedly. As CEO of the prison facility, he arranged for my permit to visit the women in the prison.

The detention center stood on a barren hill, with yellow sand and scattered rocks covering the ground. Several gates barred the inmates from the outside, and many had never seen the sea that surrounded the hill.

With a heavy heart, I entered the heavily guarded compound. It was heartbreaking to see the women gathered in the courtyard of the prison cells. A pregnant woman slept on a thin mattress. Next to her, a toddler was fussing on the ground. The mother of this child leaned against the gray concrete wall and smoked a cigarette, blowing smoke in my direction. She had given birth in prison. The women in our Bible study were of different ages and backgrounds. Some had been there for a long time, while others were serving shorter sentences. One was serving a sentence for murder.

One day, a young girl joined our group, and I was shocked to learn that she was only seventeen. As she listened to the Bible story I was telling and the practical application for our lives, she found a comfortable position on the floor and contentedly sucked her thumb, as if I were telling a bedtime story.

After the Bible study, I introduced myself to the girl, and she shared her story. She had fallen in love with an older man who was a fantastic charmer. Her home situation was abusive, and she thought she would be better off moving in with him. After a while, he offered her a trip to the tropical island of Curaçao. He told her he couldn't travel with her and asked her to drop off a package at an address when she arrived. Her boyfriend had carefully hidden it in her luggage. After the drop-off, she was free to enjoy the warm sun and blue waters of this paradise. However, the moment she landed, search dogs sniffed out the drugs, and she was sentenced to the local prison. Instead of diving into the warm ocean and enjoying the sandy beaches, she found herself sitting in a corner of a bare concrete prison cell, sucking her thumb.

What motivated her to blindly believe her boyfriend? Why didn't she see the setup coming? As I remembered my own decision to move to New Zealand to join a man who had promised so much but couldn't deliver, I felt a pang of pain. The processes of the mind intrigued me, as they seem to be influenced by our background and past experiences. The choices we make come from our wounded hearts, and although we try to avoid making the wrong decisions, we often exchange one nightmare for another.

Bart was busy at the university, and I traveled back to the Netherlands to get a certificate in multimedia. When I got back from the course, I was able to write radio programs with content that was relevant to women, children, and youth. Most programs were intended to bring the Good News of Jesus Christ, other programs were more for educational purposes. I worked at a local radio station, Radio Semiya, in Curaçao and hosted several programs. In my recording

1994: Getting Married

studio at home, I prerecorded many more programs for Trans World Radio (TWR), a global mission organization that spread the Gospel through radio. Their station and transmission towers stood on Bonaire and relayed the programs to many other places. By the end of three years, I was producing twenty-two radio programs per week. Some of these programs were presented live, while others were recorded and sent by mail to neighboring islands.

During the last year of Bart's study, we moved back to Suriname as he had to complete another workplace experience as part of his studies in civil engineering. I shipped my radio home studio across to our new house and continued to record programs for women, children, and youth. I posted the tapes back out from Suriname to the different stations where the programs were broadcasted.

After five years of study, Bart designed his final thesis—a cruise terminal for Curaçao—and presented it to the university board and civil companies on the island. He graduated as a civil engineer with excellence.

The Cold, Unwelcome

We had to make major decisions for our future. Bart's student permit did not allow a follow-on work permit, and we were expected to leave as soon as he finished his studies. As in so many developing countries, bribery was a way of life, and we were only able to stay and get a work permit for Bart if we bribed ourselves into the system. Both of us decided that that was not the way we wanted to start this new chapter in our lives.

Bart formulated his vision and stated that he would like to work for developing nations. His study had been directly funded by God through his parents' mission work. Many of their supporters had offered the fees for him to study. He wanted to honor that by giving his skills back to God in His service. As we prepared to leave our honeymoon island, once again the Old Testament prophet Isaiah spoke to us, showing us a mission statement for our lives together:

> *This is the kind of fast day I'm after: to break the chains of injustice, get rid of exploitation in the workplace, free the oppressed, cancel debts. What I'm interested in seeing you do is: sharing your food with the hungry, inviting the homeless poor into your homes, putting clothes on the shivering ill-clad, being available to your own families. Do this and the lights will turn on, and your lives will turn around at once. Your righteousness will pave your way. The GOD of glory will secure your passage. Then when you pray, GOD will answer. You'll call out for help and I'll say, "Here I am."... You'll use the old rubble of past lives to build anew, rebuild the foundations from out of your past. You'll be known as those who can fix anything, restore old ruins, rebuild and renovate, make the community livable again (Isaiah 58:6-9, 12 THE MESSAGE).*

We had no idea how this would play out in our daily lives. It was

The Cold, Unwelcome

clear we could not stay on the island, and we decided to move back to the Netherlands. This seemed the easiest way for us to get to work and start looking around for possibilities to explore opportunities to realize our vision.

Upon returning to the Netherlands, my parents lived with friends for a while and only recently had found a rental in which they settled. Coming back to the Netherlands had been difficult for Chris, and he had dropped out of school. Mum attended many medical appointments to figure out why she kept having a fever. Dad worked from home and also found it difficult to settle back in. To keep busy, he turned his radio programs into flyers and a Bible study program.

After years of tropical sunshine, we landed mid-winter in the Netherlands. The weather would alternate between clear frosty skies and dark cloudy days with icy rain. We stepped from the plane onto the tarmac on a freezing February afternoon. The fierce wind immediately chilled us to the bone.

We had no place to stay and were offered the chance to live in a small cottage on a large campground close to a national park. We arrived with some suitcases and boxes; these were all our possession as we started life from scratch. As we unpacked and hung out the few winter clothes we had borrowed from our family, thick snowflakes began to fall. It became silent around us, and soon everything was covered in a thick blanket of snow. In that first week after we returned, we shoveled piles of wet cold stuff away from our doorsteps. It was a drastic change in the environment, and within days we caught the flu and sniffled through the house where tissues overflowed from the bins.

We started to look for jobs which meant that we needed to fill out an endless number of documents to register ourselves back into Dutch society.

Bart had never worked before and needed his Personal Identification Number (PIN), and the Tax Department needed a permanent address. It was a bureaucratic nightmare. We filled in the current address of the campground, which triggered the local council to inform us that we were not to register this address as permanent living quarters. They would turn us over to the local law enforcement that dealt with illegal residential housing issues. We had a couple of days to leave the place otherwise we would be forcefully removed.

Whenever we tried to apply for government housing, we were knocked back by the long waiting lists as rental properties were in high demand. We desperately asked around for alternatives and finally found a place through a private agency. This was the more expensive option, but at least we were able to live somewhere, and within a few days, we moved into an old empty farmhouse surrounded by tall oak trees.

The walls in the bedrooms were moldy, and the windows permanently fogged up, freezing over into fascinating patterns during the night. We shivered and huddled close together into bed with double blankets. Even the hot water bottle made us feel damp. Eventually, we decided to make a bed in front of the small gas heater in the living room to stay warm.

Bit by bit, we gathered some secondhand furniture and started to work through job agencies. We waited impatiently for the summer, and when it arrived, I still felt cold. It was like we had moved into a dark place without the sun.

Bart's parents and his younger sister came to visit us from Suriname. His sister had just finished high school and needed to further her education, so we offered to let her live with us while she attended a bridging course for university. Cold and unused to the low temperatures—and completely unprepared for the reverse culture shock—she moved in. Many evenings we talked about our lives back in the tropics and the distinct cultures that we had lived in. The three of us found it increasingly difficult to see our lives continue in the Netherlands.

Colds and flu were my companions, repeated bladder infections resulted in an operation, and then I got pregnant. In my diary, I write:

3 August 1997
Today I did a pregnancy test, and the results were positive. As Bart entered the room, I greeted him with 'Good morning, Dad.' We looked at each other, not knowing what to think. This would change our plans for the future. Now we might have to stay in the Netherlands. We have been so focused on moving to another country, and I do not feel settled at all. What does our future look

The Cold, Unwelcome

like? It's a strange realization; I'm going to have a baby! I didn't expect it to happen. How does one adjust to such news? I want to share it with our families, but we think it's too soon, so we'll wait a little longer.

In the weeks that followed, I felt increasingly sick and unwell. I was also still on antibiotics because of bladder infections. Suddenly a tooth broke and I needed a dentist, but money was tight. I should have been happy, but instead I felt miserable.

After a short and chilly summer, the first autumn rains came in, and the leaves on the trees changed into many different colors. I remembered my youth and the wonderful times I had as I walked in the forest. I didn't have any energy to walk the trails, and I dreaded the wet weather and cold temperatures.

Early in September, I had my first pregnancy check-up. Excitedly, I went into the clinic, and, as the attendant looked at the scan, he kept shaking his head. "I am so sorry, lady, but the fetus has died. You will need to come next week to see if there are any retained products of conception (RPOC). This means if there is still dead tissue remaining, it can cause infection in your uterus." The cold statement kept echoing in my head: *"The dead tissue..."* With horror, I realized that in the coming week, I just had to sit patiently and await the miscarriage of my baby! Confused and angry, I left the clinic to go home and called Bart. As the week went on, nothing happened. The doctor prescribed medication to help the process.

After ten days, I woke up feeling very sick. I developed a fever during the day, and I called the clinic to ask what I should do. This triggered a panic response from the assistant, and the doctor ordered me to go immediately to the emergency room where I would be treated with a curettage procedure. The dead tissue had become infected and triggered a sepsis reaction. A sense of loss and anger washed over me. It felt like we were promised a gift that was taken away before we could even open it. I had no mental tools to deal with this, and I buried it deep inside myself, but it would come up many years later.

This personal loss left us shaken and unsure of the future. The owners of the farm sold their property, and the house would be demolished soon after. So off we went, to seek another place to live.

Finally, the sun broke through, and another farmhouse came

available in a small nearby country town. We had a few months of carefree living and explored the Netherlands during a much warmer seasons than the year before. We canoed through the marshlands in the south, walked forest trails, and visited old castles in the east. In the late summer, the heather colored purple, and we spread a picnic blanket in a hollow between the low shrubs. We read books on missionary lives in the warm rays of the ever-sinking autumn sun. A restlessness stirred within us, and we entertained the thought of looking for overseas jobs again. Mentally we were ready to pack up and travel and explore different lands beyond the horizon.

Over these last months, we collected information pamphlets and folders on different mission organizations. We visited mission fairs and had several interesting interviews for possible vacancies in different parts of the world. All these visits fortified our desire to work overseas. On the other hand, none of the organizations resonated.

A New Direction for Life

A young medical doctor who was on leave from the mission field invited us to hear about her overseas adventures. She had been recently evacuated because of the civil conflict and political unrest in eastern Congo, and she shared some fascinating possibilities with us.

She poured us a nice cup of tea and explained, "After I was evacuated from the Congo, I was approached by a small Christian international aid organization called Medair. Medair sends out volunteers who distribute aid into remote and forgotten areas of the world, where others hesitate to go. I have worked for years in the Congo, and I am sad I had to leave. With Medair, I will go back in with the capacity of an aid worker."

She explained what Medair was all about, "The mandate of the organization is to tend to the neediest who are caught up in a crisis and offer first relief and then rehabilitation programs. Many teams are sent to remote countries, besides the continent of Africa. It mainly gives practical assistance to rebuild the lives of people who had to leave everything behind because of natural disasters, war, or famine. Medair gives hope to those who have nobody to turn to."

She also warned us, "Be aware, Medair goes to the most insecure places on earth. In areas that have not been tended to by larger, non-governmental organizations (NGOs), that have access to major funding. This means you live in remote and primitive locations, and often dangerous circumstances."

As we listened to her stories, they immediately resonated with us. It seemed a fulfillment of the Isaiah 58 verses that had spoken to us when we left the Caribbean. The ideals and philosophy of this organization also appealed to us. We decided to ask for more information and contacted Medair regarding the requirements and recruitment process.

Only a few weeks later, after we had sent off our applications, we received the official invitation to participate in a ten-day seminar. This meant that we had to take part in a simulation program that introduced us to life as aid workers and ran through several projects that Medair conducted at the time.

Our hearts were filled with new prospects of an interesting future as we traveled to southern France in July 1998. We were in for an impressive and intense experience.

During the training and simulation program, we learned about angry official bureaucracy at a simulated refugee camp. We discussed the ethics of bribing and how this would affect our work in countries where people had different values and worldviews. During the day, our sleeping quarters were transformed into a shabby office where a team member acted as the landlord. He spoke a foreign language and somehow, we needed to communicate to him that we wanted to rent a place for our teams to live and work in. We learned that not all locally recruited translators had your best interests in mind. They would translate your requests very loosely and season them with their interpretation of what you tried to say in English. All these scenarios were based on real experiences in the field.

On a misty, early mid-week morning, we were dropped off in the middle of a nature reserve with just a compass and map of the area. We were tested on resilience and how we would react if we encountered stressful situations. The objective was to find a simulated refugee camp that was pinpointed on the map. Scattered scribbles on the map indicated simulated minefields around the camp, and it came with instructions to avoid these areas.

As we walked through the countryside, we were suddenly surrounded by uniformed soldiers who jumped from behind some bushes. Forcefully they pushed us to the ground. Some grabbed our backpacks and shouted, "Give us your lunch! We will shoot if you resist!" We still had to get through the rest of the day, and it meant we would go hungry. It was obvious that we were tested on how we would deal with stress on an empty stomach.

We regrouped and divided the remaining lunches so that all of us had something to eat during the journey. After walking for a few hours, we found ourselves on a deserted road. In the distance, a lone car sped toward us and skidded to a halt in front of us. Masked men jumped out and blindfolded us. Loud voices yelled instructions in another language as we were shuffled into the car and driven to a fast-flowing river. At least that was what we could hear. Pushed from the car and driven like cattle, we were forced to walk down the muddy riverbank.

Suddenly loud explosions assaulted our eardrums, and the "rebels" screamed in heavily accented English to get down. We plunged into the shallow, chilly water to wait for the bombing to stop. Dripping wet, we were ordered to hold tightly to a rope that guided us to the other side of the river. The blindfolds were ripped from our faces. With hand gestures, we were told to get away from the riverside.

We had to find an alternative route to our destination, which was the refugee camp. During these simulations, staff members observed our reactions to these situations that could easily be part of our daily challenges in the field.

The next challenge was to practice driving four-by-four on rough roads and we learned the basic mechanics of changing tires and oil. Other technical issues were simulated, and we had to find solutions to these problems as all of these could arise in remote areas where immediate mechanical assistance was not available. Shortwave and handheld radios were part of our daily communication exercises and overnight the alphabet changed to "Alpha, Bravo, Charlie, Delta..." Our names changed into Bravo Whiskey (Bart Wassink) and Mike Whiskey (Maria Wassink), using only the first letters of our names in Radio Language.

We were asked to make shelters from discarded wooden pallets, UN tarps, some rope, stones, and poles. The use of Ventilated Improved Pit (VIP) latrines was explained, and an array of otherwise useless items was shown that would help us survive in dire circumstances.

We assembled a survival kit with items that were vital for whenever we would be forced to evacuate and survive in remote areas. A condom became a water bladder that could hold up to forty liters of water. A torn T-shirt filtered Guinea worm from otherwise undrinkable water; a mirror reflecting the sun was used to transmit signals. The use of coordinates was taught to be able to communicate the location where an evacuated team had identified a possible landing zone. A magnifying glass was used to start a fire, and some fishing wire and hook made it possible to catch fish. Of course, the Leatherman multi-tool was part of the survival bag which was truly the most important treasure for survival in primitive circumstances.

Every day we attended lectures on how to care for our physical, psychological, and spiritual well-being and how to deal with tensions within the multicultural teams or collaboration with other NGOs that were working on projects in the region. We made an estimated budget for a program that had to be added to a proposal that was sent to government donors. Finances were explained and endless forms, diagrams, and spreadsheets were put before us to impart the importance of reporting back to the donors.

In the middle of the seminar, we were introduced to a field staff member who specifically was flown over to give us an immediate picture of what life in the field looked like. This also gave us a glance at the impact of the projects which Medair implemented. Our heads spun after hearing wild survival stories of the victims of war and hunger, bombardments, difficult logistical challenges, and descriptive evacuations.

Most of all, the endless suffering the teams were exposed to while they worked with the local population made us aware of what was to come. The seriousness of this kind of work made us sober, and we had to answer some tough questions about how we would react to the severe scenarios that were shared and simulated. This seminar was only the first of many other workshops and short courses to prepare potential aid workers for living in countries during war, famine, and after natural disasters and destruction. We were heading into the most unsafe places on the earth if we joined Medair.

At the end of these intense ten days in France, we were interviewed by the couple who did the recruiting. They briefly explained the background of the organization and its concise history. Medair was created as an organization in 1988 as a means to respond quickly to a humanitarian crisis. The MAF (Mission Aviation Fellowship), YWAM (Youth with a Mission), and a French medical organization joined their expertise and created the Christian emergency response team that was now established as Medair. The larger and better-known NGOs could easily respond and raise funds for the majority of groups as media coverage assisted in securing these funds. The marginalized were often left out. Many of these were Christian groups.

Medair's mandate says it all: "We believe each life matters. We relieve human suffering in hard-to-reach places. Medair is an impartial, independent, and neutral humanitarian organisation inspired by Christian faith to save lives and relieve human suffering in the world's most difficult-to-reach and devastated places."

We were nervous as we felt this was the kind of work that we would like to be involved in. If we were accepted, would we be able to handle stressful situations, were we ready to commit ourselves to this difficult lifestyle?

With great excitement, we listened as they officially confirmed that we were accepted and that openings were coming up as the crisis deepened in the areas where Medair had feet on the ground.

We Are Going!

We started more preparatory trajectories and enrolled in more courses, including those on communication, logistics, and field safety. These courses also included training on how to navigate landmines and booby traps. One specific course was given in England by the British army, which trained the participants on how to survive kidnapping and safely get through checkpoints.

Bart and I took the overland bus through the Netherlands and Belgium, using the North Sea Tunnel to get there. We bought the cheapest fare, which meant we traveled throughout the night.

It rained continuously, and, on the interstate in Belgium, we suddenly woke from our restless slumber in the uncomfortable bus seats. The terrible screeching of metal on the tarmac made us cover our ears as we witnessed the most horrific traffic accident in front and beside the bus. Eight cars slammed into each other, and drivers and passengers were thrown from their seats into the air, slamming back onto the road. The bus braked frantically to avoid the bodies, and finally slid to a standstill on the side of the road.

As we had just renewed our first aid course, we were allowed to disembark and assist the accident victims, together with some doctors who were also on board. There was a lot of blood and tears, and we had no gloves, but each of us stayed with the car crash victims until ambulances arrived.

After hours of delay, we finally entered England. We felt as if we had already entered a reality of destruction and suffering, and still had to attend British army training. Crunched up in the bus seat, leaning into each other, we caught up on some sleep as we crossed from Kent to Moreton-in-Marsh in the middle of England.

The course was as intense as the experience we had just encountered on the Belgian highway, as it focused on aiding victims of mines and booby traps. Now we were fully aware of what we were getting into and more aware of the challenges we would face in the field.

To prepare ourselves for our first field appointment, we hiked

We Are Going!

through the Alps for a couple of days with a 15 kilo backpack. This was a standard weight allowance for our destination. Little did we know this would be our last peaceful trip to a first-world country for a long time.

In a flurry of activities, we finalized our contracts with our current employers, informed our friends, families, and church about the new direction, and sold our meager belongings. The last few months flew by in a blur of events, including speeches, socializing, and preparations for our move.

On the daily news, we saw that TV reporters were flown into those places where Medair was already on the ground to provide aid. As we watched the news, it brought a new depth to our perception of dealing with human suffering. Soon we would be in those locations ourselves and bring hands-on relief instead of just watching it from a comfortable seat in front of a TV. We felt ready and wanted to go, bring relief, give ourselves, do something, and make a difference!

The telephone rang, and—with pounding hearts—we listened to the HR officer as she explained that the situation in Africa had become extremely volatile. We were asked to consider and respond immediately to the proposal of going to the war-torn country of Southern Sudan (as it was known prior to their independence in 2011) as soon as we possibly could.

The crisis was most severe in Bahr el Ghazal in southwestern Sudan. It was referred to as a complex crisis because there were several causes: drought, hunger, war, and tribal conflict. There was a government backed mujahideen militia that had been raiding the Dinka population for years. Women and children were seized and taken to Northern Sudan. The theft of cattle, looting of harvests, and burning of crops and homes had been ongoing while the civil war also escalated. The internal war for independence of the south from the north caused a major disruption to any attempts by relief organizations to provide aid. After July 1998, food distributions finally took place, and NGOs were able to enter the area.

A group of initial emergency responders traveled to a district where hunger had severely impacted the population. Hundreds of people were displaced, and children were dying daily. A small team was sent ahead to set up a base from which a follow-up team would open feeding centers and organize food distribution. Medair had secured funding and started the first response by sending food and medicine into the area. The need was overwhelming, and the crisis was far from receding. They required people to replace the exhausted Rapid Response team and develop a longer-term strategy to implement feeding programs.

Our first field assignment was to be part of the feeding program in Southern Sudan in a town called Yirol. The town of Yirol was situated in Yirol County, although this has changed names over the years. (The county is now divided into Yirol West and Yirol East, in the Lakes State, which was established by a peace agreement in February 2020.)

Finally, we stood with just our backpacks at the check-in desk at Schiphol Airport in Amsterdam. Good-byes were said, tears and prayers accompanied us to the plane that would fly us to Nairobi, Kenya, where we would be inducted.

For many years to come, we wouldn't be living in the same place for extended periods. Bart and I were strangely aware that this chapter in our lives could be dangerously brief if anything happened to us in the field. Many people prayed for us, and we compiled all the encouragements and Bible verses people had written into a little booklet which we took with us to the field. These messages would help us through the times when we might need them the most.

We entered the African continent in 1998 and wondered what day-to-day life was going to look like. The lifestyle we now embraced conditioned us to love the thrill and sensation of action in our lives. We felt we were made for an adventurous life beyond what we could imagine, and it would change us forever.

Part 6

International Aid Workers

The African Continent

Kenya is a captivating country in eastern Africa with endless grasslands, low scrub, and picturesque vistas. Wild animals ran in disarray from their water holes as we glided over Nairobi National Park in the last rays of the setting sun and touched down at Kenyatta Airport. The wet, humid heat slammed into our faces when we stepped onto the warm tarmac.

A Medair volunteer drove us through the city to the team house in one of the districts in Nairobi where we would be thoroughly briefed before departing for Sudan. The city was vibrantly alive, with the roads dirty and badly maintained, like those we were used to in Paramaribo, Suriname.

A mix of rich and poor Africans milled around rickety shacks from where general household goods were sold. Colorfully dressed Indians stood at the doors of their shops and loudly praised their wares. Old women scurried along the sidewalk, carrying large packs on their backs secured with a band around their foreheads. Young boys with vacant eyes begged for scraps of food at the traffic lights. Street markets were busy, and vivid-colored fabrics were flapping in the warm breeze. Merchants who had traveled from the villages around Nairobi sat on grass mats, skillfully weaving hats and mats from the long elephant grass lying next to them.

Nairobi is situated 1,200 meters above sea level, ensuring that the city does not have too many mosquitoes during the early evening. It has a pleasant climate as the temperature does not rise far above 25°C. During the nights, we needed blankets to keep us warm, and I had to buy some warmer clothes as the clothes I brought were meant for the sweltering heat in Sudan.

The team house in the city was a stone building properly designed for tropical weather. When all doors and windows were kept open, a pleasant breeze cooled the rooms. All windows were secured with iron bars. It had ten bedrooms and several bathrooms, although only one shower seemed to work. Water pressure in the evening was extremely low, meaning that the dishes were stacked high in the kitchen after dinner, waiting for the day staff to clean up.

During our first days in Africa, we explored the city and the nearby nature reserves. We slowly felt the African atmospheric images come to life as we drove through the surrounding countryside. Old colonial buildings with exuberantly flowering gardens and stylishly decorated living quarters of the former tea plantations brought us into the world of movies and famous writers. We visited a tea house which was the former house of Danish author, Baroness Karen von Blixen-Finecke, where the film *Out of Africa* was recorded. We visited the site where thousands of ivory tusks were burned to restrain the smuggling of ivory out of Kenya.

Both of us had to pass a driver's test customized for African traffic conditions. It was busy at all intersections, overloaded bicycles and mopeds weaved through the smallest gaps between the cars. Hooting buses were crammed with travelers and high stacks of luggage. People hung out of the windows; children grabbed their mothers' legs who, in turn, were precariously balancing in the open doorframes. Pushcarts and automobiles maneuvered inches from each other; larger passenger buses squeezed through impossible spaces of the chaotic traffic. Most cars looked like they had just been rescued from a scrap yard.

On Sunday, the city changed into a sleepy, sunny scene where nicely dressed people walked with a Bible under their arms, ready to go to church. We went to a large church, and the building was packed. Latecomers had to take seats outside on the verandas, and as churchgoers kept coming in for the service, they were directed to the lawns of the church grounds. Large speakers made sure all churchgoers would hear the Gospel message. African singing filled the cathedral as people swung to the rhythmic music and lifted their faces as they worshipped.

We felt encouraged and were amazed by how many people turned up to go to church. Many churches had such great congregations that they ran three services on a Sunday! In contrast, churches in the Netherlands had dwindled in numbers, and in general, interest in religion had ceased except for the rise of eastern spirituality. What made Christianity so attractive and real for the people in Africa compared to the faith experience of Western believers? I pondered this as we prepared ourselves for the upcoming move to Sudan.

I leaned against the headboard of our bed with pillows crunched behind my back. This would be my study place for days to come. We had to read many documents that informed us about the projects in Southern Sudan and the village called Yirol. The project director explained our role in the next stage of the feeding program that had already been going on for a while.

He called us into his small office and filled in more details: "Large C-130 Hercules cargo planes will fly over the hunger-stricken district. Wooden pallets carrying hundreds of kilos of rice, grains, and other supplies are being dropped in a secure zone that is managed by WFP—that is, the World Food Program. The Medair team currently in the field will have prepared lists of families who need the food. These family groups have been gathered from around the village. Some of these families have only just returned after they had to flee a recent army offensive. Local administrators will have calculated what amounts need to be distributed to the clans. It is your task to oversee and manage the distribution once the food has been dropped by WFP."

He continued, "The situation is stable at this stage, and some feeding centers will be closed as the number of malnourished children has gone down significantly. The local military government has asked if Medair could remain present for some time longer to monitor the impact of the food distributions and if it will last until the next expected harvest. We will be staying for at least three months to implement other programs as we await the so-called 'hunger gap' to pass. During these months, we will have more food drops in the area, and in addition to that, we will also distribute seed, and fishing and farming equipment so that the population can support themselves. We will continue monitoring the growth and weight of the children, and eventually, after the distribution and sowing of the seed, we need to measure the harvested crops. We need to determine if the harvest will cover the villagers' food needs and re-seeding for the coming year."

The current team would be replaced with new and fresh volunteers, which would be us! Bart and I were asked to become team leaders for the next period of projects in Yirol. Bart would be responsible for maintaining contact with the different beneficiaries and liaising between local chiefs, the military, and other governmental departments. He would also have to organize the different distribution sites that were pinpointed by WFP for the coming months.

I became responsible for setting up low-scale distributions of teaching supplies to schools that were scattered in the bush due to the war. I was briefed on the dire situation of education in Southern Sudan: "Many schools are either not running at all or only operational when teachers are available and have not gone off to fight in the war somewhere. Access to school materials has been cut off because of fighting and subsequently, the hunger crisis. Any teacher not displaced by the war or recruited as a soldier tries to work in their gardens. They need to provide food for their families instead of spending time as teachers in schools."

The project coordinator for education continued, "Occasionally, men come back from the front with injuries. They may have lost limbs and cannot perform their duties as a soldier anymore, which also means that they are unable to work in their fields. Trauma and loss of hope have robbed these young men of motivation and, in general, care for their communities. They divert their daily lives toward less beneficial activities instead of providing for their families or being available to be a teacher to the village children. Some have taken to producing local beer from fermented sorghum to make money by selling this or drinking it to drown out their misfortune. They are drunk most of the time."

I would find out soon enough how difficult it was to motivate people to invest in any development when basic human needs are not satisfied.

The days were filled with preparations to implement the tasks at hand. Bart received briefings from government officers on the current situation of the war and met with numerous partnering organizations and NGOs that worked in Southern Sudan. Meanwhile, I was introduced to the head of the Interim Education Department and officially became an education coordinator.

Our primary objective was to locate existing and scattered bush schools in the area, map their location, and report on their needs. Once we gathered sufficient information during the initial surveys of the schools' conditions, we would put together a proposal for the distribution of educational materials. These materials would be given to the selected schools with the potential to reopen. The follow-up stage involved monitoring and reporting on the development of the education programs in Yirol.

There were many perspectives to be considered while we lived and worked in the volatile situation in Southern Sudan. We had to educate ourselves on the background of the conflict, the names of the warring parties involved, and their objectives so we could collaborate effectively. In most projects, we would be working with the humanitarian branch of the rebel movement that was in power at that moment. We needed a large dose of wisdom and sensitivity to cultural issues and the right attitude toward military and civil leadership in the region.

Crossing the Border

Finally, we boarded a small plane that took us to the north of Kenya, to the UN staging camp at Lokichogio, a village situated at the border of Sudan. Over the years, this large campsite had evolved into a bustling semi-permanent village, serving as a gateway for all NGO personnel heading to mainly Southern Sudan. It had multiple landing strips that could accommodate large cargo planes that were loaded with tightly packed food pallets, which were then dropped over the distribution zones.

The area surrounding the original village of Lokichogio had been transformed into a massive logistical base, comprised of scattered UN tents, huts, and compounds. It served as the final stop before entering the war zone and hunger-stricken Southern Sudan.

"Loki" itself was a small, stretched-out village occupied by the Turkana tribe, who were nomadic people and frequently on the move. They lived in rounded mud huts made of grass or pieces of cardboard. Men wore loose, long gray or brown pieces of cloth around their shoulders, while girls wore layers of beaded chains around their necks, which they never removed. Without these layers, their lengthened necks would be without support. I wondered about their hygiene practices since there was a chronic shortage of water in the area.

As we approached the landing airstrip to the UN base, we saw whole families carrying all their belongings on their heads, cutting a long line through the dry grass. Where were they going? The grasslands seemed endless in all directions, except for some hills visible over the horizon. I would have liked to follow them and observe their way of life, but the region was perilous. Another passenger on the plane explained, "There is a constant danger of cattle raiders from neighboring tribes in Uganda—the Karamojong. They frequently attack the area and fight the young men for honor and fame besides raiding the cattle. You cannot go for an afternoon stroll outside the

UN camp. The Turkana tribe is not Kenya's most peaceful tribe either. You will regularly hear violent shootings at night."

The UN camp appeared to me like a luxurious camping ground. It had concrete shower blocks with running water, although we were instructed to conserve water. The showers were screened from each other by cement walls without a roof, providing an opportunity to shower under the vast starry sky. The toilet blocks had lidded plastic bowls placed over a hole in the ground. We were instructed always to cover the toilet bowls after use to limit the swarms of ever-present buzzing flies. Next to the latrines were the pipes for the vents, protruding like factory chimneys.

For longer-term team members traveling to and from Sudan, there were six-sided mud huts as accommodation. Other staff members, who stayed just overnight, had permanently erected tents. The wooden buildings were utilized as sleeping quarters for NGO workers who were permanently situated on this logistical base.

Medair had two houses, each with three bedrooms and a small living room. The fridge was stocked with cold Coca-Cola bottles, which was a treat for everyone as the water was not safe to drink. On a low wooden table stood a television, video player, and tapes for entertainment purposes if there was any time left after a long day at work. On the other side was a corner where radio equipment was set up for 24/7 access to communication with teams in the field. However, personnel usually spent minimal time in these houses as they were mostly in transit on their way into Sudan.

Main electricity was only provided until 7 p.m., after which large generators took over. The lights briefly dimmed until the generators were geared up. This was the moment most people interrupted their work and went for dinner to a large building where communal meals were offered. You just signed your name in a book under the name of the NGO you worked for. In our case, Medair got the bill.

The food was delicious, with lots of fresh fruit, vegetables, and cooked food. It was food that we would not be eating in the field. It was brought in over the road by trucks to Lokichogio, A strange feeling came over us as we realized that only a few kilometers across the border, another country was at war and in a hunger crisis.

At the administrative side of the base, large shipping containers were converted into general administration offices for the NGOs. There were about fifty or more organizations that worked from this base in their huge endeavor to assist at the height of the complex emergencies in Southern Sudan. Loki was extremely hot and had regular sandstorms. Red sand blew high on the thermal winds, and suddenly the horizon disappeared as sand and dust spread everywhere, covering everything. It entered your nose and ears, so it made sense to cover up your face with a thin cloth that everybody kept handy.

Early on a Tuesday morning, we were finally booked on a flight to leave for the town of Yirol. Everything seemed like a dream. At five in the morning, we were woken up by the monotonous drone of the C-130 planes. They took off early so they could do several food drops per day. The airstrip was about a five- to ten-minute drive from the camp.

A flight had been arranged for us, but the pilot who should have flown us, received conflicting orders, and instead he just took off back to Nairobi. "A normal situation here," according to the airport official. "Nothing works out as planned…"

Soon it turned hot as the morning sun burned on the bare sand as we watched plane after plane disappearing into the distance. Back at the offices, logisticians were frantically trying to arrange another plane as time went by. It had to be organized in time for the aircraft to drop us off at our location and cross back over the Kenyan border before dark. At nighttime, no planes would fly over an active war zone.

After hours of waiting, an opportunity arose when a young French pilot, who wanted more flying hours, volunteered to take us across the border. We received a radio call from the base giving us the green light. The Cessna Caravan's engines roared, and the young man shouted at us to buckle up. But as quickly as he had started the engine, he turned it off again. We couldn't understand all his French cursing, but we got the idea that he was very angry. The pilot disembarked, shouting through his headset, "Hey, where's my flight plan? I never received it, and I'm certainly not going without one!"

He left us all buckled up in the chairs, wondering if we would ever take off. When he returned, he fired up the engines, but another stream of curses spilled from his mouth. "What's wrong with this machine? The motors aren't firing properly," he bellowed. As the pilot became more agitated and fiddled with the instrument board,

Crossing the Border

Bart and I held hands and began to pray. Finally, the traffic tower advised the pilot to just take off and try to get back before dark!

The Cessna Caravan hobbled over the shortcut grass to the take-off track, and a short time later, we flew over the UN base. The aircraft was fitted with wings on top so we could study the landscapes as we passed the Kenyan border and entered Sudan. Above the hills, the air was unstable with turbulence caused by the warmer air rising from ground level, and we danced over the range, our already tightened stomachs tested even more.

The country stretched endlessly under us. It seemed a vast deserted land, with no signs of roads or other infrastructure. Sometimes a little green appeared, but the ground was mostly dotted by patches of colorless shrubs, bleached by the constant scorching sun. Closer to Yirol, it became a little greener as the plane followed the glistering of a river. We were in the country of the world's longest river, the Nile! Large lakes stretched far into the wetlands of Southern Sudan. These areas were prone to devastating floods, if only it would rain.

A cleared piece of reddish earth marked a landing strip, and nearby scattered huts indicated that we approached a village. From the air, we could see a ring of large square holes surrounding the village, and the pilot enlightened us by saying that these were hand-dug tank traps. We had reached our destination, Yirol. Dust circled high up into the still air as we landed, and the aircraft circled for an immediate take-off once we had disembarked.

We walked quickly to the edge of the strip, and, as we looked over our shoulders, the plane roared over the dusty airstrip and flew off into the distance again. It would barely cross the border into Kenya before the sun went down. We stood alone with our backpacks in the dry grass. Loneliness and silence descended upon us from being in the then largest country on the African continent.

In the distance, we saw a car bouncing toward us. As it swerved to a halt, the doors flung open and we were welcomed by the current team leaders, Stuart and Rachel Forster.

As we drove the uneven road toward Yirol and the Medair compound, we were briefly reminded of the background of the crisis and the current situation. Sudan had had internal wars for decades. Officially, the warring parties were the Government of Sudan (GoS) and the Sudan People's Liberation Movement/Army (SPLM/A). (This war ended in 2005 with the Khartoum Comprehensive Peace

Agreement.) Unofficially, individual warlords caused localized conflicts all along the Uganda border farther south which impacted the whole region.

Quite a few people were gradually returning to the area as Yirol was recently retaken by the Sudan People's Liberation Army (SPLA) from the GoS forces in June 1997. The signs of that battle were still clearly visible.

As I looked around, an alien environment enfolded before me. We passed the rubble of destroyed brick houses with shattered tin roofs, walls collapsed, and weeds taking over the once-cleared compounds. The buildings in the middle of the town were remnants of British colonial times, and everything had the appearance of a faded, once-Westernized colony. Here and there sat armored vehicles in several states of disrepair. A tank leaned sideways into a gaping hole on the roadside. Probably hit by a landmine. The main roads in and out of the town were all mined. Yet everywhere, we saw people living in the ruins as cave dwellers, hiding from the horrors of a constant war that had raged for decades.

It overwhelmed me; I could not regulate the onslaught of the daily, new impressions. I must write them down. So once again I began a diary and wrote into the night with the flickering light of an oil lamp.

10 December 1998

During our walks on the sandy unpaved roads of Yirol, people are constantly coming up to us, trying to touch us. In the early morning, I see women filing in rows through the tall grass as they approach the village pump. Each one of them carries a yellow water container on their head. I hear their laughter and chatter as they pass by our compound. There are always children frolicking around, and they are shouting repeatedly the Dinka word for a white person: 'Khwaja.'

The Sudanese Relief and Rehabilitation Agency (SRRA) was the humanitarian branch of the SPLA, which was the ruling party of what was then known as Southern Sudan. We were introduced to the appointed secretary who resided in a mostly shot-to-rubble brick building. A single room had survived the bombing and was set up to serve as his office. There was a table with a pile of dirty exercise books containing information about all kinds of departmental projects. Everything was gray, covered in dust and dirt, and a few broken chairs lined the wall.

Children ran freely around the place, completely naked, and women carried firewood on their heads to start cooking fires. People outside the office grabbed my hand and vigorously pumped it up and down, calling out, "*Kudual, Kudual, yin ca cool!*" In the Dinka language, it means, "Good day, I welcome you!" When we walked back to our compound, people ran up to us and started asking for clothes and other items we could give away. They pointed to my glasses and earrings as if they wanted it all. Afraid we would leave soon, they quickly wrote a note and presented us with a list of their needs spelled out: food, blankets, mosquito nets, soap, and salt. Wherever we walked, we were asked for goods. I began to wonder if it was a real need or if it had become a principle to just ask a white person, even to the point of asking for the clothes off your back.

Throughout the day, I walked the dirt road in the center of the village to better acclimate myself. Women were very busy and doing all the heavy work. They pounded maize or sorghum in a wooden pot. Rhythmically, the women lifted wooden poles and then slammed them down onto handfuls of kernels deep in the pot. After the first stage of pulverizing, sieving the particles was the next step. The women used woven mats of dried grass and tipped the crushed seeds from the pot. Chaff lifted off and flew high in the wind as they shook the mats up and down.

I asked a woman if I could try to pound some maize too, and with anticipating grins, she handed me the heavy wooden pole. I grabbed the pole and let it come down with force. With chagrin, I found out that I didn't have the skills as the maize just jumped out of the pot. All the women doubled over from laughter and chattered with each other while pointing their fingers at me. Calmly and smiling, the owner of the pot showed me how to pound, and I gave it another go.

I wished I could understand them. I wondered how they lived their life. What made them laugh? What made their lives worth living? What did their day look like, and what were their worries? And as I watched these ladies, I had the feeling that they might not need anything that I could offer. What was I doing here, and what could I possibly be to these women? I was overwhelmed and at the same time impressed with the resilience of these people who lived under so much oppression and had encountered so much suffering.

We visited the Food Distribution Center. My eyes had to adjust to the semi-darkness, and I smelled a sweet aroma permeating the air. It came from a large pot on a small open fire with a simmering thick porridge. This was "Unimix," an enriched maize, bean, and flour mixture to fight malnutrition. It also had milk powder, sugar, vitamins, and minerals added to it.

I looked around the dimly lit building, and my eyes fell upon a gaunt-looking baby. Its skin pulled tightly around the bones. Other mothers sat on the floor, their legs stretched out before them, staring at their little ones who looked like living skeletons. A nurse picked up one of the small babies and lifted her gently into a sewn linen bag that hung from a handheld weighing scale. The baby screamed as it felt unsupported in the swaying bag, her huge dark eyes looking straight up at the ceiling. After scribbling down the weight on a clipboard, the baby was put back in the arms of a malnourished mother who pushed a stretched nipple between the little one's lips. The mother looked like a tired ragdoll, silent and unmoving.

We continued our walk through Yirol, and I followed a wide dirt road where both sides were lined up with merchants trying to trade their few wares. A crippled old man stumbled to the side as we passed by. Naked children ran everywhere, some of them scared as they saw white faces for the first time in their lives. Small paths branched off to the left and right from the main road. Herds of brown cows with huge horns milled about while some boys tried to direct them through the main road. Snapping blows resounded into the air as they whipped their hides with thin branches. Some cows had bells around their necks; they looked like they were made from melted bullets pelted into sheets and bent into a shape to make rough bells.

Most herding boys had hair the color of copper. Our translator explained that this happened because the boys washed their heads under the powerful stream of urine from the cows. Over time, it changed the black, tightly woven curls into a strange tint of orange or blond. As I looked at the boys, I was shocked to see that some of them had horrible sickly white bodies. With a chuckle, the translator grabbed a small boy and showed me how they were covered by a paste of ashes from burned cow dung. They smeared their whole body with the liniment as this kept the mosquitoes at a distance.

These energetic boys looked healthy, well-fed, strong with bulging muscles, and far from being malnourished compared to the rest of the population. I asked how this was possible, and my companion said, "They feed on milk combined with blood from the cow while they herd the cattle. They also do a lot of physical training as they take up serious wrestling competitions with their peers to build up their strength. Later, when they lead the herds into the towns, they will show off their skills."

Compound Living

The Medair compound where we all lived and worked was still under development. The house was an old, half-bombed-out brick house, shaded by a few large mango trees. An English commissioner had occupied it during the colonial era. During the occupation of the Northern military, Arabs had been living in this house. After the liberation of Yirol from the GoS, the head of the SPLA took up residence in the house for a while. When Medair came to Yirol to assist in the hunger crisis, he allocated it to Medair as living quarters and a base to work from.

The roof had been patched up after a bomb had gone through and left a gaping hole. The bomb ended up on the veranda where it slammed into the concrete and never exploded. It had to be removed before we could safely occupy the house.

The house was constructed in the old colonial style. Inside, three large rooms were interconnected with a doorway, so you could walk from one room into the next. Each room also had a side opening onto the veranda that surrounded the whole house. The windows and doors did not have wooden frames anymore and were secured at night by closing the shutters from the outside. The veranda would have been screened against insects, but it had rotted away over the years.

We used the last room for food storage. In the next adjacent room, each team member had been allocated a wooden plank and a place for a metal trunk where personal items could be stored and locked away. This part of the house also functioned as an office and radio room. Next was the living room and kitchen area. Everything was just bare concrete, and the only furniture in the house was a rickety-made shelf for holding a water basin and a cooking stove. We sat at camping tables and chairs to have dinner or play a card game, and here we held our team meetings.

Surrounding these rooms was a large veranda. The side where the sun came up was designated for the men, while the side where the sun set was for the female staff. Each one of us had an individual, small white mosquito dome that was set up along the wall on the veranda. As a couple, Bart and I slept at the corner of this building, at the boundary line of the male/female quarters. There was little privacy.

We looked up into bare rafters that supported the roof, as there was no longer a ceiling. High between the rotten beams, the house was infested by colonies of bats. We secured plastic sheets above the table in the kitchen and dining area to collect the droppings so they would not get into our food. Bats released a specific odor that would stay with me forever. Some wooden beams were eaten away by termites, and others looked like they were ready to collapse. The whole house was in bad shape.

Around 7 p.m., it was pitch-black outside. There was no electricity except for the five solar panels that we switched on for the time that we ate and played a game of UNO before turning to bed at 8 or 9. We all had oil lamps that we took to our mosquito dome and a small penlight to guide us to the toilet that was built on the compound.

At night, massive centipedes traveled over the swept pathway to the latrine. I only went when it was absolutely necessary and urgent! Before I entered the small latrine, I shone the light everywhere in all corners just to be sure there were no uninvited, creepy crawlers around my feet, hanging over my head, or hiding under the toilet lid.

The moment it was dark, foreign sounds echoed throughout the night. We heard constant activity by hunting bats and other inhabitants on the veranda and around the compound. In the beginning, it would keep me awake as I pricked up my ears. Did I hear softly planted footsteps in the compound? Was there an animal on the prowl on the veranda? That screech…an owl or was it a baby that cried in the hut close by? Often, bits and pieces fell on the netting above our heads. A young bat might fly at full speed into the net as it did not detect the flimsy material, and on instinct, I ducked my head deeper into my pillow.

During the morning, it was pleasantly cool on the open veranda. The tall grass was yellowing around us, and the now broken stems made it easy to see far and wide through the African trees. We saw the lake shimmering in the midday heat. Brightly colored birds sang and fluttered in the mango tree, and the branches rustled over the tin roof. Goats scrambled around our compound, and people squinted through the raised fence of thin branches. We were building a stronger fence as the branches weren't much of a boundary to keep roaming animals out of our compound

Sitting here, I forgot for a moment that we were in an active war zone. Huts for the team members were being constructed all around the brick house so we could live in more privacy. For the roofs, we needed tall grass, and as the grass had properly dried out, it was now harvested for that purpose. The walls of the huts consisted of thin cut-off tree trunks that were collected from the bush and sold as poles. They would be placed flush to each other and later plastered with a mud paste that hardened in the sun.

The price of grass and poles had fallen, so we were building three more *tukuls* (mud huts). One *tukul* would be for the night watch, and two for the married couples on the team. Closer to the entrance of the compound, a large *tukul* was constructed. The grass roof hung low over the short walls, which were sticks half the length of the other huts. You had to bow your head to enter the heavily shaded hut. Here, we held meetings with the village people and other important leaders of the area.

After the harvest of usable grass for all the huts that were now popping up everywhere in the village, the grasslands were being ignited, and fires started all over the area. For days, a low sheen of smoke covered Yirol, only lifting when a slight breeze picked up during the late afternoons. At night, glowing embers became ever-present eyes watching over us.

Burning the earth had the added benefit of fertilizing the ground for the planting season. But it also added more heat to the already simmering hot days. Close to the main road that led to the airport, there were still unexploded ordnances buried under the sand. Often, while whole areas were being burned down, bombs went off, and explosions were heard during the night.

One day, as we drove back from the airstrip—after we had unloaded a plane of goods—another bomb exploded close by. It was common for cows to step on a mine and be blown to smithereens. The entire population grieved the loss of a cow as it was their livelihood, their status, and their means of payment for a dowry.

In the mid-afternoon, even in the shade, it was scorching hot. The wind dried you out, your tongue felt like leather, and we sipped from a bottle of filtered water that we carried around. Lunch consisted of dry crackers with a layer of peanut butter and hot tea. We were in a country where food was scarce, and we adapted.

Around five o'clock, the nurses returned from their work. A cassette recorder was placed on a lone rock, and music filled the compound. Some played badminton, and others danced to the music. Laughter filled the air, and the tension of the day subsided.

When evening approached, we strolled toward the lake. In the red afterglow of the setting sun, people came out of their huts and walked with us or talked with their neighbors and tended to their cooking fires. Children played on the swept compound with metal hoops or handmade windmills from thin tin that was formed into gleaming flower petals.

Sometimes we were overtaken by a nice, new-looking bicycle. This puzzled me as everything around was dilapidated or broken. My companion explained, "Only important individuals have been given transport like this; the SPLA pays for them." A tall Dinka man approached us and showed us his New Testament. I looked up a known verse and ended up reading aloud John 3:16. A *'Khwaja'* (white person) who read Dinka! The gathered group of people nodded, laughed, and clapped their hands.

Our local household team consisted of water bearers, wash ladies, cleaners, and a cook. They lived in the village and came in each day for domestic duties. The water bearers were young women who made a lot of fun of us. Giggling and chatting together, they pointed out the unfamiliar items we had lying around. Often, they would stop and talk with other women on their way to collect water at the well. Peals of laughter and pointing fingers made it clear they spread the word around about how these strangers lived.

The main treat of the day for our local staff was a cup of tea with lots of sugar. For some of these ladies, the amount of sugar we gave was never enough. Their drink should have been sugar with a drop of tea! They acted like mischievous children and made life difficult for others to do their work. When the tea was not sweet enough, they just threw it over their shoulders into the dirt. When it was time to sweep the veranda where our little mosquito tents stood, they defiantly sat on the edge of the wall and braided each other's hair. We had to replace some of these young ladies.

How do you communicate discipline to women who had suffered many crises and were in dire need of correction? We tried to speak about their attitude toward their duties and how to show respect to those who were committed to bringing relief to their situation.

Mama Lou, our cook, was an outstanding example of someone committed to personal growth. She showed genuine respect and was willing to expand her knowledge, and asked many questions so she could better conduct her daily tasks. Although she understood some English and could make herself clear, she asked our translator to help communicate the more elaborate conversations.

Sometimes, she would advise us when the water girls were causing trouble or when a theft was imminent, as she knew what other staff members had talked about during breaks. She told us how the staff forced her to ask us to give them things and even gave her a list of items they wanted. She had told them that such attitudes were not appreciated and that she would do no such thing! Her determination to be open and upfront was commendable.

In the late afternoon, she prepared a meager evening meal for us without meat. As she washed the few vegetables and cooked some rice, she kept mumbling to herself. She would pick up jars with spices or herbs, smell them, and sample them to determine how she could liven up our dinner. That evening, when she went back home, she immediately spoke to her husband—who had several wives and traveled between families. She shared her concern about the lack of meat and told him, "My people have no meat to eat, which is bad. You need to give them a goat."

The next day she came in with a twinkle in her eyes. With restrained excitement, she exclaimed that tonight we would have meat to eat. And sure enough, that afternoon, a goat straining against a rope was delivered. The men slaughtered it, and Mama Lou prepared a most delicious meal of goat meat and local vegetables. It was a welcome change from the tomato paste mush or a curry dish from sardines out of a tin.

One Sunday morning, I was woken by the sound of tins being banged together as if there was a procession. Just outside the fence, an enormous herd of cows was being herded through the town. Cows with bells around their necks added to the cacophony of noise. A whole cattle camp appeared to have been uprooted and was transported to another part of the area as the water holes had dried up.

Compound Living

The dry season was really dry, and sand was thrown high into the swirling, stifling air.

The new fence around the compound was nearly completed. From the flat wooden pallets from the WFP, we made a proper gate, and we painted the Medair logo on it. The white paint would hold the termites at bay; otherwise, the wood would be pulverized within a few weeks. We could now close the compound off against the free-roaming cows and goats, and it provided a boundary for people who came in to ask for help. The workers initially asked why we made it look so nice for the brief time that we would be with them. But when they saw the fresh effect and the benefit of a layer of paint, they soon asked if they could have that white paint too for their huts and walls that were made from sticks.

The People and Culture

One early morning, I sat on the brick stairs leading up to the veranda of our house. Mr. Abut Deng, our compound manager, translator, and liaison officer, came into the compound. With a sigh, he sat down and started to talk about his life. Abut was assigned to us by the Sudan Relief and Rehabilitation Agency, the humanitarian branch of the SPLA.

I was intrigued and pleased that I was granted a glimpse of his life. I asked him to tell me more about the cultural customs of his people. With a grin, he explained the role of a woman in his society. "Women do not have many rights compared with how you would see it. They are to be there for their husband, look after the kids, cook, and keep the compound. We do have organized women's groups with a strict hierarchy that states who can be a spokeswoman for the family. It is a highly regarded position among women. You would need to be respected by others and seen as worthy to be the representative of your clan."

I nodded respectfully as he looked sideways at me to see how I took this information. "And the men, what is their main activity and role in your society?" I asked.

He thought for a moment to decide what part of his role as the man he would share. "The men are travelers, and they go from wife to wife. They only have permission to visit their woman regularly if he has properly married her by paying a dowry. They work in the fields, have a trade, or are employed in the army and do not do anything that is allocated to a woman, like carrying household goods, water containers, or preparing food."

He continued, "A man would never carry anything on his head, which is for women to do. The man is mostly in transit, his adult life is taken up by visiting the different compounds where his wives live. You can only afford wives if you have a lot of cattle as good wives are expensive. The more kids you have, the better it is, as that would ensure a secure future when you are old."

The People and Culture

He further explained that a girl is married by seventeen. After a brief silence, he said, "In reality, this is when a girl is twelve. When she has had two years with her husband, she might have proven that she is worth a dowry...that is enough time to see if she is fertile. When she has produced a child, she is sent back to her mother to learn more about womanhood." Abut's face beamed as he told me, "The man will visit her regularly, and when she has produced another child, she is taken back to his compound to become his full-time wife." With an approving sigh, he concluded, "She gets to build her own *tukul* and gets status!"

I asked him: "What happens if she doesn't produce any children?"

"She will be returned to her family, and the cows that have been paid for her must be paid back. Automatically she will become a prostitute to support herself," he answered.

He told this story as a large herd of cows passed our fence, and he counted them aloud and commented that this herd was enough to buy two women. "The Dinka climbs the ladder of status when he has more than one wife, and it is obvious that the owner of this herd is a rich man! A good woman will have to be trained by her mother. She should be able to pound her maize and sorghum well, cook, and produce children. She needs to be beautiful and have respect for her husband. The community has to testify of her good character and that she is lovely, friendly, and gentle."

This was the ideal picture of a Dinka family. However, it could easily happen that a young girl was given to an elderly man. One of our water bearers happened to be married to an old man. She was very naughty, and according to the community, the old man could not handle her very well. Male staff who worked with us did not understand Medair's policy on treating the staff with so much grace. They commented, "Why do you not rattle good sense into this woman? Without a proper beating, she will never do what you ask!"

One of our young nurses and I decided to walk to a local Catholic church somewhere in the village as we heard a Mass was being held. The church was not a building, but rather rows of sticks driven into the dirt under a large mango tree next to a broken-down school. It was uncomfortable as we sat on these thin sticks that were held up by V-shaped branches.

A very dark-skinned priest in a sparkling white dress decorated with a bright-colored belt walked reverently through the pews made of sticks. Choir girls walked in line with the priest. Around their heads they each wore a band made of beads, and a cross dangled on their foreheads. Singing and swinging, they walked around the gathering. Finally, they drew up to a small wooden table at the front of the stick pews. A Bible lay open on a white cloth. A large picture of Mary and the Baby was lifted into the air.

Slowly the pews filled up with young mothers, their babies still suckling on their breasts. There were only a handful of men and lots of children. The singing of songs took up the first part of the traditional service. In the end, the priest read a Scripture from the Good News Bible. He had put quite some thought into the referring Scriptures, and I was encouraged by his message. It was so good to see how God can speak to us and is not bound by any denomination. God is not pushed inside any walls, literally or figuratively. The priest read the same verses we as a team had read the night before.

> *Therefore, strengthen your feeble arms and weak knees. Make level paths for your feet, so that the lame may not be disabled, but rather healed (Hebrews 12:12-13 NIV).*

We walked back through the dilapidated village. Everywhere in town were piles of rubble from broken-down houses. Against the walls of the ruins, tarps were stretched between sticks as shelters. The people built a little boundary around the tarps from the strewn-around, mud-baked bricks to indicate their personal living space. Larger structures lay in ruins, and everywhere were collapsed mud huts with caved-in grass roofs. More and more people came back to town after having been scattered because of the fighting and the hunger. Sometimes a family took up their residence under a tree where they tied up large mosquito nets under which they slept.

Leprosy Colony

There was another group of people in dire need staying around Yirol: a group of lepers. The mandate of Medair states that we should reach out into the most remote and forgotten areas, so we decided to visit them. I made my first visit to the leper colony on a Sunday afternoon.

They lived in an old sunflower oil factory with broken-down, rusty machines bolted in the middle of the room. The building had not been damaged in the war, and quite a few families lived within the four huge brick walls. Large broken fans hung from the ceiling, and rusted metal equipment was strewn everywhere. What an unhealthy place for lepers to live with their many festering wounds!

There were people with ragged clothes, hardened stumps as feet, and disfigured hands. Some showed me their untreated wounds. Old wounds had crusted over and were covered with flies. Many women had been married off to leprous men and gave birth to initially healthy children. Later on, some contracted the virus and started to lose feeling in their hands and feet. Open wounds were visibly infected. It was a rejected group of people, not tolerated in the townships, chased away from the water wells, and even pushed away by their people when they came for treatment at the Red Cross clinic.

My heart went out to these marginalized people. They were ecstatic to see us visit them. Quickly, a "committee" was put into place to properly give us an official welcome. The chief opened the meeting with a speech full of glorifying facts about Medair as an organization. "You came to us first to give us assistance; you made it possible for other NGOs to follow up on the many needs of our people. Our lives are in your hands. We are thankful; yes, we praise God for the arrival of you all. But we require food, clothes, and blankets. Look at our feet; they need proper coverage. We need shoes. Our children are sick and need medical attention…"

The speech went on and on, and finally, the second in charge got a chance to say something after the chief finalized his speech with, "And now I have nothing more to say."

Then it was our turn to speak, "We are so thankful that you wanted to receive us into your homes. We have been informed of your situation, and that is why we came to visit you." After these words, the gathered group of people burst out in spontaneous applause. "As much as it is possible, we would like to give you what you require. Today we brought you shoes and a large bag of maize. Of course, you all will understand that we cannot get you everything you requested as we are required to help more people in your community."

It certainly was difficult to hear of all the genuine needs and not be able to fulfill the list. We continued our speech, "We appreciate the display of gratefulness, and we are hoping you will at least receive what we brought to you today. Again, the group clapped their hands.

The chief was less happy and obviously not satisfied. He pointed to the large bag of maize. "This is not enough for all of us. Look at our hands and feet; we cannot plow and prepare the fields to sow the seeds and harvest its food. We are poor. Look at our children. Christmas is near, and they are naked. What you bring is not enough."

The time was indeed near when the people could start preparing their fields for sowing. There were also healthy men in this group who could work the land and herd their cows to grassy areas. It was a difficult matter to find the balance between giving what was needed and, at the same time, letting the population discover the joy of being in charge of their own lives and not becoming dependent on outside assistance.

We can keep giving, but will it ever be enough? We soon found out it had become a system to just approach any NGO and request goods and food. In their experience, we would disappear soon enough again, leaving them behind while we go back to our comfortable lifestyles.

At the end of the meeting, we distributed the gifts that we brought. I handed over a pair of sandals to the chief, and his face lit up. Suddenly, sadness spread over his features as he looked at the sandals and then at the stumps where his feet once were. His toes were gone; I could identify the rounded heel and a protruding piece of bone covered by thickened flesh where the feet should have been.

Another type of sandal was searched for in the bag, and these

Leprosy Colony

seemed to fit better, still looking ridiculously grotesque on his stumps. As he fastened the straps, he pointed to the stumps that had been his feet and showed us the hideous scars. He explained the wounds were not due to leprosy, but by the feasting of rats that would nibble on his feet during the night when he was asleep. He had not felt it as the nerves were dead from the disease. With a wide smile on his face, he rose with dignity from his hand-carved wooden chair and stood on stumps now shodden with sandals. The people burst out in song and rhythmically clapped their hands.

After hours of going through the meeting rituals and the distribution of gifts, we were shown around the several buildings in which the leper colony lived. Behind large reservoirs and tanks in the main building, there were tall stacks of grenades, bombs, and other combat equipment. We were specifically ordered not to photograph anything inside the building. The lepers walked casually between those stacks as if unaware just how dangerous they were. Families sat huddled together around smoky fires, cooking up porridge. Naked children played and ran around, and I wondered if they would feel anything if they walked by accident through the hot coals as some of their feet were just stumps.

Deep inside the semi-dark building, groups of young men gathered around their smoking fires. A large, chopped-off cow head lay close by, blackened by layers of flies that scratched on the rotting tissue and laid their eggs inside the hollowed-out eyes. A few bloodied legs were divided up by someone who wielded a sharp cleaver. Children watched the procedure with fascination, their tongues licking their dry lips. After the carcass was divvied up, they dished out the intestines, and everyone got a handful of squishy goo.

Back outside, the chief divided all the people into two groups. Rachel and I were invited to sit under a large tree on rickety stools. It was time for a story, and we both would be telling a different story. One group went to Rachel, who spoke about Christmas, and I talked about Abram—the beautiful story of how God wanted to have a relationship with us humans. The people applauded, and the translator told me that the people loved the story as they could identify with Abram and his nephew, Lot. They saw themselves traveling from place to place and in the accumulation of herds and the outcome of making good choices as Abram did.

The women offered to sing for us. Our translator tried to follow the musical rendering of the story. An older woman closed her eyes and started to sing about the oppression they experienced because they made the right choice by being Christians. Just like Abram had chosen to be friends with God, and although being a chief, he humbled himself before a younger member of his family. The rest of the women answered her in short outbursts as a chorus and thanked God for the good things they received while they were still in so much suffering.

As I listened, a man approached me and asked if he could say a prayer for me. The translator told me later that he had been thanking God for sending me and telling this story. He had prayed a blessing over me and had asked God if He would bring me back so they could learn more from His Word. Another man pointed to the sky, which meant that the meaning of the story was as widely applicable as the air in the sky.

More songs were sung, more prayers were offered, more speeches, and more lists of the things they required. After a good two and a half hours, we were able to go back to our compound. I was filled with joy, as I could see that God reached beyond human suffering and brought life into people's dark-filled experiences. Africa is alive.

Planning Programs

Early one morning, I sat behind the laptop in the makeshift office and read through reports, trying to comprehend all the different projects that Medair managed. I read that not only did we run programs in Yirol, but we also had feeding centers in neighboring towns. There were educational programs, training programs, and immunization programs. And of course, we still played a significant role for the individuals who came to our gate and asked for assistance. Families had traveled for days, sometimes weeks, because they had heard of an NGO that had come into Yirol County to bring relief.

During the morning, a group of people gathered in long queues in front of our gates to wait for the distribution of food and clothes. They distinctly smelled of old sweat and dried-up dust and dirt. As we scanned the group, we could see that the intensity of the hunger was declining as people looked better than in previous weeks. The feeding center was closing up soon as well, as there were only twenty children admitted that week for the Intense Feeding Program. Soon the mothers would be sent away with specially formulated food to keep up the weight of the child. I wrote another account of a day in Yirol:

> Today, a few children are sent home from the Intensive Therapeutic Feeding Center as they had reached the proper weight for height. The mothers get a box filled with extra food and clothes, kitchen gear, blankets, and mosquito nets. They go on their way with a few kilos of maize, lentils, and nutritious biscuits for the children. Everything got piled up on their heads, and—with straight backs—they walked out of the building. Another baby died during the night, although she was treated with medicines through an intravenous drip. The nurses think she died of meningitis as she continual-

ly shook and shivered as if she were having fits. I thought the baby would make it, but this morning the father came to tell us she died. There is no funeral ceremony for this baby, just a shallow grave where the child is laid to rest. A small pile of sand identified the place, which would disappear soon enough. At night, we heard the high-pitched sounds of hyenas, and I cry.

At lunchtime, as we nibbled on our crackers, I listened as the nurses chatted and reflected on their programs. Two nurses were teaching local coordinators the hygiene and immunization procedures as an immunization program would be conducted early in January. They used an abandoned mosque as a classroom. The students would learn to give injections, organize the logistics of transporting the vials as they needed to be kept cool, and keep records and a filing system.

We were also asked to learn to inject as we would be accompanying the teams when they were sent off to their locations. We used a fruit like an orange to learn how to inject water just under the skin. I tried it and felt proud after I saw the orange swell up where I administered the jab. I chuckled at the diversity of skills we developed as aid workers.

Later that evening, a mother entered the compound with a comatose child in her arms. One of the nurses got up to attend to the emergency. Each Medair nurse was on a roster for emergencies that might appear during the evening and night. Officially, Medair had handed over the clinic to the Red Cross, and our nurses had only volunteered to come over for emergencies. Medair had established a trusting relationship with the people of the village, and people preferred to come to our compound for assistance.

Shortly after the mother had been redirected to the clinic, another scream pierced through the late evening. A man with an enormously swollen hand stood at the gate and asked for help. He had sat down at the fire and put his hand on the sand. A scorpion had stung him, and within minutes his whole arm was aching and throbbing. He groaned and tried to compose himself as the pain of the poison seared through his body.

UNICEF had funded Medair to implement the education program. Back in Nairobi, during our induction period, I had been prepared to help out in this program. Rachel, our team leader, had begun the initial groundwork by handing out surveys to the district leaders who would contact the local schools and teachers. She had designed questionnaires that teachers at the bush schools had to fill in before we would even come to visit the schools. As the data from the schools came in, we understood the great need for basic materials so that the schools could function again. To prove they were motivated and took ownership of the project, we asked the communities to build a meeting *tukul* where classes could be held and school storerooms for the materials that we were going to provide.

It was also common to have a school garden that produced food for the teachers as they had not been paid salaries since the internal conflicts. And we wanted to see that some ground had been tilled so we could distribute some seeds for the garden. It needed to be fenced properly so others could not steal the harvest or allow animals to walk through the gardens and trample the crops. This also ensured that teachers were able to keep on teaching even when the planting season started as they did not need to leave their work to secure their food supply. Ownership of these projects stimulated commitment and motivation to continue even after we exhausted our support and other funding from organizations such as the United Nations High Commissioner for Refugees (UNHCR).

Indeed, before the end of the set period, most questionnaires were returned so we could make a list of the materials the schools needed to start their school term in the new year. We were pleased with the determination teachers showed, and it seemed important for the community that schools would continue even during war and famine. The war had destroyed most civil systems, and education had not been on the people's minds. Young men would go off to war, never to return, or those who did returned never got the opportunity to finish their education.

There were countless meetings with the head of education in what was called by the departments as New Sudan, which would later become independent and called South Sudan in 2011. The newly appointed coordinators were all well-established leaders within the SRRA. These significant positions were filled with people with long lists of titles that could not be skipped during the opening addresses. Their role was essential since they were in charge of setting up the schooling systems—through which teachers would be paid salaries—and organizing remunerations during the seeding and harvesting times, as teachers then could not attend to their gardens. Their job was to speak to the community so they were convinced of the importance of education and would take up the responsibility for a long-term solution to keep the teachers and children in the schools.

I am saddened to say that there were no female teachers employed—they couldn't read or write. Our own female staff also could not read or write. None of the children in our village went to school or receiving an education. They just hung around, played with handmade toys, climbed the mango tree to eat unripe fruit, and ran around dangerous surroundings where mines were still a threat.

One of our water girls watched me writing in my diary. I saw her trying to sign her name in the dirt with a stick. It was important to them to be able to print their name since every week they had to sign their salary slip. As I observed her, I could see she had never learned how to hold a pen properly. Awkwardly, her hands tried the fine motor movements, but her fingers just did not do what she wanted. I tried to remember how we were taught to hold a pencil in primary school and how to draw little circles on dotted lines to train these fine movements. I explained the principle, but without proper translation and repeated exercises, it was useless. The women just scribbled unintelligent, wobbly figures under the dotted line, the concept of making signs that mean something was unfamiliar and strange to them. I could get a women's literacy class organized next year, something to follow up on when I was in Nairobi with the education and literacy coordinator.

The days were now terribly busy, but we made sure to visit the leper colony to encourage them. When we entered their compound, they all wanted to hug us. Some had open, festering wounds. In the back of my mind, I recoiled for a moment, not sure if I could contract the disease myself. Then compassion and love for these people overcame the hesitancy, and I returned their greetings. When I talked to the nurses about it, they assured me that I would not contract the disease since we have strong immune systems. For years, nobody outside their own community would have wanted to touch them.

On our last visit of the year, they told us that they were very worried about our absence during the upcoming Christmas break. Their fear was based on the idea that we might have gotten inside in-

Planning Programs

formation that the soldiers would come back around Christmastime and would take over Yirol again. They thought that when all the foreigners had gone, an offensive attack would be conducted. Although there was a cease-fire at this moment, we did not know if this would be revoked in January. If that happened, whatever we had carried out might have been for nothing. That is the risk of emergency aid work in a war-torn country; today we build and live, tomorrow it might be destroyed, and lives snuffed out.

Soon, we would all leave for the New Year break. We distributed outstanding salaries and the "food-for-work" incentives. The payment system we kept was that each worker got a month's supply of food at the beginning of the month and a salary at the end of the month. It meant that today they would only get their salary because the food had already been given at the beginning of the month. We explained this every month, several times, and they signed their contracts, but it looked like the people did not understand—or did not *want* to understand—the concept.

While we were having our last debrief meeting with the SRRA, our workers came in ready to cause a riot because they only received the money and not any food items. Abut tried to explain it again to the staff, but tension rose as arguments grew louder and louder. Finally, Abut lost it and yelled at the people that they were just 'ungrateful dogs" who could not stop asking for more.

He stood up, took Rachel and me by the hand, and guided us away from the developing riot. He felt as frustrated as we were and mumbled an excuse, "Our people do not understand that you come to assist the whole community and not just to make individuals rich."

A few days before we would leave for a break, Bart woke up feeling unwell, and later that night, he lay sweating in his mosquito dome. His fever surged high, and he shivered violently. The nurse took some blood samples, and he was diagnosed with malaria. He felt horrible that he was now unable to help pack; the whole team was preparing to vacate the base over Christmas. Between looking after him and giving him constant water to drink, I had to clean out the storeroom in the back.

The storerooms in town also needed to be emptied, and doors fitted with locks, and even windows boarded up so the house would be available when we returned. Otherwise, we would find the place looted and occupied, and then it would be difficult to reclaim it as our workspace. In one of the last entries of the year, I wrote:

> I worked in our storeroom in the house today. It was where we stored our food, and I could see that many mice, bats, and other vermin had enjoyed themselves. The boxes of cornflakes had been nibbled on, and a trail of crumbs showed that the last packets of dried crackers had been eaten, leaving only the packaging. Under the few tins of food still on the shelves, I found cockroaches and a dangerous centipede. On the floor, a scorpion scurried toward a crack in the floor. These pests were all common and freely roamed around the house, tents, and compound. Last night, someone went to the toilet and saw a scorpion running in front of her, which dove under the doorframe into the latrine. When she opened the door, the scorpion was waiting on the doorstep with a raised tail, ready to attack. Needless to say, the storeroom wasn't my favorite place to work.

Everything got a good cleaning, and all radio equipment was stored in the lockable storeroom. We would have a permanent guard living in the compound to make sure there would be no break-ins during our absence.

The wait for our flight out of Yirol was long. In the morning, we had locked and sealed the house up. The windows were closed off by WFP bags so no one could peek and identify items to steal. Bart lay on some bags on the ground in the meeting *tukul* to be in the shade. He was still shuddering with malaria fever.

At last, we were brought to the airstrip by the International Committee of the Red Cross (ICRC) staff members, who also promised to keep a lookout on the property during our break. A MAF pilot flew us back to Nairobi, and I felt encouraged by the pilot's prayer before we took off. It was a different experience than how we started our journey flying into Sudan.

As we flew over the outskirts of the city, I saw the shantytowns of Nairobi beneath us. We flew low over Nairobi National Park as

Planning Programs

we descended into the airport. From my side of the small window, I spotted a herd of impalas grazing peacefully in the adjacent grasslands.

Coming back into the team house was now a luxurious experience after weeks in the field. It was comfortably furnished, decorated in bright colors, and cool upon entering. I had not noticed any of this when we first arrived such a short time ago. We were all relieved to take a long, refreshing shower in Loki and sleep in a normal bed in a furnished team house for the night. It was exciting to meet many other team members who worked in other field locations in Sudan. Some of them we only knew from our conversations through the high frequency (HF) radio briefings each day as we did our routine morning and evening radio checks. Some would travel to their home countries for Christmas and New Year's, but we decided to enjoy some time in Nairobi.

We visited a large cathedral for the Christmas service and joined others who had booked a nice retreat close to Hell's Gate National Park. There was a beautiful hike around the large crater mouth, and it was exhilarating to stand on the rim and gaze over the Great Rift Valley.

1999: The Startup of Programs

It was time to return to Sudan. We all gathered in the Nairobi office to listen to the latest security briefing. Until the fifteenth of January 1999, tension was high as we awaited the outcome of the national caucus for an extension of the cease-fire arrangement of the GoS.

One of the disturbing items on the agenda was that there had been a North Sudanese reconnaissance Antonov flight over the town of Yirol. These planes were known to drop bombs after they finished their initial circuits and had compiled information about people's movements in the area. People immediately fled into the bush when the plane came down low. Only a few days past the fifteenth—the due date for the extension of the cease-fire arrangement—did people cautiously come back to check if the villages were safe. Another reason people returned was that they had heard we would come back to distribute displacement kits that contain household goods.

The barren and dusty airstrip welcomed us back to Yirol. It was as if we had never left. A busy time lay ahead; we would be in the field for a stint of six weeks, and my mind was in overdrive as we planned the implementation of different programs.

We had employed new water carriers, and I liked the ladies who were now part of our local staff. They brought us jerry cans filled with cool water from the well and distributed the water throughout the house for cooking, washing clothes, and filling up the shower reservoir.

Only one lady remained from the previous team, Cholok, and she was a heavy drinker. We knew she did not have any family in town, and we knew she could be a liability to the new team. Still, we decided that she needed us the most, and that was our slogan within Medair: reaching out to the neediest. Her story was so sad; she had just had a baby, but her milk had dried up because of her drinking problem. We were able to help her feed her little one. We prayed daily for her, and she grew into the position of overseer of the young girls who carried water for us. This new responsibility stimulated her,

1999: The Startup of Programs

and she picked up her daily tasks with pride and dignity. We had a solid team that we could trust to do their duties well.

Often, I lay awake at night, just listening to the different sounds around me. Both the sounds and the silence during these long hours had a way of captivating you in Africa. I tried to identify the sounds farther away in the village. Maybe groups of nocturnal animals? Or the movement of soldiers as they regrouped? I opened my tent and stood outside on the balcony and listened to the beat of drums while absorbing the night. Through the sparse undergrowth, I noticed the flickering lights of campfires all around the town. Dancing people were singing after a binge-drinking event of locally brewed beer. Sleep was far away when I heard gunshots, and I made sure I had the "run bag" close to me in the tent in case we had to evacuate suddenly.

Before the war, lions hunted in the region, and the local staff told us that a leopard now lived near our compound. The feline animals had fled the sounds and terror of the war and were returning to their territories. For a few nights now, something had been stalking our roofs. The muffled thumps, scratching, and hissing made my skin crawl.

Before going to bed, we all stood leaning on the crumbled balcony of the house with a cup of water to rinse our teeth before retreating into our mosquito tents or mud huts. As we brushed our teeth and spat into the bushes, a team member suddenly shouted, "Something is staring at us through the bush! It is a baby leopard! Can you hear it growling? It is small but moves like a shadow!" I tried to penetrate the black night but couldn't detect any movements. That night, after we had all gone to our tents, we heard a loud commotion. Branches on the mango tree were sweeping frantically back and forth, and we heard growls and hisses. Whatever cat-like animal this was, it was terribly angry and had very sharp claws.

A team member who had worked late into the night entered our side of the veranda, unaware of the commotion. Urgently, we whispered through the thin gauze of our mosquito dome, "Get back into your tent! We think the leopard has returned and seems very aggravated." The animal let out a scream, and more rustling and scratching could be heard. She froze on the spot as the four-legged visitor jumped from the tree onto the roof. She screamed at the sound of screeching nails; it was losing its footing on the tin roof and sliding to the edge. We all breathed a sigh of relief when we heard it jump to the tree. Finally, the noise receded as it ran away through our compound.

The next morning, we excitedly told the story to our night guard. He promised to hunt it down and kill it because it had tried to enter the chicken coop and had woken him up too. He did just that the next night and showed us a silky furry carcass that proved to be a genet cat. These are cat-like animals with long sleek bodies. They have spotted fur, a ringed tail, large ears, and a pointed muzzle. The beauty of the pelt made it a wanted animal. The guard was enormously proud of his kill and made a nice bracelet from its hide.

It was another early morning, and the first light dispelled the shadows and created patterns on the netting of my mosquito tent. The light grew brighter, and the sky turned grayish pink. In the stillness of the dawn, some tropical birds started their song. A goat bleated in the distance. Minutes later, the sound of cattle bells told me that a herd of cows passed our fence. A rooster crowed; others soon joined him to mark the beginning of a new day. I had tied our rooster at the utmost corners of our compound as I did not want to be woken up before 5 a.m. The branches of the mango tree filtered the light of the upcoming sun. A cool morning breeze gently stirred the leaves. A baby cried in a nearby hut, and then some rattling in the kitchen cleared the last cobwebs of sleep from my head. The first team member was making a cup of tea and humming a song.

In the compound, logisticians started our cars. These had to run because they powered up and charged the batteries for the base radio. The first task of the day was to perform a routine safety check on the vehicles. Next, we had to wake up the night guard so he could open the compound gate. It became a running joke that we had to wake the guard up, even though he was supposed to be the one opening the gate and waking up the staff! After splashing cold water on my face and drinking a hot cup of tea, I was ready to begin our proposed daily routine:

    6 a.m.   Radio check and breakfast
    7 a.m.   Devotion and team meeting
    8 a.m.   WORK
    1 p.m.   Lunch for those who are around and in town
    2 p.m.   Rest during the hottest hour of the day
    3 p.m.   WORK

1999: The Startup of Programs

5 p.m.   Return to base and relax
7 p.m.   Dinner and debrief
8 p.m.   Showers; turn off solar power
9 p.m.   Bedtime

Seldom did the day turn out to be so nicely organized. More often than not, the scheduled plans were not half realized by the end of the day. It was not possible to be back on time for lunch, and we often worked late into the night as we processed the gathered data into reports.

The moment the sun hit the bare sand in the compound, the temperature soared. By the time it was nine o'clock, sweat poured down my face, and I tried not to think of the rising mercury in the coming hours. Or dream of a simple fan to cool my face. And forget about a cooled, air-conditioned room. This heat was draining. During the hottest time of the day, it was difficult to concentrate, so we would lay still in the shade. This way we conserved some energy for later in the day.

By listening to BBC World Radio, we learned that the cease-fire was prolonged until March. This was confirmed by a nurse who had been in Loki for intense training for the upcoming immunization program. With gusto, we started to arrange the details to implement several programs that we had planned for the coming months.

Security issues were always discussed and on the briefing agenda, both in the morning and evening. During the day, we remained on alert to any changes in the normal activities or behavior of the townspeople. For a few days now, a new NGO in a gleaming four-by-four cruised through the town. With a little investigation, we learned that they were a de-mining company. This meant that the roads around Yirol would be cleared of antipersonnel mines, large anti-tank mines, and other ordnances that were still lying around. So now and then, we heard explosions that rock the ground.

As they briefed us on the progress, we found out that last year we had been driving over a road that had an anti-tank mine buried in the soil. We were never more aware of how much we needed God's protection as we went about our work. They even found several mines mounted on top of each other for better detonation and more destruction. They could not remove the bomb and take it to another place without risking the lives of their team members, so they exploded it on the spot, leaving a huge crater.

The dry season was at its peak, and all the animals were herded deeper into the Sudd Wetlands to find sufficient water. The children stayed behind in the little townships, and food became even scarcer. We received reports of outbreaks of meningitis, and soon we were treating several babies for this disease.

The situation got worse as the weeks went by, and soon WFP recognized the looming crisis and organized food drops again in Yirol. Medair was asked to be in charge of distributing the food after the drop. We identified a drop zone at a safe distance from the town. The boundary had been marked where pallets should fall when dropped from the plane. We scanned the sky expectantly and right on time, several planes appeared on the horizon. As the sound grew louder, we could see the huge black letters *UN* (United Nations) painted under the massive wings. Identifying these letters was reassuring, as the Antonov planes from the GoS had the same sound when they did their reconnaissance flights over the village. It was an impressive sight to see the huge white C-130 cargo planes come in from the Kenya border.

On their second pass, the planes roared low over the drop zone, and large hatches opened up the belly of the plane. At the right angle and at the right moment, the pilot would pull the raging machine in a steep incline. Pallets loaded with tightly packed sacks of grain began to slide through the opening. The falling load rumbled until it thudded on the ground. The logisticians started up the cars, driving towards the dropped pallets. Locally appointed distributors started to unpack and carried the sacks to the distribution sites in town. We would need to continue the feeding programs well into March. Each day we received more reports of insects that had destroyed the small sorghum (a staple crop) harvests.

To enhance our life style and make it more homier, I decided to extend our chicken flock. We had a young rooster and some hens, so we expected fresh eggs and chicks. One morning, a very thin man poked his head through the sticks of our fence and held a tied-up bunch of chickens high above his head. He sold me three chickens for a piece of soap, and as he spread the story that I was buying, we got more donations and gained two more roosters. Every morning, I found myself feeding them and collecting eggs for the team.

1999: The Startup of Programs

A local carpenter made a true palace for our feathered friends so they could be locked up during the night and protected from the elements or theft. Unfortunately, the roosters soon started to fight, and I had each one of them tied up at the far end corners of the compound. Our free-range hens could visit these males whenever they felt like it.

The dry season provided many opportunities for scorpions and snakes to enter our compound. Young boys helped us by cutting down any vegetation around the house to ensure that no garden waste piled up for snakes to find a cool hiding spot. However, a huge snake found a hollow under the mango tree while we were away, and it came out the moment we had chickens roaming around. Killing the well-fed snake was a horrible scene to watch. The men pinned the head between a forked stick and then bashed the head until it became a mushy pulp and waited for the body to stop wriggling.

The team was in high spirits. The break had been good for morale, and since the programs were still in planning mode, we all spent more time together, which led to getting to know each other better. I worked closely with Rachel and now felt less intimidated by her vast array of studies and education compared to my meager accomplishments in that area. Until now, I easily got stuck dwelling on my feelings of inadequacy. But working together as a team helped me to appreciate the skills and knowledge of others and learn from them. We complemented each other as we worked on designing the women's literacy course, and I enjoyed her sharing the bigger picture as she explained her approach to the course.

Rachel was good at communicating with all the stakeholders of the different parties involved, and she knew how to ask questions and zero in on priorities. She took the initiative and discerned how to apply the information she had gathered from the SRRA capacity builder and adjusted the course accordingly. She functioned as a liaison between the country education coordinator, other NGOs, and their programs, all with the overall outcome of the project in mind. I learned that effective communication between different operational levels is a skill that has many benefits. It requires the ability to speak to higher authorities about the benefits of the just-designed literacy program and later switch to the worker on the ground, conveying the information in lay terms.

In the case of the education program, schoolteachers had different perspectives on the school distribution program. They had other motives for being part of the program than the Educational Department of the newly formed government. Rachel maneuvered skillfully through all the different parties involved.

As we established ourselves in the community, the people renamed us with local names. The new Dinka name for Bart was Mobur (the white bull), and I was named Akir (brown and white cow). Another name that people used for Bart was "leg-leg," which meant he never walked fast. Well, in this heat, none of us were ever in a hurry.

Compound Boys

I got to know two young high school students who received some education during the prolonged war while they were boarding in a Catholic School in the district. They had come to us with the wish for a job, as school was not starting up again until it was proven that the cease-fire would hold. They carried a letter of introduction from their teacher in which he wrote that the boys should not be idling around and should seek employment. These were intelligent boys, both with impressive life stories.

During the hottest hours of the day, I sat with them and talked about their culture. In return, they taught me Dinka, and I shared some Bible teachings. Their English was not good enough to read the Bible, so a children's Bible with pictures was a suitable alternative. Faithfully, they studied the stories, and every day they had some questions about it: "How do I become a good leader?" "Can we talk about Moses today?" "How do I know if God really exists?" "What is the Kingdom of God?" "How come a local medicine man can heal people too?" "How do you overcome bad spirits?"

I tried to answer these questions from the Bible. And as we talked about the Kingdom of God, I explained the Gospel. The conversation was in limited Dinka and simple English! In the end, I asked if they knew for sure if they were part of that Kingdom by speaking out a prayer in which they asked Jesus to enter into their lives and be their King. They had never heard about this concept of Christianity before, and both boys wanted to be part of this eternal Kingdom. In prayer, they invited Jesus to come into their lives: "Lord Jesus Christ, I Daniel, thank you today in January 1999, that you sent our sister Maria to tell us about all these things we didn't know..." As I listened to their prayers, I did not hear a classic sinner's prayer, as we sometimes get taught in church, but I am convinced that God heard their hearts. They stumbled over the unfamiliar English words, mixing them with Dinka that I could not follow.

A few days later, I asked the boys how they felt after praying to

God, and one of them responded, "I'm so happy inside and relieved. Bad spirits have gone." Another boy then asked an interesting question. He was confused about why the letter to the Galatians said that circumcision was no longer necessary, given its importance in the story of Abram and the covenant with God. It seemed to me that these boys had a better understanding of cultural rituals than we do in the West. We looked through the Old and New Testaments, and I explained that God is interested in the circumcision of the heart and that a new covenant had been established through the blood of Jesus Christ, so that all nations on earth could enter into a relationship with God. The boys nodded and exclaimed, "Now we understand!" I enjoyed these sessions and felt that this Bread of Life was as important for these people as the food we distributed for their bodies.

On one particularly hot afternoon, I asked the boys to tell me their stories. Daniel, now seventeen, was born in 1982 and lived in Yirol. His father, an influential official, had built the hospital that now lies in ruins and was in charge of the oil factory where the lepers now lived. He had twenty-three wives and many children, including Daniel, who never knew his father personally as he divided his time between his wives. His father died young from high blood pressure.

This large family once lived in the house we now occupied, and Daniel felt as if he was working in his father's garden. His mother was his father's latest wife and, after he died, she traveled to Ethiopia with Daniel and his sister in search of a better life and education. However, the war soon broke out in Ethiopia, and while Daniel was at a boarding school in a neighboring village, his mother fled with his sister from a bombing that destroyed their house. She ended up as a refugee in Kenya. When Daniel was sent home, his mother and sister were gone. He spent four years searching for them throughout Ethiopia before returning to Southern Sudan and finally arriving back in Yirol County.

Martin was also born in Yirol County. His father died early in his life, and Martin had no recollection of him. According to custom, his mother automatically became the wife of his father's brother. Martin had more siblings from this uncle.

When the war broke out, his mother decided to leave this man in search of a better future for her children. She enrolled Martin in the same Catholic school as Daniel, and she earned her living by cutting grass and selling it at the market. The year that Yirol was liberated, his mother went back to Yirol. This meant that schooling would end for Martin as he was not allowed to board the school without family around to support him.

Martin came to us to ask for paid work. He was fourteen years old and living off WFP food distribution. He was a determined young man, and at this early age, he had decided what he wanted to do with his future. This did not include just survival and living in poverty. He was very keen and intelligent. The local school had nothing to offer him anymore, so he was set on earning enough money to support his studies outside Sudan.

It was so sad to see how destructive the effects of the war was on these promising young teenagers. Many such men would never have the opportunity to get a higher education and therefore were never able to rise above their situation. They had a taste of education and it had left them with a desire for more. Sudan could not give it to them at that time in their lives when it mattered most. Southern Sudan was not yet recognized as an independent country, and school systems were still in development. There was no officially established Education Department for the southern tribes at that time.

There were glimpses of hope, as the next story proves. Before I left for Nairobi, I received another letter from a young boy in the village. I leave it as he has written it:

> Dear Mum Maria,
> Cordially, and best greeting to you in the Name of our saving God. Dear mother, I am really in need of your help. You still remember me from my other letter. I am Daniel Maker. (A different Daniel that worked in our compound.) The thing on the ground is, I need help: My father died in 1988 in the war, as well as my mother on 30th April 1998. We are left with our aunt. We were born seven, and now our aunt cannot manage to take care of us seven children and pay our school fees. Also, you know the predicament situation the Sudanese people are leading, especially orphans. So, my aunt decided to take me to Kakuma (a refugee camp just across the border with Kenya) where my other aunt is. I am always pondering where to get a Migration Card. I

am imploring you to help me get this special card during your leave for Nairobi. I could help to get 500 KSh on the spot for you to bring it for me. My aunt and I went to SRRA previously, and they remarked that at least I can send the money and help me to fill it out and send me to Kenya Kakuma. In my absolute understanding, I hope you will do so for me. I think I have covered most of my letter. I hope to get reliable results and thanks.

 Yours in spiritual struggle,
 Daniel Maker Mayek

 After losing touch with Daniel for many years, we finally reconnected in 2022 when I found his profile on the Internet. As a teenager, he had immigrated to Australia after spending almost a decade in a refugee camp. Today, he is a successful litigation lawyer and the principal solicitor of Mayek Legal in Victoria, Australia.

Team Changes Ahead

The founders of Medair, Erik and Josiane Volkmar, were planning to visit us in the field. Rachel and I decided that painting another Medair logo on the ruins of the stone water tank in the middle of the compound would be a fun exercise and would make the couple feel at home when they arrived. So, we painted the half-crumbled tower in the middle of our compound with the colorful logo and fastened a flag on top of the highest standing stone. How proud we felt to present our organization to the world around us. We called it "our war statue."

During the meeting with our visitors, we heard that our current team leaders, Stuart and Rachel Forster, would be transferred to another team in Kampala, Uganda. Medair had set up a support base there to assist with programs in Congo and northern Uganda. This meant that Bart and I would become team leaders here in Yirol.

It was a daunting idea for us. We had not been in the field long enough to know what was going on in so many aspects of the work. We had only spent a few weeks in Nairobi being briefed and a few months in the field, and suddenly we were asked to take up the major responsibility of leading a team and managing the programs. This was nerve-racking. I certainly was not confident. And the old self-doubt raised its head. How could I be of any good when most of our team members had higher education and more experience? I felt insignificant and wondered if others saw more in me than I did.

As Erik and Josiane were preparing to leave, they prayed with us and asked the Holy Spirit to come and anoint us for this new role. We needed wisdom, strength, and understanding. Only God could reach beyond my limitations.

While I lay sweating in my hut (we had moved into our *tukul* once they were finished) during the midday rest hour, I was thinking about it all. I saw the stark blue sky, felt the hot wind, and saw the shimmering lake in the distance. My eyes followed the moving branches of the mango tree as they swayed with the wind. The branches reached the ground as the heavy fruits were ripening. I thought of the boys, and I saw them thumbing through their English Bible to answer the questions I made up for them. I thought of the twenty-five women who would soon be learning to read and write, and I realized that this was my place for now. I truly felt alive; I was able to do it! We were allowed to make mistakes. HQ was aware of the enormous pressures and demands of life in the field. We had the support of the team and the country director in Nairobi. We would learn as we went.

I focused on learning the Dinka language, and it paid off as we visited the many stakeholders of the different programs. The women's literacy course would start shortly, and Rachel and I needed to visit the first schools that had applied for the education program and distribute the subsequent school materials. We needed to make sure that the school compounds had been prepared, which was a requirement to qualify and participate in the program. The first thing we would distribute was material to make uniforms for the students.

At the same time, once we arrived at the locations, we would investigate whether there was a need for an additional seed distribution after the meager harvest. If people had been using the earlier distribution of seeds for eating instead of sowing, we would simultaneously distribute food. During March, we planned to reopen the food distribution centers and the feeding centers if we detected malnutrition in the areas where we went to look at schools.

We also had permission to build an alternative shelter for the leper colony so that they would not be living in the oil mill with the treacherous storage of ammunition. The chief had thought we would not return after Christmas, and his relief was visible when he welcomed us back. It really impacted me when he said. "You are people of your word. You do as you promise. You have come back to us."

All these programs required more team members, and so the team would grow from eight to about fifteen international staff members. To me, this was a large group to lead, and it scared me as this would drastically change the team dynamics.

Part 7

Rural Sudan

In Search of Bush Schools

There were no roads to where we needed to go. Sometimes, it might be a wide sandy strip that had been used as a road during better times. Mostly, we followed small tracks through the low scrub. We visited nine schools over the course of a week, driving as far as we could and continuing on foot to walk from village to village through the narrow paths that connected the far-spread huts.

If we were able to drive to a village, the car would be battered by the dried-out stalks of the previous sorghum harvest. The car swerved from side to side as we avoided deep potholes or tree stumps, only to get stuck on a hardened anthill. Then suddenly, we entered a swept-clean compound with a hut built high on wooden stakes. It even had a small upper veranda of dried mud. On top of the grass roof, a meager harvest of sorghum and maize was spread out to dry.

Some women were weaving grass hampers and baskets, and others were pounding maize in a hollowed-out tree trunk. Farther in the shade, a young woman lay on a mat and fed a baby. Some children ran toward the car and started yelling their greetings. Smaller children tried to hide when they saw white faces behind the window. Toddlers wobbled and faltered as they ran into the stubble of sorghum stalks, crying loudly for their mothers. This looked to be the true remote Sudan.

As we swerved through the hot and dry land, I suddenly saw a water hole where some women pulled up large calabash gourds. The dried-out and hollowed-out fruits were used as drinking bottles and utensils or for other similar usage, like storage containers or even as musical instruments. A long row of these hardened shells was ready to be filled. The top was secured with a plug of grass. These gourds could take 2-10 liters of water depending on their size and shape. After they were filled, young girls came and lifted the gourds on top of their heads and disappeared to their distant huts. Children, goats, and cows all mingled around the water hole, and I wondered how clean the water truly was.

Farther down, we were surprised by a troop of baboons that crossed the road and took their time as they observed the strange sight of our large, white four-by-four. Then suddenly, they ran off in a hurry, using their long arms and legs as they disappeared into the dry shrub.

We smelled the strong scent of burning bushes in the wind. During the afternoon, the hot wind picked up, and a small whirlwind of dust rose from the dry sand. Soon, we were immersed in thick smoke, and a bushfire outran us on one side. The wind blew it across the path, and before I knew it, we were engulfed by high leaping and bouncing flames. I was worried about the tires as we smelled burning rubber.

We left the fire behind us and entered another clean-swept compound. It belonged to a small bush school. We recognized that it was a school by a fence around a large hut, but this school had not done anything else to prepare for the new school term. There were no sticks dug into the ground to hold branches for the school seats, no blackboard standing against a tree to write on. Some schools used a flat wooden pallet from the WFP when they distributed the seeds and food sacks. After a coat of blackboard paint, they had a blackboard. Other schools were using a sandy patch of sand to write instructions in.

From there, we walked farther into the bush to another small school. The sun was hot on our heads, and soon thirst plagued us. We did not see the locals drink anything during the day, yet our lips were parched, and my tongue felt thick. I was not allowed to take any photographs on this trip as the coordinator explained to us that the people were ashamed of their poverty. They had experienced the Western world piling pity on them. Westerners had shared pictures of their naked children and rundown country in their newspapers. They still have their dignity.

Among the many schools that we visited; we picked out those who were motivated to get their education back on track. In April, classes would start again, and our visit had stimulated at least some local teachers to set up the school properly. We planned to distribute the school materials, uniform materials, and seeds for the school garden before the start of the new term. The packages we ordered and would distribute contained pens, pencils, rulers, sharpeners, exercise books, an alarm clock (to ring for the start of classes), and erasers.

In Search of Bush Schools

A second distribution would take place once we had proof that the schools had reopened in April. Whatever we were able to give, it was never enough, but at least it revived the teachers' motivation to start teaching again.

Getting education up and running was still a major problem, and local authorities were desperate to stimulate the teachers and students to become more serious about it. They needed new, strong, and educated leaders in the future.

Our requirements for schools to enter the distribution program were that they first built a storage facility to keep the materials safe from theft and weather. It meant we would visit the participating schools several times to see how they were doing in implementing these demands.

Unfortunately, only nine schools from the twenty had built some sort of storage room when we came to check their progress. We made sure we sent a message ahead of our next visit to tell them we were coming to deliver part of the promised materials and that we wanted to see their completed facilities. We were obliged to give the SRRA and local authorities our schedules, so they knew about our movements, which made planning crucial.

The school zones were often totally abandoned when we arrived, and there was no teacher in sight. When we asked the people, they had many excuses, "We are very sorry, the people aren't willing to spend time making the storeroom." Or "We can't help it; the authorities didn't give us a piece of land to build on!" Another excuse we heard was, "The people are still in the swamps and will return only when the rains set in"; or "We do not have water to build the mud walls for the huts." Or even, "You didn't tell us you would come." I understood the excuses except that most teachers were at the meetings a few days ago when we reminded them again about the conditions of being part of the distribution and the possible dates for the follow-up visits.

One of the very remote schools was situated across a lagoon. An old fisherman offered to take us there. He had one eye, and the other was a festering mass of pus. Still, he handled the dugout tree "canoe" with care and skill. To keep the canoe stable, we were ordered to sit very quietly on our knees, precariously balancing the narrow boat. Brown water, smelling strongly of fish, soaked our clothes. Between my knees, I saw wiggling maggots. After half an hour, my legs were pins and needles. To top off this adventure, we needed to get out of the canoe when we were still meters from the shore. That meant we waded through infested waters to get to the shore, and I wondered if I would end up with Guinea worm as this was still prevalent in Southern Sudan.

The Guinea worm larvae ended up in the waters where cattle bathed, and where they infected the water with their feces. You could ingest the larvae by drinking this water, which was why we always filtered and treated our water. Guinea worm was nearly eliminated in most of the world, though we knew it was still here in Southern Sudan. Initially, you would not know you had contracted it. As it grew into a worm inside your body, it needed to come out...one day. Usually after a year, you might notice a growing blister somewhere, often on your legs. The blister would burst, and the worm would slowly work its way out of your body over a couple of weeks. It could be meters long! This was the painful and disgusting bit; typically, this became a festering wound with lots of flies attached to it. When the worm came out, you were not to pull at it as it would break off and die. It then calcified in your body, causing complications later.

Once, I saw a child with a dirty rag on his leg, and I asked him what the problem was. Shyly, he showed me how the Guinea worm was treated. He would wind the worm around a small stick, and each day rolled it around as it inched out. The filthy cloth kept the stick and worm safe from being bumped against or broken off. I shivered as I gazed into the open, oozing wound on his leg.

While we traveled around, we were in the process of mapping unsafe roads for a de-mining NGO to come and check. We needed safe access as we journeyed through the area in search of schools, and for when we returned to distribute food and seeds later on as well. I was aware that many unexploded ordnances were lying around.

On this particular day, I drove behind a de-mining car that was showing me their newly made tracks that led around a mine-infested area. With clammy hands and a pounding heart, I tried to follow the large four-by-four that sped through the tall grass next to the existing road. Soon, the lead car turned around and left this part of the track to check another side road. Casually, they waved me on toward the flattened grass track. I was on my own, and I was apprehensive as I weaved through the bush and tried to follow the new track.

The official road next to it was in bad condition. Long thick grass grew on the median, already spilling over the edges into the deep gullies that were created by the previous rainy seasons. Driving on this became a treacherous exercise, as the car could easily get stuck as the wheels slipped into the steep trenches. In time, the old road would be taken over by the undergrowth. I tried to keep away from the edge as I looked for the new path. Sometimes I lost it and had to retrace back until we saw the freshly flattened bush trail again. I held my breath as some of our guides jumped out of the car to scrutinize the tracks to make sure we were on the right path. Later we understood that this was really necessary as some antipersonnel mines were found close to the edge of that road.

The last school on our list was situated in the village of Panakar, and this visit would take the rest of the day to get there and be back on time for curfew. As we approached the village, I noticed that this last bit of the road to Panakar had not been used for some time. We radioed in, "Mobile one to Yankee Lima Base." (This was the call sign for our Yirol compound). Within minutes, we heard our call sign back over the radio, "Yankee Lima Base to Mobile one, go ahead." I answered, "Hello, this is Mike Whiskey. Please advise if the road toward Panakar has been swept clean of mines yet, over?" The base radio squeaked and crackled, and then came back, "Yankee Lima Base here. We checked around and NEGATIVE! The area has not been swept yet! We strongly advise not going ahead. There are still four unaccounted mines on that stretch. Over."

"Thank you, Yankee Lima Base. Everything is Oskar Kilo (Okay). We will turn around and continue the survey at a later date. Will contact you again soon. Mike Whiskey, out." To be safe, we decided to leave this visit for now and drove through to the next village, Yali.

As we entered this village, it was deserted and eerie. Ruins of small buildings were scattered about, and dead-straight palm trees rose between the white patches of the piles of crumbled, sunbaked bricks. Hot wind sighed through the fingered leaves, and a baboon family had a picnic in the shade of the low re-growth of thorny scrubs. It was incredibly quiet, parched, and hot. It made me uneasy; why weren't there any people? I did a tight three-point turn on a small patch between two small tracks, hoping there would not be any mines. Everyone in the car held their breath, and all of us were completely drenched in sweat when we finally returned to our camp just before dusk. A sigh of relief came from the other team members, glad that we made it back safely.

Life and Death

Medair had officially handed over the management of the medical clinic to ICRC. We would only be helping out during an emergency and available to stand in if their teams were on a break. We also had funding to start rebuilding the old hospital into a more permanent facility.

On a quiet Sunday afternoon, we were sent to assist during an emergency delivery. No one from the ICRC was present in Yirol at that time, which meant we were on duty. Some of our nurses left for the hospital to check on the young mother's status. They called in by radio and reported that the lady had been brought in because she had already been in labor for a long time. The delivery was complicated, and we needed to bring equipment for a forced delivery.

As we entered the shaded room, the mother lay on a blood-soaked mat with the afterbirth wrapped in a dirty cloth on the floor. This would be buried close to where she lived. The baby had arrived just before we came in, and I could feel the nurses' urgency as they inserted a drip into the exhausted mother's arm. The baby lay floppy on a rusty clinic cot and was not breathing well. I watched as the tiny, light-colored boy fought for his life. He shuddered and breathed raspy in and out, then lay still for a long time. Another nurse tried to insert a little tube into his mouth to suck the mucus from the airways. Glucose was injected directly into the umbilical cord, and in the meantime, another nurse breathed into his little mouth. The top of his head was out of shape, and his face seemed swollen. He had been stuck for a long time in the birth canal, and I was worried he might have brain damage from oxygen deprivation. I prayed the boy would survive.

Then we turned to the mother. She had cultural scarification on her forehead and around her belly button, telling us she came from the Nuer tribe. The nurse had aided the birth with incisions, and now the mother needed attention. Nurses who came to work in the role of aid worker had to do much more than they were taught during their formal education. I had profound respect for these nurses as they made decisions that, in Western cultures, only a doctor was allowed to make. Often these nurses would return home to get more training or do midwifery, so they felt more adequate to deal with situations in the field.

After suturing the episiotomy, the baby was placed on the mother's breast, but he showed no interest in suckling. A wooden bench next to the bed held several local women who had been watching the procedure. One of them took the baby and stuck her tongue into his mouth, sucking his saliva and squirting it out of the window in a powerful arc.

Side note: A few weeks later, after Bart and I returned from a short R&R in Nairobi, we inquired about the mother and baby. We learned that the other women, all married to the same man, had noticed that the baby's head was shaped oddly. They attempted to push and massage it back into a more normal shape, but an hour after this treatment, the baby died.

Late in the afternoon, after attending this birth, we returned to our compound. As the sun's last rays shone down, we saw a woman sitting under a mango tree with a little boy in her lap. She had been waiting hours for us to return. The little boy appeared to be sick, and she only wanted the Medair nurses to tend to him. The woman visited our Kenyan nurses regularly since she also came from Kenya. She had lived in Nairobi's slums before marrying a Sudanese soldier and moving with him to Sudan. They had traveled for weeks in an open truck to reach Yirol, where her husband was recruited into the local army. He left her behind with his elderly father. Their home village was deep in the Sudd, Southern Sudan's wetlands. The young mother had brought another daughter with her and now resided with her old father-in-law in a ruin near Yirol. She expected her husband to return shortly from an army assignment so they could continue their journey to his village.

The little boy was well-fed and clean, but now lay still with closed eyes in his mother's arms. We asked the mother about the boy's health, but she only mumbled incomprehensible words while keeping her eyes fixed on him. We sensed her fear, and the nurse reached out to feel his pulse and touch his head. The boy had a high fever, and the nurse hurried back to her room to retrieve a stethoscope. Suddenly, the boy opened his eyes wide, then slowly shut them halfway. Holding my breath, I watched the little boy's chest and waited for the nurse to return. When she got back, she lifted his eyelid and rested her hands on his torso. But it was too late; the boy died in front of us. The nurse searched for a heartbeat with the stethoscope, but to no avail. The mother rocked back and forth as if in a trance, holding the limp child high in the air and moaning softly.

The woman walked out of our compound, and we could do nothing but watch her disappear into the darkening evening. The following day, we visited the family in the ruins. They were packing their meager belongings as the old father decided to bury his grandson in his own village, Adior, an eight-hour walk from Yirol. The mother sat in a corner, rocking back and forth on her feet. The little girl stared at us with tears streaming down her dirty cheeks, chewing on her already bleeding lips. We decided to help and drive them a few kilometers toward Adior. The small body was wrapped in a sleeping mat, and we drove in silence along the uneven tracks.

Close by, a bushfire had started and added to the strange atmosphere. Everything was covered in smoke, and I heard the fire crackle as the grass next to the tracks caught fire. After an hour's drive, the sandy track stopped in the middle of the bush. Deeper into the shrubs was a cattle camp, and children ran toward the car as they heard us approaching. We handed over the wrapped body to the mother and then formed a circle around the woman, her little daughter, and her old father-in-law. We said a prayer, but I don't think she noticed anything around her. She just stared blankly into the bush and rocked her dead baby.

The old man started to walk away; he was very thin and bent over and leaned heavily on a stick. The small girl picked up a bundle with their personal belongings and placed it silently on her head and followed the old man. She was only eight years old, and she kept dropping the bundle as she repeatedly turned around to watch us. Nobody gave her a hand as she stumbled and rearranged the bundle back on her head. Her dress was many sizes too big, and it was kept around her slight posture with rough ropes. To me, it looked like they disappeared into endless nothingness. There was no path that showed them the way. I felt strangely empty as I went to the car and turned back to our compound. I wanted to cry, but it was not my grief to grieve. Still, emotions flooded my soul.

Another short break came up soon after these happenings, and

I longed for the brief relief from encountering so much suffering. Medair had mandated that when working in a complex crisis, team members would be asked to take a short leave every six weeks or so in the field. This way, burnout and identification with the people and the traumatic circumstances could be prevented. Medair cared for our well-being, and these breaks kept the team in an emotionally healthy state. Indeed, so many impressions weighed heavily on us.

Back in Nairobi, we booked an overnight train to Mombasa in Kenya. This was the train track that was constructed in 1896 by the British in their then East African colony. The track runs from Mombasa, Kenya into Uganda. It was also the train track where the two man-eating lions made history by attacking the coolies (laborers from India). Later that story was the basis of the 1996 movie *The Ghost and the Darkness*. The trip was a little like stepping back into history. A diesel engine pulled the long train across Kenya, and everything was still operating in the English colonial style. The staff that attended the passengers wore patched starched uniforms, and dinner was served on unpolished, battered silver plates. As we ate in the dining car, our compartment was transformed into sleeping quarters, again with starched white sheets and stiffly tucked-in blankets. We slept to the cadence of the steel wheels and the gentle sway of our wagon as it rattled through the night.

The next stint in Sudan would be even more stressful as we took over team leadership and would be responsible for the safety and running of programs.

Women's Literacy Course

Clouds gathered on the horizon, and throughout the day, the faint rumbling of thunder came ever closer. The sun set early, and bright shafts of the last light flickered from under the thick layers of clouds. Soon, darkness took over, and the first proper storm of the season was unleashed. Lightning lit up the sky, and strong blasts ripped through the branches of the mango tree. Unripe fruits popped like heavy stones on the ground, and one of the tents under the tree collapsed as the wind snapped the wooden poles. The canvas tarp flapped wildly in the wind and then sailed off. Rain came like a thundering train through the scrub, and within minutes, the parched ground changed into a mudslide. We had to yell instructions to each other as we ran around to secure loose debris that rolled through the compound. Suddenly, the rain changed into huge hailstones, and we sought cover inside the house. I was amazed at the power and havoc this storm wreaked in such a brief time.

After two hours, the storm reduced in power, and we assessed the damage. Everything dripped, most tents were flattened to the ground, and mattresses were water-soaked. Our mud hut was leaking badly. In some places, the fence around the compound had fallen. We attached a plastic sheet over our mosquito nets in the hut so we would stay dry during the night as light rain continued to fall.

Before we left for our last break, we had prepared the women's literacy course, and Rachel had started the course while I was in Kenya. Now it was time I took over since Stuart and Rachel had left to set up the new base in Uganda. It was a huge challenge to take on this role and lead the women's program. I had to step out of my comfort zone as I felt so insecure and felt inadequate. How would I be able to teach appropriately if I did not even know enough about the culture of these women? Another thought occurred: How do you start an adult literacy course without being patronizing? I could not just start with pre-primary examples and the use of kindergarten pictures that had no association with their adult lives! I had to come up with some alternatives that were both appropriate and fitting for this group of adult students.

We had been given a sagging mud brick building in the middle of Yirol with a tin roof to use as a school facility. Rain would increase over the coming period, so a dry place was paramount. There were no windows or doors to protect against the heavy rains. Nor was there any other furniture to set up a proper classroom. Nobody cared as this was a momentous day for them.

There was one woman who had been to school before. Although her English was limited, she was still able to translate for me. Another NGO had also trained her to be a traditional birth attendant (TBA) as most women would not want to go to a clinic to give birth. She proved to be my greatest asset over the course. The first day started great with speeches and singing by the carefully selected group of women.

After the proper introductions, which took an hour already, I wanted to start the first lesson. Soon the women began to talk loudly and point toward the translator. Aggression surged through the group, and a full-blown fight between the students developed in front of me. I asked what was going on, and my translator, who stood aside, explained the age-old story of the effects of jealousy in the hearts of people. A woman had accused the translator of not doing a "proper job" and that she should not have that chip on her shoulder by pretending and acting as if she was the only "educated one." Apparently, the women disagreed on the position this translator now had in comparison with those in the group who came to learn to read and write. Many of them were the wives of prominent chiefs of the area.

I felt so sad as tension rose between the women. They scratched, bit, and tumbled over each other in a chaotic frenzy. I just sat down to observe; I could do nothing to defuse the situation since I did not adequately speak their language. I silently prayed and then decided that I would close the class for the rest of the day due to improper behavior by *grown* women.

While the class was in upheaval, I slowly took down the posters and flashcards from the walls and returned them to the storage boxes. Some women started to cry, and the translator walked out of the room. I was at a total loss as to what to do next. I felt vulnerable and threatened by the aggression taking place. Before I knew it, emotions overtook me, and tears started falling while I quietly put away the equipment.

Suddenly, the class became silent, so quiet that I turned around to see what caused this sudden change. The translator had slipped back into the room and was softly talking to the women. The women immediately stopped fighting and turned to watch me with wide eyes. Their faces showed shock as they realized I was crying. Soon, all the women were wailing and sniffling. What had happened? The translator told me the women were stunned because they understood they were the cause of my distress by raising such a ruckus.

It opened the opportunity to talk with them on a much more personal level. I was not an educated, white, and powerful teacher anymore; I was just one of them, overwhelmed by emotions. I walked back to the small table I had brought with me, and we talked freely about what had happened. Instead of teaching the ABCs, I told the story of the Sower and the Seeds. I related this parable to their own situation. How the good seed of receiving education could fall on several types of soil in the mind. If it fell onto the shallow ground of a jealous heart, the weed of anger and disunity would take over the good seed. I explained that what I had just witnessed were thorns and thistles overtaking the good seed. Although all the women had the desire to learn, the soil was poisoned by jealousy. Seeds could not grow in such a place.

Slowly, the women came forward, and as they stood in front of me, one of the older women asked if we could pray together and ask God for forgiveness. As they started to pray, the translator explained to me how they begged God to forgive their bad attitude. They started to say blessings over me, begging me to continue as their teacher. Some asked if God would take away my sadness and replace it with happiness again. Then the women burst out in song, a beautiful melody filling the small building, and I tried hard not to start crying again. I was exhausted that day, but I realized we had bonded more strongly than I would have ever imagined.

The next day, as I walked down the road to the classroom, the women formed a long line in front of the entrance and started singing and clapping their hands rhythmically. Immense joy filled my heart to see such a public display of unity, and I shared my happiness with them. This set the stage for the coming five weeks with this fantastic group of women. Every morning, we started with a small Bible reading and devotion. Their faces were intent and full of anticipation of what they would learn that day.

One morning, as I was sharing the Word of God with the women, a small, brightly colored bird flew into the room and briefly settled on my shoulders before taking off and sitting on a rough stone on the windowsill. It started to sing loudly before taking flight again. For a moment, the class sat in total silence. Then, they all stood up and started to sing a harmonious song. The translator informed me that the women thought that the Holy Spirit had just come in and visited the school; they concluded that Jesus was now present in the room.

Back at the base, many other activities demanded my attention. As I reviewed our staff issues, contracts, and reports that needed to be written, and programs that needed to be overseen, I realized that I loved living in Sudan and loved the work we were doing. I felt alive, and the challenges stretched me.

The work was diverse and constantly changing. When a small MAF plane arrived, we would drive to the airstrip to offload the plane, then soon after we organized a meeting with the workers for the upcoming extended program on immunization (EPI) and polio vaccination campaign. Our gas fridge broke down one day and needed to be repaired since it would store the vaccines. New solar panels needed to be installed on a wooden rack next to the house. The panels could not go on the roof because they would reflect sunlight and be easily detected by Antonov bomber planes. During the weekend, we socialized with other NGOs and organized a goat for a barbecue or played volleyball competitions. We had a soccer game on the village oval with the local men and boys or went out for a picnic. Life was busy and I loved it.

As I worked on planning the programs, I looked out over our compound. A group of little children threw stones at the now-ripe mangoes on the tree just outside the fence. The tree decided to give up one of the wanted fruits, and with loud applause, the mango fell between the boys. As they sliced the juicy treat with the sharp edge of a lid from a tin, two birds of prey dived in for a bite too. Panic spread among the young boys as the birds swooped down and hammered one boy on the head. The mango was forgotten, and the tree was once more a silent statue in our garden.

Women's Literacy Course

We were always aware that we worked in an active war zone. As I taught the literacy course, I listened and watched the women, picking up information on the latest news around Yirol. The moment they were restless and kept walking toward the door to look up into the sky, I knew that there was military activity that we had not been privy to. Sometimes, an Antonov plane flew over extremely low, and then all the women ran for cover or hid in a nearby bomb shelter. I ended up giving them a lesson in bomb security, telling them how they could avoid shrapnel by lying flat on the ground as the fragments would fly upward.

I caught a cold and lost my voice. I was sure it was because of the many sniffling and snotty noses in the classroom. I constantly reminded the ladies not to sneeze into each other's faces and not to spit on the floor, as this seemed to be the custom.

It was wonderful to have a mud hut. Bart and I had a place where we could be alone and discuss issues that needed some privacy. The hut was round, and we had a bed made from wooden WFP pallets, a small table, and two camping chairs, so we could drink coffee together without interruptions or curious faces pressing through the fence. The freshly cut grass roof smelled of the sun, and the gray-plastered mud kept the hut cool and in constant shade. We shared the hut with many other occupants like mice, lizards, and centipedes, but I felt safe with the mosquito net tightly tucked under the thin mattress.

On the last day before the women graduated from the literacy course, my TBA translator was called away from the lessons to a hut where a woman was delivering a baby. After an hour, she returned and took me by the hand to visit the newborn and the mother. Together we walked the sandy path to a hut. Under a nearby tree, a group of other women was chatting away. I had to bow low to enter the hut, and a mosquito net hung from the stick rafters. My translator opened the netting to reveal a very satisfied young mother on a woven mat on the floor. A small baby wrapped in a cloth lay close to her.

The mother unwrapped the baby, and although it protested, she proudly showed me a beautiful little baby boy. Then she soothed the cries by gently pressing it to her breast. His hair was still damp, and already little curls were standing up, the skin silky smooth and light in color. It was so good to see a healthy mother, happy with her healthy newborn, born in a lowly mud hut in the middle of Sudan. I left the hut in wonder; war cannot take away the miracle of life. As we walked back to the school, a totally different sound came from another hut. A child screamed with long squealing outbursts. A mother appeared from the hut with a wailing toddler, holding him in front of her. She had been cooking their porridge on an open fire, and the pot had fallen over, spilling the hot liquid over her naked little boy, right between his legs. I kept telling the translator to pour water over the burns, but people were gathering around the mother in a panic. Finally, I got through to them that the boy needed to get to the clinic for treatment. Slowly, an unorganized procession formed to accompany the injured boy and his panic-stricken mother. How quickly happiness and suffering alternated in this country.

Then the women's literacy course ended, and the community organized a graduation ceremony that was a proper feast and party. The women had received an intensive introduction to literacy over the last five weeks. Most of them could recite the ABCs and could point out the individual letters when asked. Simple word formations were being created, and one hundred English words were repeated. A few women picked up the principles of forming English sentences.

The exams were taken seriously and consisted of ten dictated letters and five words selected at random. I would write the word on a blackboard and leave one letter out, which they had to fill in. Then a reading test followed, and they had to write in their exercise books. To stimulate continuous learning, I encouraged each of them to keep writing words down. They could copy words from the WFP sacks or from the side panels of the NGO vehicles that passed through the village. They could even recite the ABCs to the rhythm of the pounding of corn, to reinforce their knowledge of the alphabet.

I was filled with motherly pride as I looked upon the group of graduating women. Medair donated a goat to accommodate the festivities for that night. Various parts of the goat were prepared in different ways. There were boiled intestines, roasted legs, stews, and broiled meat. I sat among the group of women and ate slimy green vegetables that had been prepared on a large banana leaf on the ground. The soft leaves were pounded into a green slick as if they were hardened, unbending stalks that needed to be reminded of their place in the food chain. Normally, green vegetables were not part of the diet.

The party only started two and a half hours later than indicated, so I took my time eating the bits that were offered to me as I waited. I gathered that the whole procedure of graduation would last much longer than I anticipated. I engaged in faulty Dinka, and the women "oh-ed" and "ah-ed" at the white teacher who could speak their language.

Violent noises suddenly startled us. I could not see what was happening as it took place in the tall grass farther away from where we were feasting. A fight was going on, complete with slapping, yelling, and crying.

Earlier that afternoon, I had witnessed a fight where a group of men and women were at each other's throats. One man was so aggressive that he destroyed a stick fence around a hut, then started to beat himself, throwing himself on the ground, scooping up a handful of dust, and throwing it in the air. We were warned not to come too close to that particular compound as the people knew this man was armed. Now, during the evening, the aggression had accumulated, and the man was running around with a gun, wanting to shoot anybody who would try to calm him down. Despite the danger, another man tried to approach him to take away the weapon, but it went off and a bullet shot the owner through his hip. This finally shut the man up, and in silence, a group of people carried him to the ICRC clinic. Although I was shocked, nobody else seemed to be. Most people were still chatting away, preparing the slimy green mass and roasting the goat.

I was asked to open the meeting with a speech. That meant the first introductory speeches were delivered by others and lasted more than thirty minutes each. Although I had spoken publicly before, this specific meeting made me nervous. There were many officials—army personnel, chiefs of other villages, local authorities, the elders of Yirol, and the husbands of the wives who had graduated. In most speeches, Medair was addressed as "the mother and father of all NGOs," and then the programs were listed that we had initiated. After that, we were profusely thanked for saving their children from hunger, and now we had given yet another blessing to the people. We were the first NGO that was willing to strengthen their women in their position by giving them an education. It felt as if we were given credit for providing a university degree to these people, and in my mind, I recounted the five words these women could now read and write.

The little building where we had been teaching was dedicated and promoted to become a future school and was given a special name. A name that everybody would remember for years to come since it would be called the school of "Maria Akir Marial"— my full Dinka name. The speaker continued to tell the listeners that from now on, my name would be remembered for generations to come, and it also showed my full Dinka status. I was a daughter to the mothers, a sister to the Sudanese people, and a mother to the children of Yirol. I felt very honored and humbled, though I did not believe myself to be of such worth. These words lifted me up, and I stored them in my heart.

After all these diverse speeches from the many officials, night had fallen, and the sky was filled with millions of stars, adding a soft glow to the celebration. Little fires were lit around the groups of people who lived under the mango trees scattered all over Yirol. Small children walked freely through the partying group, and their little hands grabbed whatever food was given or dropped by the people. We ate sour-tasting pancakes and chewed on tough pieces of meat. Most women asked when the next course would take place. I could not promise anything as we were dependent on funding and donors who needed to approve an extension to the education program, which was seen as a development program rather than relief.

The timing was not good either, as the season of preparing the soil and sowing was starting soon. Most men wanted their wives at home to assist in that process.

Stirring Encounters

The long rainy season should have arrived by now. The men were either repairing or making their wooden plows as well as training their oxen. It was fascinating to see how the local smith fastened the treated leather strips with hand-forged nails that were hammered into the wooden tool attached to the plows. Young bulls were arranged in front of the yoke, and young men were instructed by the elders on how to train them. They must make deep and straight lines in the still dry and dusty soil. By the time the big rains arrived, the team would be trained.

The wind became stronger every day, and dust devils raised the sand high into the sky, obscuring the bright sunlight. There were days when no clouds were seen, and people looked worried at the horizon, speaking out their anxious thoughts: "Will the rain come? Will this season of seeding happen? We pray it will come soon so the hunger period will end, and harvesting will bring better tidings for the population." We all looked forward to the rain. The last storm was an experience, and we were told it would be like that in the wet season.

One Sunday, after we had visited another team, we returned just before curfew. We passed by the hospital to check on the faltering gas fridge in which the vaccines were stored, as they would spoil if not properly cooled. The moment we entered the hospital compound, we noticed frantic activity of people and nurses running around. We jumped out of the car and asked what was going on and if something had happened while we were away. A nurse stopped and recognized our Medair logo. She said, "Please come quickly, we need all the help we can get. Four children have been injured by a mine explosion!"

There were many types of mines still around. We even saw landmines being used as tables inside huts. They seemed harmless and normally would only explode on heavy impacts, such as a loaded truck driving over them. However, these four children had been playing with antipersonnel mines in their compound. They had placed this smaller device against a tree and were trying to hit the fuse with well-aimed stones. It exploded violently, and the children were hit in their legs, arms, and torsos.

Two children lay on the hospital floor, and two were on rusted cots pushed against the wall of the ward. They were all wrapped in layers of gauze to protect the open wounds from infection. One was unconscious, and a boy of about seven years screamed incessantly from the horrible pain. His stomach, arms, and legs were all swathed in gauze, and soon blood seeped through the bandages. Our nurses got to work straight away by bringing in drips. It was heartbreaking to see the mothers trying to comfort their suffering children. They touched their heads and said prayers over the writhing bodies. The children kept calling out for their mothers to ease the pain. I wondered how these women could endure yet another trauma. On their faces, emotion could not be detected, as if resigned to the suffering that had been part of their whole life.

The week ahead was fully planned with endless meetings. As I sat in the large meeting *tukul*, I sighed, wishing I could be outside working on some reports. The deep sound of many drums echoed in the distance, slowly moving closer. This could be the moment to escape the ongoing tedious speeches. I asked if I could be excused to take some photos of the large procession of young men who came to show off their strength and the conditions of a large herd of cows. I got a supervisor to come with me for safety purposes, and soon I was surrounded by a mass of dancing young people.

They came from several cattle camps and entertained the village with their competitions of wrestling, stick fights, and the presentation of young marriageable girls. These girls wore brightly colored Ankara sheets of material (African wax print fabric) draped around their shoulders. The wind blew open the split ends of their covers, and I could see the string of beads around their small black waists. Their hips were smeared with glistering fat, and the sun deepened the colorful display as they shuffled their feet to the beat of the drums.

The young men were powerfully built—with straining muscles and well-fed bellies—from eating beef and drinking the rich mixture of blood and milk. Their calves were painted white from the ashes of burned cow dung, and intricate patterns were drawn into the white layer. Dust particles swirled high into the air from the stomping of their feet and the shuffling of cow hooves. Around their waist hung leopard skins that swung around powerful legs as they jumped higher and higher.

My white face stood out among the dark faces, and soon the dancing crowd surrounded me. My companion translated the song they invented while they danced. Dark sweat-covered faces pressed into mine, and they pulled at my hands to come and join the wild dance. I declined and instead asked permission to take photos. I felt privileged to stand among these powerful young people of Southern Sudan. In their dance, they included me as a guest and stranger to their land. It was an honor to witness this cultural happening.

After this event, it became known to the extended villages that there were white women in the district, and Bart often received offers for me. I was worth more than a hundred cows, according to tradition.

I loved strolling along the dusty main road of our village. Whenever I walked around, a group of children ran toward me to shake hands and tried out the little English they knew. During one of these saunters, the kids pointed to something behind me and pulled my arm to show me what made them so excited. "Another *'Khwaja',*" they shouted. I turned around and was shocked. A small boy, maybe ten years of age, walked toward me, and he was white—ghostly white. When he shook my hand, I noticed his eyes were a wonderful shade of green. He was an albino, and in his heavily accented English, he asked me for a cap to shade his eyes. Red blistering patches covered his body. The sun beat mercilessly upon his unprotected skin, and his firmly woven blond curls were dirty from accumulated dead skin flakes. The children were greatly entertained by my surprised face. They accepted this boy as a full member of the clan, and they informed me that both his parents are truly black! Happily, they continued the soccer game they were playing.

One morning, I was woken up by the head of the district police. He needed my help to check out a situation that was brought to his attention earlier that morning. Someone desperately needed our assistance. Sleepily, I walked with him to the large mango tree in our compound. An exhausted-looking young man covered with dust sat against the rough bark. He looked up at me with wide questioning eyes, full of trust. Next to him, on a cow skin, sat a little boy gnashing his teeth. He was just a sack of bones, crying and moaning without tears. A little heap of humanity in desperation.

The man had walked for days to come to us for help. The mother had died a month ago, and the father did not want to care for the boy. The young man under the tree was his uncle, the brother of the mother. He decided to take the boy, and he started the journey to Yirol because he'd heard there was help. We decided to assist this little boy by feeding him twice a day with the special Unimix which we had been using in our feeding centers during the height of the hunger. For the next four days, the young man appeared exactly on time in front of our gate.

Early the fourth morning, I walked over to the man with the steaming tin mug who then handed it carefully to the boy. I also brought high-energy biscuits and special formula milk, plus an Oral Rehydration Solution (ORS) drink to give to the boy during the day. The uncle's dark eyes were full of gratitude as he gave the mug to the little boy who stretched out both his shaky hands to gobble it up. He smiled and smacked his lips. After he finished it, I took the mug away, and immediately the child started to cry, and his bony hands stretched out for more. When I shook my head, he started gnashing his teeth again.

Sometimes he crawled after me on his hands and feet as he did not have the strength to get up. His buttocks stuck out with two small sharp hunches nearly bursting through his thin, tight skin. He cried and whined until he got another mug with foaming warm milk that he gulped, spilling it down his chin and chest. We had to fight to get him to drink with one little sip at a time. His little stick-like fingers were like vices around the mug. As I aided in letting him drink the nutritious milk, I saw it gushing out at the other end. The child was extremely sick, and after four days, the young man and child did not return. The usual spot at the gate was empty, and I asked around. The night guard told me that I did not need to come to the gate with milk anymore because the child had died.

At the end of emotionally charged days, Bart and I would escape the compound and walk to the lake to see the sunset. As we took in the brilliantly colored sky, we watched the final rays gradually dance away, succumbing to the darkness of the African night.

It was close to Easter, and the local church welcomed the episcopal bishop of Yirol. He had come to encourage the people and bless them before Easter. He announced a day of fasting on Thursday, and everybody was called to pray for peace. Nobody was allowed to drink locally brewed beer. He proclaimed, "No food, no beer, no tobacco, just water!" In the days leading up to Easter, we attended the church services that were conducted randomly in the bush. On Palm Sunday, the people guided us in a procession to this bush church. It had been made according to the instructions of the Old Testament for the feast of tabernacles. Everyone sat on the bare ground, and those who would partake in communion were placed under the shelter of large leaves and dressed in white robes. They all held hand-carved wooden crosses.

The procession started in the center of town and walked through the whole village. People held palm leaves, and young men carried large drums. We heard their singing and drumming far off as they approached the waiting people who lined the roads. When the lead group passed, people on the side joined in and answered the singing in chorus and clapped their hands. Once everybody was seated in and around the little bush church, the preacher stood up. These kinds of services took hours and hours. We came home from these services more exhausted than from our daily tasks. Yet, it was a pleasant break from the constant pressure of running the programs.

As a foreigner in charge of a relief program, it was a delicate balancing act to both provide aid and empower local communities to take on responsibility for themselves. It was a challenge for the people to communicate their needs while preserving their dignity. On the other hand, when we brought the requests to the donors, we had to resist the urge to inject our own opinions and focus solely on what was most crucial for the survival and well-being of the community.

Our local education coordinator received a summons to the administrative office in town a few days later. As the notice was highly unusual, he anticipated trouble and decided to bring someone with him as a witness. Later, they reported that they were made to wait for at least forty minutes before the newly appointed head of security burst into the room, shouting in Dinka. He complained that the two hundred exercise books distributed to twenty schools were not enough and demanded that we provide more to serve the officers. It became clear that our distributions were being taxed by the army for their own use, a fact that donors would not want to hear.

As our team member recounted the story, our unease with the

new head of security grew. Working under a hostile leader in a wartorn country was already risky; could we trust this department to inform us of any insecurity that could threaten the safety of our team? The days that followed were full of new challenges, and we pushed hard to get the planned programs underway. Bart and I were tired and on edge. We longed for a break to put all the pressure of being team leaders on hold and get a perspective on the local situation. It was increasingly difficult to stay neutral and detached from the people that we served.

During general table discussions with team members, we started having conversations in which we communicated our opinion of the war and how it was managed. We passed judgments on the local leaders around us, and tensions between the different international staff made us feel that we were pulled in all directions. It stretched our perspectives and challenged our paradigms. Medair was so right to put compulsory R&R into the schedule for all expatriate staff. We now understood the need for it and were looking forward to the break that came up for us after a full-on, eight-week period.

Team Dynamics

Refreshed, we returned to our team in Sudan after a five-day break in Nairobi, only to find even more problems awaiting us. The temporary team leader we had chosen to fill in for us had the most challenging time because relations between our national and international team members had escalated.

An international team can consist of many nationalities, and our team had Kenyan, Swedish, English, Caribbean, German, and Dutch members. The composition changed continually as some would end their contract or go on a long break, R&R, or were sent to other locations where Medair was working. This made for interesting times of learning to adapt, accept, and appreciate different perspectives and worldviews. We had to learn proper conflict management and engage in self-reflection to test our contribution to the team's challenges. One Medair slogan often came into focus during our discussions: "Unity in Diversity." Practically speaking, this required spending time with each other to establish working relationships. The only team time we had together took place after dinner, during a game of UNO or while preparing food. Often, team members just wanted to take a short shower and go to bed to read a book until the kerosene lamp ran out of oil. Sunday was spent either going to a church or staying in your hut to be alone and catch up on personal correspondence.

We started to take time to speak to each team member, and we discovered that most friction and tensions came from personal problems or past experiences that triggered a sharp response that then seemed to overflow into the team spirit. All of us had a story and were burdened with hurts from the past, which if not dealt with, activated long-forgotten memories, and caused stress. Under pressure and discomfort, unhelpful behaviors were brought to the surface. This could just be that we were overly tired or had a difficult day. Different personalities and cultural values came under scrutiny, and depending on the personal conviction of why we were doing this kind of work, the discussions could be quite heated. It might seem trivial to the reader, but some issues could determine if your stay in the field was bearable or not.

It happened that some Kenyan team members were on salary while the expatriates were on a small allowance, as most of the international aid workers were volunteers. This created a division in attitude and the approach to the work. Some wanted the normal working hours to be respected just as they would have been in a regular job, yet others wanted to work until the light faded, putting in as many hours as possible to get the job done. Some were driven to get up early and stay up late because we worked in an on-alert setting that demanded a response.

As the evening wore on, those who had been working used up all the battery life of the solar-powered lights. This left others who wanted to read or play games in the dark. Predictably, arguments broke out. The solar panels were only intended for night trips to the toilets or for emergencies. Those on salaries argued that solar light was free energy and that buying extra batteries for their flashlights was expensive and not reimbursed. Indeed, some could afford to have their personal items sponsored by their church back home, while others had to pay for everything out of their own pockets. Adding to the tension was the fact that bringing extra batteries would exceed the already limited weight allowed on the small MAF planes.

Another problem arose that in any normal circumstance would never have been an issue. We used perfumed antibacterial hand soap for washing our hands. Suddenly, these were rapidly disappearing, and our stock did not last until the next supply plane was due. On a Sunday, we saw some team members using the cakes for washing their clothes, simply because the clothes smelled better as opposed to using the local hard block soap which did not foam or smell nice. Bringing in extra soap on a small MAF plane would just add to the cargo bill and, as practical European-thinking people, we thought it was a waste to use hand soap like that.

The desire for better-smelling clothes made me reflect on the importance of meeting individual needs to feel appreciated and valued. The team members' use of different soaps provided a sense of normalcy and comfort, helping them endure the challenges of life in the field. It also prevented them from becoming too immersed in the constant, disheartening poverty they encountered daily.

We arranged another team meeting to regroup and hear out all accumulated grievances. This cleared the air and opened our eyes to the varied reasons why people reacted so strongly to seemingly unimportant issues like the use of soap and solar batteries. Or, for others, to understand why priorities were given to the usage of equipment, utilizing everything as economically as possible. All our equipment was donated by donors for the implementation of the programs, and ultimately, we needed to give an account for everything.

It was often late at night before Bart and I could catch up on our individual adventures. Sometimes, we stood on the broken-down balcony and watched the galaxy pass through the sky. The wind had died down, and it was quiet. Opposite our compound, a family lived in a small hut. During the day, we saw the children play on fallen tree stumps and dig in the dirt around their hut. One night as we shared highlights of the day, a piercing cry came from their place. We couldn't tell if it was a child or a woman.

Then the sound changed into a high-pitched scream. After a short silence, we heard the monotonous humming of a traditional healer before the screams turned into spine-chilling guttural animal sounds. I got goosebumps as it dawned on me some ritual was taking place to placate the ancestral spirits of the Sudanese family living so close to us. Bart and I prayed for God's presence and protection, we not only served people in need but also shared the Gospel of light by bringing peace through Jesus Christ, often through just our actions.

One early morning, as I was writing in my diary, I heard some kids giggling as they spied through the stick fence. As I looked on, I saw a woman with a load of cooking utensils balanced high on her head, walking on the small path in the direction of the lake. At some stage, she stepped aside from the trail and squatted briefly. A small child of about two years followed suit, and I saw waste flowing from under the buttocks. I sighed and got up to teach a lesson in hygiene to the children who were watching me.

I got many lessons in return. They would chat with me about all kinds of cultural gems. "Do you know why meat from a chicken is only eaten by old men? It is because a chicken devours insects that will come into its blood and then into the meat. When young men eat that kind of meat, they will get insects in their blood which will make them weak and itchy. So young people eat cow or goat, and old people eat chicken." I wondered if that was why we got so many chickens as presents as we drove around to different villages. Were we considered old people?

In Dire Straits

Another NGO conducted a food distribution in Yirol, and since I had not had the chance to see how this was implemented, I asked permission to observe and take photographs. It was particularly important to get permission because when large groups gathered like this, the military was on high alert for any interference, disturbances, or riots. On the day, a large group of people sat around the ruins of a school. Patiently, they were waiting for the village chiefs who would allocate the amount of food according to each head of the family that was selected earlier to receive aid. Large WFP bags were stacked high on the concrete veranda against the shot-through walls of the school.

Women would be the carriers of these large sacks that were 50 kilos each. Men sat around watching the distribution and discussing more essential business. The sacks were placed from the elevated veranda upon the head of the waiting woman below. She then brought the sacks to the place where her family group was waiting to have a sack opened and divided portions between the households. I was wondering how a lean and often very gaunt woman could carry such a load. As I pondered this, a woman received a bag on her head and staggered while trying to find her balance. Suddenly her head snapped backward, and she fell into a heap on the ground, groaning with pain. She had dislocated her neck, and Bart was asked to take her to the clinic. I tried not to show how upset this made me.

I took some pictures even though I was extremely nervous. I did not want to give the authorities a reason to think I was spying. Especially when I saw a large group of soldiers receiving food. This distribution was funded by donors with specific instructions that it must be given to the people, not the army, thus I restrained myself from taking too many pictures of anyone in uniform.

The roll in the camera was full, and for safety's sake, I returned to the car to replace it. I carefully rewound the spool and replaced it with a new canister. A loud knocking on the window startled me. As

I looked up, a tall, angry military man surrounded by soldiers, commanded me to open the door. My heart pounded in my throat, and I felt color rush to my cheeks. He yelled, "You don't have permission to take photographs! You are a spy of Northern Sudan, and you have been taking pictures of military equipment, which is forbidden!" All the while, he tried to open the locked doors of the car. More people joined the uniformed group, and soon the car was in the middle of a large angry mob. I tried to get out of the car, but the doors were now pressed shut by the packed crowd. I opened the window and requested some space so I could get out and explain what I was doing.

Indignation rose inside me because I knew I had been given special permission by the SRRA secretary appointed to Yirol and certainly was not spying. And with the rising of adrenaline levels, my courage came back. I stepped out of the car and asked first if he could identify himself. Then I explained that I had been given permission by the SRRA secretary of Yirol who was in charge of this distribution. I knew I needed to be very polite so as not to embarrass him in public. That would give him more reason to intimidate me or order me to give him my film, which I was not willing to comply with. I looked him in the eye and assured him that I was fully aware that I could not photograph anything military. He suddenly backed down and started to stutter during my firm counterattack, looking around as if to see where he could find more support. He then grabbed a young man by the arm and appointed him to be my guard and guide. The young man was instructed to report directly to him if I did anything suspicious. And with that, he disappeared into the crowd.

My heart still fluttered wildly, but as the people dispersed, I grew calm again. My new guide explained to me that this was the newly appointed head of security for the region and that he was trying to establish his superiority and position. Later that day, I met the same man again as I walked around and took pictures. This time he was very polite and shook my hand and even gave me suggestions for good spots where I could take my photographs. I understood that we could either be assisted by him or hindered in our work in the coming weeks.

In the days after the distribution, we heard more from him and witnessed his outbursts and mood swings. It made us aware of how precariously dependent we were on the goodwill of the local authorities. He was sometimes angry, then overly polite, then distant before suddenly turning amiable and accommodating. Since he came to be in charge, I did not feel safe walking through the village. Even other local authorities warned us to be careful in our dealings with him.

Yirol was restless. Just before we left for another R&R, we observed increased military activity. Unexpectedly, we saw Asian people climbing on an abandoned tank and rummaging through the inside and engine compartment. It looked like they were mechanics, as a bit later we noticed them working on the engines. They were North Korean mercenaries sent to rehabilitate cars and tanks. It looked like they secured a contract to repair these for the war effort. These vehicles could be transported back to the front and used for war purposes. A few days later, repaired tanks roared through Yirol, and a convoy of other military cars was towing away more damaged vehicles. Was there another offensive planned? Was the Northern Army closer than we knew? Because we were so focused on meeting and dealing with our own team issues, we were less alert to what was going on around us. And the weekly UN security updates and reports from Lokichogio did not always come through.

Shortly after our return from our R&R, we were yet in another meeting. Suddenly the compound guard rushed into the meeting *tukul* and yelled, "Get out of the hut! Get to the bomb shelters, the Antonovs are coming!" We stumbled from our wooden benches and rushed to the door while a coffee mug crashed to the floor. We got stuck in the small wooden door opening as too many wanted to get through at the same time, and I scraped past the low grass roof. People scattered over the compound ran toward the shelters that were evenly spread from the main buildings. An exceptionally low-flying Antonov plane—flying lower than I have ever seen—came into view, and the low drone of its large engines rumbled above our heads. It was expected that the plane would circle three times and then drop barrel bombs (improvised unguided bombs).

Panic-stricken, the people fled into the open spaces and flung themselves onto the ground. Many ran toward the large bomb shelter we had constructed just outside our compound, which had once been a swimming pool. Others jumped into the so-called foxholes that we dug inside the enclosure of our compound. When we slid into the shelter, the cellar was packed full of frightened villagers.

Dust danced in the light of the opening, and some people

peeped outside into the sky, waiting for the loud explosions of falling bombs. After some minutes of silence, someone climbed out to have a better look, only to rush back inside as the sound of heavy engines swelled into a roar. People pressed into each other, and women began to moan. A small child clung to my legs, and I felt his whole body shake. My stomach cramped up, and I needed to go to the latrine.

After a tense moment, the drone of the plane disappeared, and I tried to get out of the hole to reach the toilet in time. People chattered excitedly among themselves, and suddenly all of us felt united in sharing the tension of the moment. Everybody dispersed and went back to the places they came from, and I heard some relieved laughter in our compound as I went into the tin shack latrine.

Then suddenly I heard a loud cry, "The planes are back!" The Antonov planes had done a large circle over the area. The heavy engines shrieked as the plane accelerated into a descent. Bart hammered on the flimsy toilet door, urging me to get out and get into the bomb shelter at once. I hurried and nervously stumbled back underground. This time we waited longer, and every time the plane came down low, we expected explosions. But nothing happened. Anxiously and silently, we sat for a long time in the dark shelter. When we deemed it safe, we emerged from the underground cover and tried to continue our daily tasks, but my legs shook for the rest of the day. This little visit by the Northern Army influenced the rest of our stay; we tasted the danger and saw the alertness in the eyes of the people as if they were hunted prey.

The incident made us more aware of the volatile situation, and we acted accordingly by preparing our run bags, parking the cars under tree canopies, covering our solar panels to minimize detection, and repeating safety instructions to our team. One of the local workers reported that the planes dropped pieces of paper over the area instead of the expected bombs and concluded, "We think they were testing the wind direction and made surveillance photographs of the area." Our compound manager added, "It is their pattern to come over very low, test the wind, and come back in a few days' time when the people just start to relax again after such a display of power. They like spreading fear."

We decided to make another bomb shelter on the other side of the compound within our fence so that we had quick access to shelter if the planes returned. Our logisticians spent days digging, and just as they finished, the plane did return. Together, we jumped into the freshly dug foxhole and looked up into the sky where the plane circled several times above the town. Again, no bombs, but by now, we were highly strung and tense. Would they or would they not bomb the town, or was it just a display of power?

Still, it did not divert us from performing our duties and putting into place the preparations for our programs. Surveys were still conducted, and children were measured for height and weight wherever we found communities in the bush. As an extra precaution, we now never went alone and had two expatriate team members on all trips. We also always traveled with our locally appointed counterparts from the SRRA and a local driver. This meant that our capacity to spread teams over the many programs also halved.

In the days that followed, our alarm clock sounded at 5:00 a.m. to get us up and prepare. Still half asleep we had breakfast and silently loaded the cars with weighing scales and little swing girths so we could weigh babies and toddlers. HF radios, satellite telephones, solar panels, our run bags, lunches of dry crackers, and lots of water were securely stowed on the roof rack. Only after 6:00 a.m. was the light strong enough to see our surroundings, and we drove the first half-hour in the dark. In the early light, women were already busy pounding maize in wooden pots, and older children fetched water from the well or murky ponds, carrying the calabashes upon their heads.

We dropped several teams off at small villages and locations where the immunizations would take place. I was staying behind in one village to assist, and the driver continued to drop off the rest of the teams. The car drove away, leaving us in a cloud of dust. Immediately, a sense of loneliness enveloped me in this vast land, where the dense shrubbery surrounding the isolated huts appeared impenetrable.

Upon arrival at a location, the first action was to identify where the chief of the village lived and announce our arrival. The scattered teams in the area would only be in contact with the base again at 1:00 p.m. for a scheduled radio safety check.

The chief guided us through the village, and we went from hut to hut to ask for the children to be weighed. Soon, I lost all sense of direction—the grassy bristled fields, the gigantic anthills, huts, and scrub were all interchangeable and spread in an unstructured manner alongside many small tracks in the bush. In every hut, we asked how many children were under the age of five, if they were having health problems, and whether they had been immunized or received any food from the latest distributions, and how much was left. That way, we could calculate if there was enough food to last the rest of the season before a possible harvest.

The small group of children was herded into a clearing where our team set up the equipment to measure and weigh them. Many of these little ones had never seen a white face. When I came onto the scene, they started to cry, and in panic, they scattered and hid under the low scrub. The toddlers screamed and kicked as they were put into the girth and hung suspended between heaven and earth on the hanging scales. When they were stretched out on the measuring plank to determine their length, terror set in, and their howling soon saturated the air.

The moment we arrived at the next clearing to set up for the next group of children, the bush telegraph had already spread the news that we were on our way. I saw a three-year-old little girl running to hide in the bush, screaming and yelling. Her older sister ran after her, and laughingly she pulled on the stubby legs that stuck out from under the branches. Sometimes I needed to pull the mother away from all the hollering and shouting to hear her answers for the questionnaire. After the ordeal and the turmoil of having measured and weighed the children, many mothers comforted their sobbing babies by hoisting them into the cow skin and offering them their breasts.

At one o'clock, we searched for a clearing and set up a large antenna to initiate our scheduled safety radio check with the base. People looked on with wide eyes as we opened a little box in which the satellite phone was hidden. Soon the speaker crackled loudly, and we started the check: "Mobile one to Yankee Lima Base…" "Yankee Lima Base to Mobile one." Bart's voice sounded different through the speakers, but I recognized him. "Hello, this is Mike Whiskey, everything is Oskar Kilo. We are doing fine, and our location is (and I gave him our coordinates)." Later, we would set the radio up once again to give the coordinates of where we were so the car could find us back in the bush.

Every day, we followed the same routine, and we fell into bed with the screams and cries of the many children still resounding in our ears. Each day was hot and dusty as the rain still hadn't arrived.

In Dire Straits

We walked for hours from village to village, assessing the situation. Soon, we finished in the villages and would go even farther into the bush in search of the cattle camps that were always moving about to provide grazing for the herds. We knew that many more children were traveling with the nomadic herders of Sudan.

The Cattle Camps

It was still dark when we arrived at the edge of the vast swamps of the Sudd. We drove carefully over the rough terrain where there were no tracks or roads visible in the beams of the car lights. Our guide knew where we were going. Everywhere around me were swaying fields of long, dried elephant grass. No trees, no scrub, just endless golden fields of grass. So now and then, the car hit an anthill or thick clumps of grass.

After about an hour, a large dust cloud appeared on the horizon. It hung suspended between the grasslands and the endless space above. In the middle of nowhere, a large cattle camp had set up residence. A stream meandered through the grassy fields, and clumps of small trees grew as they had their roots deeply embedded into the water. It was full daylight now, and the people in the camp had woken up and were about their tasks.

Their shelters were rudimentary and clearly temporary. A few sticks were haphazardly planted in the ground, with leaves woven between them to provide shade from the scorching sun during the day. Low poles were arranged around the living area, with a cow tied to each one. Young children crawled around these poles, collecting the cow dung that had accumulated overnight. With their small hands, they rolled the often-still-steaming dung into balls and covered them with the surrounding fine dust to compact them. These were then stacked into mounds that were later burned. Throughout the day, the little shelters were invisible behind the thick smoke emanating from the smoldering piles. White ash covered the ground and, when a breeze stirred, it lifted the ash, creating a long-lasting cloud that obscured the outline and details of the camp.

Within the hour, we were all caked with the dust from those ashes. It blackened our hands and faces. Our clothes turned an indistinct gray; my hair hung in matted clumps around my face. Between the huts, the wind blew the dust onto the porridge that bubbled in the clay pots and into the water puddles in which both kids and cows

The Cattle Camps

scrabbled in. Children grabbed handfuls of the ashes and rubbed it over their whole bodies, resulting in strange-looking, ghostlike figures that floated through the dense, clogged-up air. Soon my eyes began to water and sting, and I could not even read the small numbers on the scales and measurement labels. How could people live in these circumstances for more than a day? There was no protection against the heat or any other weather conditions. There was no division between animal and human living quarters. Dust lay thick as a blanket over the entire camp.

At the end of the morning, I escaped the cramped area where we conducted our survey and stood at the edge of the camp, gazing over the vastness of the grasslands. The air above the plains simmered in the blistering heat. Cows grazed aimlessly, from grass clump to grass clump; they seemed to hover through the heat waves that rose from the ground. We walked to the trees next to the little stream to rest for a while before we finished our survey through the camp. Our driver had crawled under the car to find a respite from the heat and parked the car close to the trees, so the white roof would not attract attention from the air in case an Antonov flew over the plains.

Just as we settled down to rest, a car approached with great speed. It was an old, battered military jeep. Uniformed soldiers jumped out of the vehicle, all with taut faces, and then to my great displeasure, the new head of security arrived. Last week, he had asked us for assistance in moving three wounded men who had been in a serious fight in the cattle camps. We had to refuse his request at that time because of our policies, which had made this man furious, and he had stomped out of our compound while uttering threats.

And here he was again; he knew every move we made. A soldier marched up to us and barked, "You are commanded to leave this area immediately!" Politely we asked, "Please could you clarify why we are being hindered from doing humanitarian work for the needy people of Sudan?" This was too much English for this soldier, and he returned to his commander. Soon, another soldier walked up to us and firmly declared in his elaborate English, "This camp is now empty and devoid of men, so there is no need to do humanitarian work any longer. All the men have gone away for a meeting. We also have now concluded, at this moment, that the children are all in their huts as they all got the measles!"

We tried to keep our faces straight as this was the most ridiculous excuse we had heard. Besides, we had just been in the camp for the whole morning and knew very well that everybody was present in the camp. Regardless of what we were thinking, we decided to do what was demanded of us. We did not want more animosity from him, so we packed our gear and went straight to our car to return to the base. Befuddled, we navigated the long way back to Yirol. Everywhere this man turned up, we were blocked or hindered in our work. I wondered what this meant for Medair and the continuation of programs around Yirol.

One of the other NGOs in our area organized a picnic and games afternoon. None of us felt like going because we thought it might provoke the security officer to make rounds in his district. He'd continued to prominently follow all our movements and test us to see if we kept to the rules.

On the other hand, those types of informal, social meetings were important to catch up with the other aid workers and their programs. It was an opportunity to network. To be on the safe side, we informed the SRRA and its Security Department of our plans. To my dismay, the head of security stated that he would be present to monitor our movements. This meant that we could not freely discuss any sensitive information or share our experiences with the other aid workers while we tried to relax and have some fun. As soon as we arrived at the chosen spot, the head of security set up his canvas chair, and like a king, he sat on his throne and observed us from a distance.

When the light started to fade at about 5:00 p.m., the organized games were not yet finished. The invited officials and some soldiers were still racing and competing against the other NGO team members. We knew it was against the security and safety policy to be mobile after dark, and we had to be back on base before curfew. The ever-watching head of security scrutinized the outcomes of the games and kept casting glances at us as we packed up. We had decided to get going and got into the car to leave. I felt an unease rising inside my chest, suddenly aware that we might have been set up by the head of security to test us to see if we upheld the rules and curfew.

We were the first NGO to leave the party and were careful to follow the previously made tracks through the tall grass. We tried to rush through the plains to get to the main road leading to town. In my peripheral vision, a sudden movement caught my attention. Behind the distant tree line, which was a natural boundary of the

The Cattle Camps

grasslands and a small forest, camouflaged figures were running to hide behind trees.

Just before we entered the opening into the tree line, piled-up tree trunks prevented us from going any farther. This barricade had not been there before. Soldiers jumped in front of us and demanded we get out of the car. One angry soldier told us that we had violated the rules by not asking permission to go out for the day, "We were not informed or made aware of your presence in this area, and because of this violation, you are demanded to take soldiers back to Yirol in your company car."

His specific demand confirmed my suspicion that we had been set up. Like with the request to transport the wounded, we were tested to see how we would react to a request to transport soldiers. To give in would be a blatant misconduct of the set rules by the SRRA and our own policy within our organization. We answered firmly, "We apologize, but this is a demand we are not able to comply with. We are forbidden to carry military equipment or soldiers."

While we were talking, the other NGO vehicles approached. They also tried to get back to their compounds before the curfew. The moment they spotted us talking with soldiers, they skidded to a halt and turned into another track away from the roadblock to escape the situation, but to no avail. Some soldiers ran toward them with guns ready and shouted for them to come toward the blockade. The new arrivals stopped, but the soldiers were taken aback when they saw the passenger in the front seat—the smiling and very satisfied-looking head of security, their superior! Smugly, he told all the soldiers to mount this car and demanded the driver to drive everyone back to town. It was a sick play of power, and we followed at a distance, not wanting to provoke him to make us take on soldiers too. I was relieved that we had adhered to all the rules when we were outside the town boundary so we could not be accused of being insubordinate. At last, we entered the main road, and I felt safer, and my heart settled into a normal rhythm. As a team, we decided that we would not be inclined to attend any more picnics or parties for a long time to come.

The days that followed had a much more relaxed feeling to them. Bart and I sat on the veranda in the evenings as the sun slowly set behind low layers of clouds that covered the horizon, promising rain. In an explosion of colors, the last rays of light touched the quiet water of the lake, mirroring the sky. It felt as if we were watching a movie. Men returned to their huts after their baths in the lake, and women started small cooking fires. The smoke slowly rose into the now still air. Young children pulled cows and goats on rough ropes back to their compound and tied them to small stumps next to the huts. It was a life that I did not know, a life in which we played but a small role for a limited moment in time. We tasted and felt, heard and saw their life only fleetingly, then the curtains were drawn, and we returned to our own lives, and the movie ended.

Then we got the news the head of security would be transferred. A new commissioner had been appointed in our district, and we were looking forward to a more approachable authority. We would also get a visitor from the Medair's office in Switzerland to experience field positions in Medair. This was one of the great advantages of working with Medair; they made sure that everyone in the office would get an opportunity to visit the field, so they saw how the office-bound decisions affected those in the field. Our project director was planning to visit and introduce the latest programs that needed implementation. For us, it meant fresh input in our fieldwork and a fresh perspective on the programs. It was May 1999, and officially it was the rainy season.

R&R and the Wet Season in Rural Sudan

Mombasa, another R&R, and this time we rented a small hut at Diani Beach directly on the beach. We slept in and had a large breakfast of nutritious food. We read books and ate our dinner with oil lamps. The slapping of the waves put us to sleep at night, and birds woke us up for another peaceful morning. We felt far away from the war-torn country of Sudan. As we talked through our Sudan experiences, we also filed them away. The wind whispered through the palm trees, and I completely relaxed. Next to me stood a large glass with cool fresh juice, while I watched a column of camels slowly approach on the sandy beach. The camel driver nodded his head at the same rhythm of the large, flattened feet of the camel as it pummeled the sand. Hawkers tried to sell multicolored cotton sheets or hung these on branches in an overwhelming display of brightly flying banners.

As the camels passed, dark clouds piled up on the horizon. The sea changed its smooth ripples into louder and higher waves that were then dumped onto the beach. The rain arrived in sheets and cooled the temperature while we swam in the still-warm sea. Once the sun had completely disappeared, a group of monkeys came to entertain us as they swayed on their long tails and traveled from tree to tree. The eyes of a stray cat lit up in the low light as it waited for any food scraps from our table.

Returning to Sudan, we resumed our immunization efforts with a focus on the children in cattle camps located deep inland. To reach them, I had to drive slowly through low bushland, often off the beaten track. During one of these drives, we hit a tree stump and lost a side mirror. We decided to have our local guide walk in front of our car to guide us through the difficult terrain.

Finally, we reached the "*Tudj*," which was a large plain where we expected to find cattle camps. The last rains had made the ground soggy, and I could not see any obvious tracks made by cattle or their herders. Here, the grass had grown to meters high, and we were surrounded by new, juicy-looking green shoots. Watching the ever-moving grass in front of me made me dizzy, and we asked someone to sit on the roof and shout directions. Although it looked even, the ground had treacherous and hidden potholes that could pop our tires. After hours of driving, we saw smoke from campfires spiraling into the still-damp air. It was a small camp where grass had been burned away to ease moving cattle around.

The rickety little shelters were a pitiful sight. The children were ghostly white from the smeared ashes over their bodies, the natural mosquito repellent. In this camp, old women shuffled on their knees through piles of half-dried cow dung, turning the patties every few minutes to dry in the early sun before more rain would render the dung unusable for fuel for their fires. The horizon changed into a cauldron of black clouds, and we would have to leave the plains before the rain started. We only had a few hours to get all the children in this cattle camp immunized.

I foresaw the possibility of the car getting stuck in the mud the moment the rain reached the plains. Under the only tree that was in the vicinity of the camp, we quickly set up the table and equipment. Soon, long rows of mothers with their babies came walking from the camp. The mothers were getting a tetanus injection while we weighed, measured, and registered the children who had received the immunizations.

Soon the upheaval started. At first, the children were very curious about what was happening all around them. Quickly, the scene changed, and it looked like a torture session. Within half an hour, all the children were screaming and crying, some after the injections and some in anticipation of the jab. After a few hours, we were completely exhausted and ready to pack up to return to base.

As we loaded the car, the sky darkened even more. An hour into the journey, heavy rain made it impossible to see more than a few meters ahead and identify the waypoints we used earlier. To find our way, we drove close to the forest edge until we found a breach in the tree line. From there, we followed a small track into the woods, and I eventually recognized the area. We soon reached the main road.

The experience helped me realize the huge challenge faced by local medical teams in keeping track of the immunization records of nomadic communities. Staff traveled on bicycles, carrying vaccines in cool boxes. Immunization cards were issued, but there was no digital database, and all records were kept manually in exercise books. To help, we organized a workshop to explain how to set up future immunization programs, the benefits of proper record-keeping, and managing the equipment. This ensured that Sudan remained free from preventable diseases.

The following days, water bucketed from the sky. Roads changed from dusty paths into rivers of mud. Any travel became a serious challenge. While we waited for the rain to cease, I took time to sit and talk with our staff. Whenever I came back from Nairobi, I brought some Bibles with me in the Dinka language. I had to be careful who I gave them to, as we were not allowed to evangelize, distribute religious material, or conduct organized religious activities. These restrictions were part of Medair's policies which aimed to maintain neutrality and respect the local cultural and religious context in which we provided assistance. Most translators and interpreters were from the SPLA or the SRRA and were connected to the interim government. Given this situation we exercised caution when discussing topics related to religion. To continue supporting the local church, our approach involved distributing only only administrative items such as paper, pens, typewriters, and envelopes.

Southern Sudan's conflict was not only between the warring tribes, power struggles over natural resources, and the war for independence from the north, it was also related to the religion of the south. Southern Sudan is predominantly Christian and animistic in contrast to the predominantly Muslim in Northern Sudan. In the Muslim faith, one could claim to be a Muslim without adhering to the faith. Our staff was wondering if the Christian faith functioned in the same way. They asked, "What is the difference between *being* a Christian and *calling* yourself a Christian." This gave us the opportunity to talk about our faith in, and relationship with, a living Jesus Christ.

As the rain eased off, we were asked to bring an old woman back to a cattle camp. She had broken a hip and had recovered in the village, but she preferred to be in the camp with her grandchildren. It allowed Bart to experience a visit to a cattle camp, so we decided we could do this favor. From a lopsided hut, a bony old woman appeared and limped to the car, carrying her belongings on her head. She wore a knitted baby bonnet pressed on her graying hair and a heavy cattle scent traveled with her. In the corner of her mouth dangled a copper pipe which billowed out an even more foul-smelling smoke from tobacco mixed with cow dung.

For generations, life in the cattle camps had followed a set pattern. Children, young herders, and old people survived on a diet of milk and meat, living in pitiable conditions. It was difficult for me to understand why people would choose to live in such circumstances, but I realized they had no comparison to another lifestyle.

Tradition dictated that older women could only visit the village for three days, after which they were supposed to return to the cattle camps with the young kids. Breastfeeding mothers kept their babies with them in the village, but after weaning, they went to the cattle camp and were looked after by their grandmother.

If a younger woman wanted to see her older children in the camps, she could only stay for a few days before returning to the village to tend to her compound. Women needed to be available when their husbands came around, so they could cook and be ready for domestic or fieldwork.

With a carload of people, we left town in a direction I had not yet traveled. I noticed a long horizontal line of square holes in the ground which we carefully avoided. These were the holes we could see from the air when we flew into Yirol. We had already heard that these were a series of tank traps, part of the former defense line.

Majec, our local official accompanying us, started to talk. His left hand lay scarred and crippled in his lap. "Ah, I think back to the time of the offensive of Yirol." He nodded, and his eyes scanned the horizon, recalling the events. "I was a tank commander and had just driven over a landmine with my tank. It exploded right under me." He pointed to his maimed hand. "I dove my tank straight into one of the dugouts we just passed. These were our defenses against invasions by enemy tanks." A brief silence followed, then, "Yes, the defense was meant for the enemy, but I got stuck in it myself!" A slight smile played around his lips as he continued, "Do you know how I got out of it? I fired one of the missiles which made the tank jump from the trap, landing me right in the middle of the Arab line of soldiers!" He grinned as he described the shocked faces of the Arabs. "The other tanks had seen this maneuver and did the same. The Arabs scattered in panic and left even their weaponry behind. Within a few hours, Yirol was liberated, back in the hands of the SPLA."

We drove on, crossing a rising river without a bridge. We eventually arrived at a small, dirty camp that was similar to the others I had visited. We slipped and slithered through the mud as we helped the woman get to her shelter. Her hut was made of a few cow hides, fastened and stretched between sturdy sticks. Soon we would no longer be able to visit these camps as the plains would turn into swamps and the rivers would become too wide to cross.

Seed Distributions and Leaving Sudan

Bart was in charge of the seed distributions after large bags weighing 50-90 kilos had been dropped by cargo planes. Ahead of time, Bart had met with local authorities to make the distribution a just affair. The district leaders provided lists of households they supervised to determine how much seed each family would receive. The distribution took place at the old hospital site on elevated concrete slabs to prevent spillage or getting the seeds wet since the ground had become a muddy mess. Bart called out clan leaders' names and distributed appropriate amounts of seeds to be divided among family members. It sounded like a simple and organized procedure, but it was mayhem.

Just imagine that around the building, a multitude of people were pushing and shoving each other. Names were being shouted out, and upon receiving their portion of seeds, people would complain loudly about the quota and demand more. The steady rain soon added to the pandemonium. Large groups pressed together under a tin roof for shelter. Multicolored wraps were held out, under which women and children huddled together in an attempt to keep dry. In a short time, the thin material got drenched. Locally appointed police wielded branches to unsuccessfully keep order amidst the chaos. Children were often the ones being flailed with the sweeping ends of the sticks, and their screams mingled with the shouts of names, angry demands, and instructions from the police.

When someone tripped while carrying a sack, which consequently split open, children grappled through the mud to gather the spilled seeds. A man in a military uniform grasped the ear of a young boy to intervene in the theft. The boy wriggled, squirmed, and tried to escape and with his bony legs kicked the man between his legs. This made the soldier angry, and he dealt another blow to the boy, who ducked away and disappeared into the crowd. While he was dealing with the boy, another boy dressed in rags crawled between

Seed Distributions and Leaving Sudan

the booted feet and gathered the seeds. As the boy clamored away, an old, bent-over woman grabbed the rest of the spills and tried to run away from the angry soldier, who lashed out at her. She quickly stored the seeds between her dangling breasts so nobody would dare to take them from her.

Amidst this mess, Bart stood like a solid tree and directed the mob, undisturbed by all the surrounding commotion, and continued to tick off names from his list. I respected this tall, white Dinka who provided the seed for the teeming masses.

In the days after the distribution, people were forking deep furrows over the now wet and pliable earth. Soon, the seeds would burst forth from the steaming warm soil. And we prayed with the whole team that it would bring fruit and life to these people, so the hunger period could be officially called off by August.

The new commissioner had arrived. The entire village ran out to greet him as he was also the army commandant and had been part of the liberation of Yirol County. A white bull was pulled forward and stood majestically in the middle of the road. In front of Bart, who had picked up the commissioner from across the river, the bull was sacrificed.

Days after the commissioner's arrival, the town was still celebrating as people commemorated their first anniversary of freedom with lots of gunshots. Every evening, a large goat was roasted, and food was shared in abundance. I had no idea where it all came from, but people were elated. Sports festivities were organized, and other NGOs got invited to take part in the soccer matches and races. The women danced, young men competed in wrestling, and we enjoyed being part of this celebration. Bart got assigned to a soccer team; he was as tall as the Dinka players. I felt proud of him as he managed to play for a team that he could not even understand. I was assigned to the fast-walking competition, and although I started well, my legs were no match for the long legs of the Dinkas.

Then a theater piece was performed in which a group played the recapture of Yirol. Food was everywhere: sour pancakes, the green mush of local vegetables, and roasted meat, all served with crunching sand that hurt my teeth. Later that night, we were invited to the official dinner with the local authorities. The sky was covered in thick clouds, and lightning flashed overhead. As we walked back to our compound, thunder rumbled through the quiet night. Throughout the night, rain drenched the grass roof of our *tukul*, dripping incessantly on the plastic we tied above our mosquito net.

During the week, I went with local teammates to visit some of the selected schools to distribute more school materials and seeds before the heavy rain would make it impossible to reach them. We managed to visit four schools before the sky darkened again. We had to be quick before the rain came and made the roads impassable; nobody wanted to get the car stuck and risk not coming home before curfew.

Hurriedly I drove the car over a narrow footpath made by women between the well and their huts to reach the last school located farthest away in the grasslands. Although the flattened grass made the journey a little easier, the dark clouds gathering in the sky indicated an imminent storm. It soon became evident that we wouldn't make it home in time. Before we reach the last school, daylight disappeared, and it became like dusk around us.

Strange green light simmered over the surrounding bushlands. Then thunder burst forth, and lightning arrows flashed straight to earth on the right and left of us. Fiery balls of tightly packed sparks rolled over the clumps of shrubs as the electrical storm unleashed. Then the rain swept over us. Water pounded on the roof of the car, and I could not see through the windows. The powerful water changed the small footpath we had followed into a river within a few minutes. There was no way I could continue and visit this last school. My only goal now was to get out of these grasslands and get us home safely. I felt the car sliding from underneath me, and soon the tires did not find solid ground. We were stuck. I looked down from the window and saw the tires had been sucked up to their rims in the thick mud.

I pushed the door open and got out, but the undercurrent of the swift-flowing water swept my legs from underneath me, and I fell flat into the muddy water. I frantically tried to grab the vehicle's step bar, but the water had reached the threshold of the doors and started to flood the car. I slipped back in the stream and gashed open my thumb on the sunken sharp grass stalks. It bled profusely, and I thought it was a good sign, so I let the water wash over the cut. Once I gained footing, I saw that one tire on the back was completely in shreds. I had not even felt the tire blow out, but it explained why we got stuck. With a combined effort, we tried to change the tire, but any attempt failed as the strength of the water slipped the jack from under the chassis.

I was so cold and shivered, my teeth chattered, my hand hurt, and the wound throbbed. The storm raged directly overhead, and the thunder was deafening. Next to me, lightning struck a tree. I began to pray as I felt hopelessly exposed on this grassland. Finally, we got the tire changed, and with a squealing engine, I tried to get the car out of the rut. Instead, we created a deep hole that the torrent eroded into a deeper gully. The car came briefly adrift, then mud scraped under the chassis, and soon we were stuck again.

Just as suddenly as the storm came upon us, it stopped. The rain changed into a gentle drizzle, and the surrounding earth began to steam. From nowhere, people appeared, and young men gave us a hand by scooping the mud from underneath the chassis to free our car. Local kids emerged on the edge of the plain to look at the half-sunken car. I radioed our predicament to the base and asked for another car to come and pull us out. Bart informed me that it would take him at least an hour to get to our position by which night would have set in. He would inform the authorities that we could not make it before curfew.

I settled in for the long wait and looked around me. A group of people had gathered, and all were shivering in their soaked clothes. My eye caught a young boy who stood at a distance, watching the commotion. He was very thin and naked, perhaps eight years of age. He kept his right arm at an odd angle, and as I came closer, I saw a broken bone protruding from above his elbow. He was shaking, and his teeth were chattering. The bone had been in this position for a while as the skin had closed around the wound and had kept the bone in place. The rest of his arm was alarmingly swollen. I asked the bystanders where his mother was, and soon a young woman stepped forward. A small girl held tightly to her tattered skirt, and a very tiny baby was pressed against her bare breasts.

My translator explained that the boy had broken his arm when he had fallen from a tree, and they had never considered coming to the village and asking for medical help. I told her to come with me so the boy could receive treatment. Most probably, he would have to be medevacked to Loki hospital in Kenya as his bone needed to be reset. The mother went back to her hut and returned with her pitiful belongings: a wicker basket, a sleeping mat, and a paper-thin blanket in which she wrapped the baby. The car radio beeped, and I received the message that Bart also was stuck in the mud somewhere. We would have to wait even longer before he could come and rescue us. The night set in, and millions of stars appeared in the sky. It was pitch dark here in the bush, and I felt small in this immense country. Finally, two lights appeared in the distance, and the onlookers clapped their hands as Bart bumped onto the road. To my surprise, other members of our local team jumped from the car as they all wanted to come and rescue Bart's wife! Bart brought dried fruit and nuts, which slowly revived us. The water had receded a little, and with the help of shovels, we were able to dig more mud away from under the chassis. Soon Bart was able to pull us out of the dip. The track was slippery, and we slithered from right to left over the path. Several times we got stuck and helped each other whenever one of us stalled. It took hours before we even came to the main road.

The poor mother and her three children had never been in a car before, and she got carsick and vomited all over the floor. The permeating smell made me feel sick too. We opened the window, and I asked the translator to convey the message that she could vomit out of the windows, which she frequently did until we arrived in Yirol. In our storeroom, we rummaged through the bags of clothes that we had to distribute among the needy. We got her a new blanket and some clothes before we dropped her off at the clinic. I was exhausted when I finally dropped into bed.

The project director from our headquarters in Switzerland came to visit us and permitted us to build proper quarters for the leper colony. We planned to build a clinic, treatment rooms, residential huts, and a small school. We started with the distribution of specialized shoes and proper medication against the leprosy bacteria. This was to be followed up by providing training for lab assistants and nurses who would work full-time for the colony. After we established these programs, a Catholic mission organization was lined up to take over any further development stages.

As we talked it all over with our project director, he also informed us that there were more programs being planned at other places, in other countries. Bart and I had a longer leave coming up and sensed that major changes hung in the air for our future.

Then, I got terribly sick. My whole body cramped up as I kept vomiting. My strength faded quickly. The wound I incurred during

Seed Distributions and Leaving Sudan

the storm was infected, and my stomach did not cope well with the antibiotics the nurses had given me. I needed to be medevacked, and we booked an MAF flight to pick me up and fly me to Nairobi. As I waited for the plane to arrive, a radio message came through from another team who had their base north from Yirol. It was not time for our regular radio checks, so this had to be an emergency! Indeed, just north of us, our coworkers had been bombarded and had fled into the bush: "Mayday, mayday Yankee Lima Base, could you function as a relay station, over?" Their next message came through, which we relayed to Loki, "We are not able to contact base from our position. We are out of drinking water. Immediate evacuation requested." They continued by giving us their coordinates so that an evacuation procedure could start, and a second plane was sent to pick them up.

I made it to Nairobi but had to stay a little longer than expected because my stomach took some time to settle with the new medication. My still swollen thumb had to be treated in hospital as a nasty red line started to creep up my arm. The wound had to be cut open again to get the infection cleaned out.

During this time, I attended some workshops in Loki where Bart and I also visited the Red Cross Hospital where we sent medevacked patients. As I walked through the wards, a bright smiling young boy skipped toward us. He held his plastered arm high while pointing to us and thanked us profusely in Dinka. He was the boy we took back with us after the fierce storm and subsequent rescue.

As we had sensed, our time in Sudan came to an end. We were approached during our break to consider another location, far from Sudan. Our time in Sudan was too short; our hearts were still with the people. We had to come to grips with having to say good-bye to our local friends and team members.

Each subsequent good-bye took a little more from our hearts, and we needed some time to let go to give ourselves all over again in the next location. This was the life of an international aid worker. Somewhere out there, beyond the horizon, more experiences and adventures waited for us. Our journey had not ended yet, and I looked forward to everything it had in store for us. First stop, back to the Netherlands for a break and catching up with our family.

Part 8

Back to Europe

The Balkans: Kosovo and Its History

My head reeled; we truly were called upon to be pilgrims and nomads as we traveled from one end of the world to another, between extremely distinct cultures.

The founders of Medair invited us to their place in Switzerland to inform us about a new crisis that had emerged while we were working in Sudan. We had to shift our focus to a completely different situation than what we had been dealing with in Sudan. We were sitting in their living room, enjoying a glass of wine while they told us about the situation and how Medair was involved. They were asked to provide aid in Kosovo after the intervention of NATO.

The Kosovo conflict—between Albanians and Serbs—received a lot of attention worldwide during the years 1998 and 1999. Years ahead of the intervention of NATO, animosity had been bubbling before exploding in a horrific outburst that resulted in the massive destruction of Kosovo.

During the early months of 1999, NATO had acted and launched a military intervention against Serbian forces. This included attacking militias and other armed groups who were responsible for horrible acts of ethnic cleansing of the Albanian population in Kosovo. The Serbs systematically destroyed housing and property from any Albanian they could identify, killing as they went. This left many places in Kosovo in ruins; the infrastructure, roads, houses, and economy were destroyed.

Bart had done his studies in engineering and architecture, and his knowledge would be invaluable for the Kosovo reconstruction projects[4]

After the briefing visit to Switzerland and a short break, we left the Netherlands again. It was early summer when we flew to Rome and stepped in and out of taxis, giving us only a glimpse of this historic city. There was no time to linger and explore this amazing place.

Early the next morning, we left our hotel and boarded a military plane that flew us into Pristina, the capital of Kosovo.

As we approached the airport, I was unprepared for the war zone scene before me. All the briefing in the world could never compare to real-life imagery. British and Russian helicopters and armored tanks were parked in rows next to the runway. The surrounding buildings were heavily damaged, and armed soldiers in uniforms that identified which country they came from were present everywhere.

To get to Peja, our new station, we had to drive one and a half hours west through the devastated landscape.

Destruction spread in every direction and increased as we approached the outskirts of the city. A former chicken farm next to a Serbian tank base was completely bombed out by NATO. It was believed that this had been a radio control center. We carefully drove around that area as there were still unexploded ordnances sticking out of the ground.

Soon we drove through a riverbed—because the bridge was destroyed. Traffic was chaotic, and piles of debris and rubble lay everywhere along the edge of the road. Obviously, driving was the biggest hazard at this moment in time. Next to the roads, and sometimes randomly in and between the rubble, were more signs that warned of unexploded ordnances, mines, or booby traps. Every kilometer we drove, the heavy scent of charred timber and burning debris clogged the air.

It was early June, and the only birds we saw were black crows. Their constant caws and cries were maddening as we spent the first few days reading up on the history of the Balkans and their fascinating story.

Milosevic, then president of the Federal Republic of Yugoslavia (now Serbia), and the members of the Orthodox Serbian minority of Kosovo "had long objected to the fact that Muslim Albanians were in demographic control of an area held sacred to the Serbs. (Kosovo was the seat of the Serbian Orthodox Church as well as the site of the Turkish defeat of the Serbs in 1389 and the Serbian victory over the Turks in 1912.)"[5]

The rising tension between the two ethnic groups provoked the political leader Rugova of Kosovo, to encourage his supporters to a more radical uprising. They argued that their demands for recognition could not be secured through peaceful ways. In '96, the Kosovo

Liberation Army (KLA) rose up and attacked the Serbian police and politicians. This went on for a couple of years and turned into a full-scale guerrilla war. At that stage the international world had not yet addressed the upheaval in the Southeast of Europe.

"The Yugoslav and Serbian forces responded with a ruthless counteroffensive and engaged in a program of ethnic cleansing"[6] of the Albanians. This caught the attention of The United Nations (UN) Security Council, and sanctions were imposed. Unfortunately, the violence did not stop.

On the twenty-fourth of March in 1999, NATO engaged in airstrikes targeting the Serbian military. In response, Yugoslav and Serbian forces drove out all the ethnic Albanians from Kosovo, resulting in hundreds of thousands of people being exiled to Albania, Macedonia, and Montenegro. As they forced residents from their homes, they systematically destroyed their properties.

"The NATO bombing campaign lasted 11 weeks and eventually expanded to Belgrade, where significant damage to the Serbian infrastructure occurred."[7] This resulted in the signing of a peace agreement that stipulated Yugoslavian (Serbian) troops must withdraw from Kosovo and allow the ethnic Albanians (close to a million) and another half a million internally displaced Albanians to return to their properties. Now the roles were reversed, and most Serbs left the region as they feared retaliation from the returning ethnic Albanians. Because some Serbs remained in Kosovo, the UN sent peacekeeping forces to Kosovo to keep the two groups from attacking each other. The territory was divided into military sectors that were administered by different NATO armies, much like post-WWII Germany.

Fast forward a few years, after we had left, Kosovo declared its independence from Serbia in February 2008. "(Yugoslavia had ceased to exist in 2003, giving way to the federation of Serbia and Montenegro, which itself dissolved in 2006.) Although the United States and several influential members of the European Union chose to recognize Kosovo's independence, Serbia did not."[8] Serbia continues to lay claim to the territory.

First Crisis Responders

A flood of NGOs came into Kosovo in response to the humanitarian crisis. Medair had already been established in the neighboring country Albania and was present on that side of the border when crowds of ethnic Kosovar Albanian refugees crossed the border to escape the NATO bombing campaign. Medair provided blankets and medical attention and started a soup kitchen at the border. We heard horror stories from Medair team members as they witnessed killings and shootings right up to the border as they assisted the families who ran toward safety into Albania. Some were killed right in front of their eyes. As soon as the refugee crisis started, it abated, and the reverse happened! The moment the peace accord was signed, all these refugees wanted to get back to their homes. Their mass return to Kosovo caused even bigger problems as most of their homes were destroyed. This was all still happening when we entered the scene in June of '99.

The first survival stories we heard came from our driver. He told us about how a relief organization came to assess a small village in the hill country. Before driving over the road to the entrance of the village, they asked a de-mining team to see if there were any mines left. They were shocked to find eight anti-tank mines that would have blown them to pieces.

Our first on-the-ground briefings were about the complex history of Medair in this region as they were already implementing the program on both sides of the border, and we had to be trained in mine and booby trap awareness.

The current programs were in their infancy, and different proposals for reconstruction were still being written. These proposals aimed to provide a thousand families with a heater, building materials, roof sheeting, a door, and plastic window sheeting to keep the rain out of the damaged structures. The objective was to ensure that one thousand rooms would be dry and livable by the beginning of winter. Part of this program would mean opening at least three distribution centers from where we could distribute construction materials to the urban and rural communities. Timber was the main commodity and was in great demand.

We still needed to identify suppliers who could deliver vast amounts of building materials. There was not yet any import of wood, and no timber mills were functioning. The area that we covered for reconstruction was divided into the city districts and the smaller villages that surrounded the city. Although it was still summer and warm on the European mainland, we already had to consider the upcoming autumn storms and the severe cold of winter.

The whole of Kosovo had been divided into different UN army sectors. There was the Dutch sector, the Russian sector, English sector and the Italian sector…and that was the sector we operated from. We were never short of all kinds of pasta and pizzas in the local restaurants, and here we developed our love for cappuccinos! For a good, strong cup of tea, our English team members preferred to visit the English sector.

Medair had been renting a house in the town of Peja while they worked on another relief project prior to the escalating Serbian-Albanian conflict. The team had to evacuate at the same time as the Albanian population fled from the Serbian death squad who hunted the Albanians and went from house to house to burn and loot.

Medair came back with the returning refugees and found Peja mostly destroyed. It was a sad picture; huge modern houses were reduced to rubble with burned rafters sticking into the air like black skeleton fingers. With difficulty, the team found the street where they had been living earlier that year. Most neighboring houses were turned into rubble, but to their amazement, their previously rented house had been unscathed! How did this Albanian-owned house escape the devastation unleashed by the Serbs on the other houses? The team told us that they had been praying for protection during their time in Albania, and when they returned, the neighbors filled in the details.

The Serbian Militia had entered the house and looked at the beautiful carpets and decorations. They looted the place, and instead of setting fire to the house as they did to neighboring houses, they decided to flood the upper floor by opening all the water taps and so ruined the expensive interior. They then went down to the basement where they spray-painted graffiti on the walls and set the large oil heater alight. The basement burned out, but the house was spared as it was soaked with water! By replacing the carpets and repairing the water damage, the house was ready to accommodate the team again.

To my amazement, people were already setting up their restaurants, businesses, and markets between the shambles and the mess of a destroyed city. We could go out for dinner in the city, and we ate on terraces with our backs leaning against highly stacked sandbags with barbed wire on top. Soldiers patrolled the dirty streets where little shelters popped up. Most shelter tarps had the huge sign of the UN stamped on them.

I got my first impression of the magnitude of the devastation when I went to a household goods distribution. This was called the "shelter program," which meant we would distribute hygiene buckets to nineteen villages in the surroundings of Peja, plus shelter materials like the well-known blue UN tarps which functioned as tents.

Those hygiene buckets had been put together by Tearfund, another Christian organization. They had asked households overseas to donate towels, soap, shampoo, Band-Aids, toothbrushes, facecloths, etc. Each bucket also had a small letter of encouragement written by the families who had put the buckets together. We prayed that these little drops of hope would lift the spirits of the people.

The extent of destruction was overwhelming. The Serbian Militia had employed diggers and bulldozers to flatten Albanian properties after burning down the houses so they could not be rebuilt. On street corners, large notice boards were nailed on wooden poles, and often a group of people could be seen scanning the lists of names on these boards. My driver explained, "If the notice has a red border, it means the names listed there are of those found massacred somewhere in the village. If the poster has a green border, it contains the names of those who have died from natural causes." The ones with a red border had the longest list of names.

Animosities were still happening between Albanians and Serbs in some villages as not all Serbians had left Kosovo. During the nights, we would hear a lot of shooting and often would not know the reason as we never got official reports. We stayed on high alert, always trying to find out from our local staff members if something big was afoot to which we needed to act. Like in Sudan, we all kept a curfew; no getting out of the house after dark for our own safety.

A family invited me to come and visit their enclosed property.

Within the stone walls, three houses were totally destroyed, and large shelters of canvas replaced their living quarters. Piles of rubble surrounded their makeshift campsites. Some children were climbing on top of the rubble and creating a slide. We were offered a small, strong Turkish coffee, with a thick layer of coffee dregs on the bottom. Under the blue sheen of the UN tarps, we were directed to sit on thick Turkish carpets that covered the ground. A lady motioned for me to follow her inside another tent, and she showed me beautiful drapes and tablecloths of fine needlework the women had been working on. An old lady in traditional clothing smiled at me with a toothless smile. She got up and handed me a pair of handmade knitted socks to keep me warm for the upcoming winter.

Initially, I was supposed to work alongside one of the longer-term team members who had returned with the refugees from Albania. The intention was that I should be trained to take over the Finance Department. Unfortunately, that never happened as team dynamics and relationships within the team were a huge challenge, and some were not willing to hand over their programs. Instead, I was placed on the team that worked in the immediate surroundings of Peja and was initially assigned other duties and assisted in setting up the base.

The setting in which we found ourselves was so vastly different from Sudan. Once again, I was in for some serious stretching of my abilities, and I would be confronted with some negative core beliefs about myself that influenced my relationships within the team.

The team was expanding as we got closer to the different implementation phases of the massive reconstruction programs. With the extra Medair volunteers arriving in quick succession, we needed additional accommodation, and we rented a second house for which I was responsible for furnishing. This meant lots of logistics, facility management, buying white goods, and searching markets for food supplies.

The first house we had initially come back to also served partly as the office. The floor level was assigned for office work; the rooms upstairs were sleeping quarters. Bart and I ended up in the attic, which was comfortable and large. We had our own wood stove and made the space into a small living room so we could spend some time alone. The only window in the room looked out over the blackened ruins of the neighbor's house, and there was always the distinctive, permeating smell of burned wet wood. It is printed into my memory, and every time I smell this particular smell, I am taken back to the immense destruction in Kosovo.

During those first weeks, I spent hours roaming the badly scarred city to find the necessary household items to make the two team houses more livable and comfortable. The day started by hunting the many small outlets that had some merchandise. I looked for beds, sheets, and mattresses. Every day shops added something else to their stocks, and finally, I was able to buy a toilet seat and toilet paper. It took a little longer for more luxurious items like bath towels, a vacuum cleaner, and lamps.

With a quickness that amazed me, the makeshift shops on top of bulldozed rubble started to get their supplies in, and a diversity of other items became available. Lots of goods arrived via the border of Turkey. To my surprise, the most advanced technical equipment became rapidly available, plus everything to do with fashion: beautiful leather shoes, expensive clothes, and fur coats were sold within weeks of our arrival. Even beauty salons popped up, enthusiastically visited by some female team members and translators.

The power supply was still very unreliable. We had only a few hours of electricity each day on which we could work on computers to set up worksheets, plan documents, and draft reports. We used generators to cover the hours when there was no power so that the batteries of the laptops could be charged. Cooking was done on the old-fashioned wood burner in the kitchen, and we employed a local lady to make our meals. The generator itself kept me busy as it needed regular maintenance, and I continually had to find out where diesel was sold.

The local markets were already selling fresh produce. Somewhere, there were crops being harvested, and the surplus was sold in the markets. Some surviving cattle, which had not been shot to pieces, were auctioned off. As I walked through the stalls, I could smell where the designated area was for the butchers. I walked quickly to the middle of the market where a cow was just being slaughtered. Strong men hung the carcass on wooden structures to bleed out. Then the customers pointed out the piece of meat they desired; the butcher cleaved into the carcass, and the chunk was weighed, paid for, rolled in newspaper, and handed over to the buyer.

As I had mentioned, traffic was hazardous. Lines of smoke-billowing, honking old cars, heavily loaded lorries with stacks of construction timber coming from the borders, all milled together in the barely cleared streets. Navigating slowly through the congestion, I tried not to hurry as that would inevitably frustrate me. The moment I saw an opening in the traffic, an oil-squirting old tractor or a flat trailer pulled by a mule blocked the crossing. With a deep sigh, I opened the window to let the warm air calm my nerves.

One afternoon it looked like we were permanently stuck at one of those bottlenecks in the city. I stepped out to see what caused the chaos. Two huge timber trucks had tried to pass each other and got stuck and were tightly squeezed together. They could not move an inch without ripping the covers from their loads. Jumping from their cabs, the drivers were yelling obscenities at each other.

An old farmer took the opportunity to spur on his horses which pulled a cart full of household items and tried to cross the busy intersection. He weaved between the cars and vehicles that were all hooting and waving wildly to everyone to get going. As I returned to the car, the horses bolted and charged through the traffic with the cart bouncing up and down. The contents were dangerously swaying from one side to the other. Suddenly the horses changed direction and came straight toward our car. The owner shouted and whipped his horse until it skidded to a halt. Suddenly, the large head of a profusely sweating horse, with bulging eyes, protruded through my window, centimeters from my face. The gaping mouth was pulled back by its reins, and I looked straight into the greenish dentures of the horse. It made for great jokes and laughter later at the dinner table.

Taking Over Leadership

In Philippians, Paul says, "But one thing I do: Forgetting what is behind and straining toward what is ahead, I press on toward the goal to win the prize for which God has called me heavenward in Christ Jesus" (Philippians 3:13-14 NIV). This verse helped us to get through the first weeks as we were meant to take over the leadership of the Kosovo team. It was indeed difficult to leave behind our team in Sudan, and I tried not to compare the team dynamics from which we came. We realized that the trauma the people of Kosovo had gone through was vastly different from the Sudan crisis. We needed to find new compassion for these victims of war.

It dawned on me that I identified much more with the Kosovars as ethnically we were so closely related. This was what we would have experienced if a war broke out in a Western country. These people here were European, educated, and possessed initiative that defied any dependency on international aid. The people were keen to work and rebuild their houses with whatever they received. Their gratefulness toward the aid organizations was motivating, and each distribution looked as if we were part of an annual farmer's festival. To be part of these distributions was heartwarming.

As motivated as the local people were, I soon found out that establishing a working relationship with the international team was a great challenge. Our program directors had asked us to take over the leadership when we were briefed about Kosovo. The team was emotionally exhausted and dealing with division among its members, so they needed positive input and spiritual encouragement.

Medair HQ had been informed about our leadership style in Sudan and thought it appropriate and beneficial to propose that we come in as new team leaders. They hoped it would bring a fresh perspective and new insights to this team. Initially, we would work with twelve expatriate staff that were all highly educated and had been involved with several missions in different countries prior to Kosovo. Some had gone through traumatic experiences in Chechnya, Chad, and Albania. Some of them had been kidnapped or had been part of a sudden evacuation. Others had lost team members to horrific accidents or were exposed to horrendous personal maltreatment inflicted by the militia. Compared to these stories, our experiences in Sudan were a piece of cake. We felt sceptical about whether our input as team leaders would assist in changing the existing frame of mind.

I was made responsible for the Personnel Department of the Kosovo projects. I had to conduct interviews and appraisals of the international team members. I was touched by their stories and experiences as I familiarized myself with their personnel files. These people were able to identify with the Kosovar people as some of them had been exposed to horrific firsthand experiences themselves. They could be of profound influence and able to spread hope to those who had undergone similar difficulties. Their background would be of immense value to our team as well, informing us on how to approach certain situations. I found out that most of the trauma they had gone through had not been processed yet. We saw serious cases of accumulative stress disorders and burnout Spiritually, these team members had hit rock bottom and had lost vision.

It resulted in members trying to isolate themselves and pulling out of any attempt to build up a new team spirit. Only three team members agreed to join us for prayer and a short devotion at the beginning of each day. Some would not even communicate at all and just did not turn up at team meetings. The argument was that they had too much work to do and were under time pressure to deliver. There was a defiant attitude and no desire to grow into a team or put effort into the development of new programs.

Soon the lack of team spirit manifested itself negatively. People lashed out at each other as there was a lack of trust and a common goal. There was no social and spiritual support from each other, and this was a dangerous situation to be in as a team. We were fighting a spiritual force that attempted to spark the disunity we experienced. We were as divided as the Kosovars were among their people; we mirrored the local animosity in our team. This made us feel weak and ineffective as leaders.

Several days in a row, I came across a member silently sitting in a corner of an empty room, crying. Another member walked around with puffy eyes, closing the door the moment she entered the office and refusing to let anybody enter the room for hours. We noticed that one young man started his day with a shot of whiskey in his first cup of coffee. Others were withdrawn, silently doing what they were supposed to do after which they went back to their own rooms at the end of a busy day without speaking to anyone. Some held onto their projects as if they were their own brainchild and chided everyone who tried to "interfere."

When a newly arrived team member tried to contribute an idea to a colleague, an emotional response would follow, "Shut up if all you can do is criticize. Besides, I am in charge of the program!" I thought these innovative ideas were fantastic as the new team members brought a fresh perspective. Unfortunately, they were not received as such. How could we make this team function as a unit and implement a high-quality program?

I wondered how our input could change all this. Yes, we had a good working team in Sudan, but I did not think we had much to do with that. It just worked well. There, team members had anticipated the scope of the programs and had thought about the dangers, the spiritual impact, and the challenges that could arise from working with a culturally diverse team. In Sudan, we had indeed great devotions and were able to encourage each other spiritually and had respect for the different views that team members brought to the table as they all had different denominational backgrounds. I was not prepared for the challenges that this team presented. They were a previously established team that had experienced great insecurities and traumas together. It made it difficult for new members to connect.

As I tried to get to know each team member as part of my role as a personnel officer, I came across stubborn, closed-off, and defiant attitudes. The moment I tried to discuss the progress of the programs, I was accused of criticizing or told to stop telling them how to do their job. When asked to report back from daily activities, it was perceived as interference, and they responded defensively. Some even resorted to withholding information that was needed to set up a new proposal to the donors or held back statistics to finalize a report. They would personally draft their reports and send them straight to the PD at HQ, without copying us into their correspondence. The initial team separated themselves from the new arrivals and were perceived as acting superior, which divided the old group and the newbies.

This was the reason I never got the opportunity to be trained in the Finance Department, which had been HQ's original plan when we were sent to Kosovo. I was sad as I felt blocked from developing another possible skill within the humanitarian aid work. I tried hard not to take their responses personally. It showed me the importance of having initial in-depth talks and screening processes with the Personnel Department before employment as an emergency aid worker. The constant stress, exposure to the trauma of others, and having to function in insecure areas or extremely volatile circumstances could be triggers. It could set off reaction patterns that are a result of unresolved issues in our past lives.

Reflection:

As I look back on this period, I remember how pressure started to build up deep in my chest. Team members were unwelcoming and had turned inward to deal with their own traumas and inner conflicts. I experienced this as personal rejection, and I allowed negative thoughts of inferiority to take over, creating an inner war. I compared myself to all these well-educated, traumatized, and overworked people. I became self-centered and lost focus on the needs of the people we were helping. It triggered the pain of childhood wounds and the rejection by my peers, workmates, and overall society. I felt unable to reach out and discuss matters objectively or be of constructive assistance to my teammates. I stepped into an agreement with the age-old lie that I was not good enough.

A Positive Change

We desperately needed spiritual input if we were to survive this new challenge. The first few Sundays went by, and although we tried to read and meditate on our daily devotions, I felt spiritually dry and lonely. Then we tried to organize a Sunday service with the team, which did not resonate with any of the other team members. We asked around to see if there was a local church that had survived the war. We found a small evangelical group that had a Sunday church service at five in the afternoon, which we tried to attend as often as possible.

It was a highly motivated group of people with a true testimony of what Christianity is all about amidst great oppression and difficulties. Sixteen members of this local church had stayed behind in Kosovo during the ethnic cleansing and bombings, looking after elderly people who were trapped in their houses. It was encouraging to see how these enthusiastic Christians grabbed the opportunity to spread the Gospel to their returning neighbors, who were often traumatized. It was this faithful group who, with the assistance of a visiting Youth With A Mission team (YWAM), organized a Gospel concert one night.

That concert night was truly a miraculous experience, and we witnessed a historic moment. This would not have been possible during the Serbian occupation, as ethnic Albanian were not allowed to hold public meetings. The concert was organized in a large indoor sports hall. Most windows had been blown out by a bomb explosion, which had flattened a nearby militia base. Ceiling panels hung dangerously loose, swinging from torn metal frames. Outside, it was pouring rain. We huddled into our jackets and sang praise songs in an unknown language to us, with hundreds of young people who celebrated their freedom. This was an encouraging experience for me, and it triggered a serious discussion later on in our team.

The debate started with a more general discussion to find out what everybody's actual expectation was of working in a Christian organization like Medair. The questions arose, "How are we seen by the communities? Are we any different from other NGOs? Are we professional Christians or Christian professionals?" This triggered an exchange on the motivation of why team members volunteered to be involved in the Kosovo project in the first place. Was it just a job, a humanitarian duty, or an opportunity to be a Christian witness? This discussion emphasized the importance of understanding why we worked in volatile situations that we did not create and had no personal benefit from intervening in.

I tried to make sense of the philosophical discussions that subsequently arose that night. One team member argued, "We can't be seen as a mission organization since we're not allowed to evangelize in this Muslim-dominated country." The counterargument was, "But Medair isn't classified as a mission organization. We're a professional international aid organization with Christian values as our foundation. One of our main values is neutrality to the conflict, regardless of the religion involved, or whether it aligns with our worldview."

"But," objected a new team member, "I read in the description of our core values that we are supposed to spread hope as we are founded upon the Gospel that promotes reconciliation and unity through Christ!" Another team member scoffed, "Whatever our core values are, it is not appropriate to have, or even be part of these daily Christian devotions we now hold every morning!" Next to him, a tall young man stated, "I certainly do not agree to invite our local staff to these morning devotions; they might be Muslims and be offended by our Christian jargon."

The intense discussions at the table continued, "I came to Medair with the conviction to just be Christ-like in my compassion to people; I would never initiate a conversation about my faith in God to a Muslim." From the other end of the table, someone overruled the last comments, "But we can answer questions of our local staff, and I have had many discussions with my driver last week. That way, I was able to be a witness and openly preached the Gospel." Some smirked at the idea of openly preaching, "Preaching is for missionaries who set up churches. No! Aid workers are the hands and feet of Jesus."

Another girl, who had experienced some traumatic events when serving with Medair quietly said, "I lost that zest to be Christ-like.

Really, if you were honest, you would agree you were just working from an idealistic point of view of doing humanitarian work. It makes you feel good about yourself. After you have seen enough suffering, you will get disillusioned in your true motivation." Someone softly answered, "That would take away the drive I feel, and I had hoped to make a difference in people's lives!"

This threw a shadow over the conversation. One of the older team members reiterated, "Guys, we are all just doing a practical job, and maybe you come from a Christian perspective, which is fine for you, but don't idealize or spiritualize humanitarian aid work." After a brief silence, he added "You can have a private religious conviction, and that has nothing to do with the job of aid workers, as this is just a universal service to humanity which we are all called to do."

Then the discussion shifted, and one team member confessed, "I struggle with my faith. There is no answer to the suffering. I feel overwhelmed by witnessing the suffering that is happening worldwide in the name of religion. Here in Kosovo, it is between Orthodox Christianity, Catholics, and Muslims!"

After a long silence, a team member concluded that it was important to show compassion to those we served when they were so downtrodden by suffering. That is what Jesus would do if He was walking among these people. And regarding our own team, we should show unity among diversity because our common faith in Jesus made this possible. We should be an example and a witness to how we implemented programs without corrupt practices, as was the case in so many countries and even within the aid community.

I had indeed identified three main religions in Kosovo: Albanian Muslim, Serbian Orthodox, and a minority Catholic. None could stand the other. The division of the local populations played itself out within our teams. I wondered if we had been exposed to this spirit of division, and through our weaknesses and brokenness, we opened a door to allow the division to become part of our team too.

After this discussion, we organized a board game night at the end of the week. We prepared a meal together and watched a comedy on our video recorder, which was running on the generator. For the first time, it felt like we were trying to function as a true team.

I also learned at this time how working with a task-oriented team can be vastly different from collaborating with people-oriented team members. Through the time we spent together on the Kosovo projects, I came to appreciate those driven and task-oriented personalities. I saw the potential of the highly professional delivery of the programs and their significant impact on the local community.

The Programs

The first installment of donor funding from the Swiss government was handed out in June, and we had arrived in the middle of the set-up of this first shelter program. We aimed to have the one thousand rooms ready by the onset of winter, and we were now at the beginning of August 1999. The moment we had finalized the plans and got permission from HQ, we started contacting suppliers to purchase all that was needed to rebuild warm and dry rooms to a livable standard.

It meant we put together three engineering teams to go out into the villages to find houses that were still repairable and safe to live in. Bart kicked off the project by identifying one hundred houses in the city of Peja. To give an idea of the cost, we procured timber and reinforced plastic roof materials, and household equipment to build at least one dry, warm room per family. This cost a total of 3.5 million USD and we spent it over five months. It was funded by the U.S. Agency for International Development (USAID).

These were immense projects, and the more statistics we got from the surveys, the larger the follow-up proposals to the donors seemed to grow. We needed so much more funds, and nobody foresaw the impact of sending off such large proposals to the donors. If approved, we had to start planning the implementation of the next phases of follow-up programs while still busy with the first phase.

Suddenly, all team members became extremely busy from early morning till late at night. Even on a Sunday, we ended up working, briefly interrupted by a church visit or a walk.

Rebuilding a roof frame to a traditional design using timber required a huge amount of wood. Once the timber was distributed, we moved on to distributing other materials, such as rolls of reinforced plastic for temporary roof sheeting, wooden battens for the window frames, and transparent plastic to cover windows, doors, and wood stoves.

In the evening, we sat behind our laptops to feed this infor-

The Programs

mation into an MS Access spreadsheet that was designed overnight. An off-duty special forces officer volunteering at Medair, dedicated himself to designing the growing spreadsheets. One early morning, I found him sleeping on the office floor as he kept working through the night.

Roof structure designs were drawn up by the engineers, and discussions took hours to find solutions on how roof plastic could be attached to the rafters. It needed to be fastened in such a way that the nails would not create leakages, and the joints were watertight. It needed to be strong enough to withstand the autumn storms and assessed for durability so that it would not tear up when heavy loads of snow rested on top. We even discussed how to prevent crows from picking the material apart.

Bart headed up the urban team with local engineers, drivers, and translators and surveyed the suburbs of Peja to assess each house as to the extent of the damage. The engineers had to determine if the assessed building substructures were still strong enough to carry the new roofs. Often the concrete beams and columns were severely damaged by fire and explosions. The damage assessment tool given by the UN indicated the severity of the damage to each house. A class one house was not structurally damaged, like our team house, up to level five class, which meant that the house was a write-off and not livable.

In the evening, architectural drawings were drafted for the more permanent roof structures that could be built after the winter. Bart managed ten local roofing teams which were assigned to rebuild one roof per week. Depending on the severity of the damage, these structures would cost anywhere from three thousand to five thousand Deutsche Mark (this was before the Euro) each! And every transaction, whether it was buying the building materials or paying the salaries of the local staff, was done in cash!

During a coordination meeting with other NGOs, we were thrilled that Medair was assigned to work in the district in which the little church was based. We were able to assess the neighborhood and assist the Christian community there.

Now the search was on for suitable distribution yards within the city and villages. We frantically searched for more timber suppliers. Most other NGOs were doing the same for their areas, so securing a supplier was quite competitive as each tried to find its trade route and importer.

A few days into the rat race, Bart got flagged down by a young man who was terribly upset. Before the war, he started an apprenticeship for an electricity company, and they were now busy going around the city to repair the high voltage power poles and lines. His colleague had just received an electrical shock and needed help. Thinking it to be a minor incident, Bart and his translator followed the apprentice to the place of the accident. When he arrived, there was a huge crowd, and then he saw a man hanging upside down from a power pole four meters from the ground. His back was strangely arched in his safety harness. His left hand was shriveled, and his face was blue. He had died because the isolation of the high voltage cable had failed. Some men got ladders safely installed to get the body down.

That night during a prayer meeting in the church, we heard that this man had survived as a soldier in the war. He had seven children, and his wife was pregnant with number eight. We were all very disturbed by this incident. After so many years of oppression and war, he lost his life while volunteering to re-establish electricity for the people in his neighborhood.

The programs were at full blast. In three villages, we identified large distribution yards that soon were filled up with rows of timber, piles of battens and stacked plastic rolls, ready to be handed out. At each location we needed over a thousand cubic meters of timber. A truckload carried about forty cubic meters, meaning we needed at least thirty truckloads. At any given time in a distribution yard, timber was stacked high and could be worth over a hundred thousand Deutsche Mark (DM).

I had found my niche in all these activities and was made responsible for distribution yards in several villages. After a day of demanding work in the open, I processed the inventory and entered the distributed timbers and building supplies into the database. Through this system, we were guaranteed one hundred percent traceability of each piece of timber to each household, something the donors loved! Updating the data spreadsheet kept me busy until midnight.

After this initial stage, we ran out of timber suppliers, and once again our logistical team set out to see what came through the borders from Bosnia, Montenegro, and Macedonia. We got reports from the logistical team that there were kilometers-long queues of trucks at the border crossings waiting to be released into Kosovo.

Our soldier on leave, who also managed the database, would scour the city on a bicycle and approach truck drivers carrying timber. He would randomly buy their loads straight from the truck. He dealt with drivers from Bulgaria, Hungary, and Austria, making late-night deals at the office. Sometimes he encountered Serbian truck drivers, and he would direct these to some village distribution yards to offload. They would only do that in the middle of the night as they freaked out when they heard that it was for an Albanian village! We had to guarantee their safety and would travel with them to assist in offloading the timber. The drivers were high-strung and fidgety, looking around every other moment while working frantically so they could get out of the village as soon as possible.

During the day, construction started all around us, and we saw in people how rebuilding their houses gave them hope. Most of the locals were so thankful, and many gave us small presents or asked us over for a meal or a strong Turkish coffee. Some offered us a strong alcoholic beverage called *raki* which we politely had to decline.

If we got complaints, it was because the doors that we supplied were plain and dull in comparison to the doors they had before! Theirs had been handcrafted into intricate wood panels with sculptures and uniquely designed door handles or stained-glass windows. These people were used to wealthy living and were determined to restore their lifestyle to their former state as soon as possible. When we distributed roof rafters, the plain and roughly squared ends of a beam were overnight transformed into beautifully carved shapes. Sanded and polished, they showed great craftsmanship.

Destruction Everywhere

As we crisscrossed the country, the aftermath of war created palpable silence. Large mounds of rubble with blackened beams looked like piles of broken bones. Shot-off tree trunks stood like beacons next to deep bomb craters in the pockmarked scenery. We avoided the already rusting bridges, carefully choosing the lowest point of the river to cross over. As we crossed riverbeds, unplowed farmlands on both sides added to the feeling of abandonment. Most villages had sandy access roads which would become muddy tracks by the time the autumn rains came.

Destroyed factory buildings that were inhabited by screeching black crows watched us suspiciously as we passed. Stinking, smoking, uncollected household rubbish was piled everywhere, and swarms of birds circled over the garbage. On one of the electricity poles next to the road, a fresh piece of paper was stapled with a lengthy list of names of bodies that were found in a mass grave close by.

Most houses in the villages that we visited had bullet holes in the plastered walls. Inside the houses, everything was completely burned out, and only the outer walls were still standing. Floors had collapsed where grenades had exploded after being thrown through the window. Roofs were caved in, and roof tiles were scattered everywhere. I stepped gingerly through to the kitchen area of one house, where glass and broken crockery scrunched under my feet. Some windows had been exposed to flamethrowers, and the intense heat had fused the glass together into odd-sized glass balls. The yard was once a well-taken-care-of orchard, but now grappling grapevines have overgrown the garden beds. Thistles spread their sharp, prickled tentacles everywhere. In the car park, a burned-out Mercedes stood as a reminder of the once-rich life the owners had.

A little later, a farmer guided us through his house and showed me a pile of charcoal paper in a hole in the wall. It had been a makeshift safe where he had kept two hundred thousand DM as he did

Destruction Everywhere

not trust banks that were owned by the Serbs. Now, all was burned to ashes.

Farmhouses farther into the hills looked untouched until we came closer. A large chunk of each corner of the structure had been taken out by huge bulldozers, as if the backbone had been broken and was precariously waiting to be pushed over. The house was unsuitable to live in; a strong wind could crumple the house into a pile of rubble. This would be classified as a level five house and declared uninhabitable.

Wherever we went people received us with great hospitality and then the recounting of stories started. These stories were so intensely sad, and I did not know what to do when emotions overtook the storyteller as they described the rapes, shootings, massacres, and torture. Even the animals suffered. One family left their cattle behind as they ran for safety. When they returned three weeks later, they found the cattle emaciated. While giving them some water, the cows dropped dead in front of their eyes. Other farmers were lucky as they had shooed the cattle into the hill country. When they went searching for them, some surviving cows had calves, although others were blown to pieces as they had stepped on mines.

Landmines were everywhere, especially around the school grounds. The school buildings were booby trapped. The hospital had to set up a special unit for mine victims who came flooding in, mostly children. As they innocently ran into their homes, they would trigger a booby trap. With happy laughter, they ran into their gardens and would activate a tripwire attached to a mine.

A girl of about thirteen ran up the stairs of her home after returning from the refugee camp across the border. They had fled the cruelty of the militia, leaving behind everything they owned. It was the only house in that village that had not been destroyed. As she jumped the stairs, she found her lost teddy bear sitting on a step. When she picked it up, a well-hidden booby trap got activated, and she lost both her legs. Children spotted shining pieces of metal between the rubble, and by picking them up, it triggered the mine buried between the broken household items. As I listened, I felt sickened because the children were the target of inexplicable hatred.

As I talked to the head of the village council, he apologized for his nervous demeanor. While the man recounted stories, he lit another cigarette with the burning tip of his previous one. His son was being held in a Serbian prison. He had just recently been captured, and his father had heard rumors of the horrible treatment given to Kosovars. I followed him as he walked toward a small hill in the middle of the town. Twenty-two little mounds rose from the neatly mowed grass, all with freshly painted crosses on them. In addition, straight wooden poles stood at the head of each mount with a crumpled piece of paper attached with a photo of the dead. One of the little hills covered the body of a murdered two-year-old.

One sunny afternoon, I distributed construction timber to a young man. He walked up to me with his leg in a contraption. His speech was halting and stammering as he told me, "It has been shattered by a bullet during the fighting." He was jittery, and another farmer who also collected materials pulled me aside. "Be careful, after he came back from the hospital, he has displayed unpredictable behavior. He fights his own war in his head." Mentally, he had never recovered. While I measured and counted the lengths of wood for him, he suddenly pulled his pistol from his pocket and aimed it at my head. I froze on the spot. A moment later, he holstered the weapon again and continued our conversation as if nothing had happened. So many people had been broken by this war, and I felt such compassion and sadness at the horrors of war.

Safety was a major concern. Shootings and heavy detonations occurred frequently during the night. In the hills, explosions vibrated the air, and houses were still being set on fire. A safety report stated that Serbian-occupied houses were often targeted by mortar attacks. Their houses had to be guarded by NATO as the Albanian guerrillas continued to attack at night. Serbian citizens were secretly transported and relocated to guarded compounds to protect them from revenge attacks by ethnic Albanians.

One morning, I was getting some supplies from the city when loaded buses were escorted through the city in a heavily protected convoy. This was very unusual, and through the chatter on the HF radio, we heard that the NATO escort had lost its way and ended up driving Serbian refugees through the Albanian center of town!

Slowly, they made their way through the chaotic traffic. The moment the fleet was spotted, people on the streets were overtaken by blind hate. Violence erupted as the angry mob stopped the NATO vehicles and tried to attack the buses. Albanians who stood at the roadside threw stones and rotten fruits at the buses that had blackened windows to protect the Serbian travelers. A cordon was formed, and the Serbian refugees were herded into a nearby NATO base while the angry mob literally flattened the vehicles.

Every Serbian Orthodox church had a NATO tank in front of the building. Generally speaking, most Serbians would be Orthodox Christians and would want to visit church services if possible. Kosovar Albanians were waiting to get an opportunity to destroy the church since, to them, this was a symbol of Serbian oppression. Consumed with hate, fear, and sorrow, people walked the streets, constantly on high alert.

The projects were in full swing, and the pressure was turned up to deliver the people the right building materials to get that dry, warm room ready before winter. I worked with thirty-five local team members, and it was a race against time as summer turned into autumn. Sometimes I got the opportunity to talk about my faith. One local worker wanted to know who Jesus was. For the remaining time in the car, Bart and I shared about our faith. The driver asked, "Did you try to convert people during your other missions in different countries?" And I answered, "I just shared my life and abilities with those who needed assistance." Then I added, "I cannot separate my faith from my actions. I believe that faith in God's love for all people is the framework from which I do my work. I want to share that love around."

Much later, I overheard a conversation between our local workers who were comparing the different organizations with whom they worked. All organizations did their utmost best to distribute according to the funds they had been assigned from donors. From Medair, it was said that they did what they had promised and handed out products of quality that were good for long-term use and not just a temporary solution. They also observed how we resolved team conflicts. One translator said, "I am so impressed. All of you come from different countries, and you have disagreements, but you solve them and extend forgiveness. This is not done in our society."

Political unrest stirred as the citizens were listening and being influenced by Serbian-controlled radio broadcasts. Loud voices blared through the speakers in the cafés. "We will fight through the winter, and we will not give up until all of you are under our rule again!" As a result, the people became impatient and started roaming around looking for more building materials so they could start making their houses more secure. They began to beg, walking from one agency to another, pleading to come to their village first. "Please put us into your system and hurry up the process, we are cold and need shelter!"

Materials were getting scarce; it was harder to reach our targets and get shelters organized in time. In the hills, the cold had come too soon, freezing conditions made us aware of how vulnerable people were as they awaited aid. We heard a story of a family who lost a baby during the night because of the cold. Some families did not have winter clothes and even walked barefoot through the early snow in the hill country. We sent teams to check out these stories so we could concentrate on the neediest among the population. The situation seemed to be as it was reported.

Winter, Change, and Hope

The weather was changing. A crisp-smelling wind blew in from the mountains. Nights became very cold, and after the first frost, the leaves on the trees around the hill country of Peja turned golden. It was stunning scenery as we drove through the mountainous terrain, visiting the more remote villages. We had already assisted in the reconstruction of houses for seven hundred families, and we still had funding for more. The mercury dropped and suddenly, one morning, we woke up to the quiet of a snowed-under city. Seeing the sunrise over the white-capped mountains behind the hilly countryside was breathtaking. Inside the still half-restored houses, people panicked as many did not have any means to heat their houses.

Winter had Kosovo in his grip. Temperatures plummeted even further, and snow kept falling and falling. Meters of snow piled like a blanket over the destruction of the war. It became silent in the city, and villages slipped away from our radar as the roads became inaccessible. Various parts of the UN's army divisions had access to snow-clearing equipment but not in our Italian division. The connecting roads into adjacent sectors of the Dutch, Americans, and British, were half a meter lower than the roads leading from our Italian area. They had been cleared from the compacted layers of snow by a snowplow. The compressed, packed down, and now frozen snow added to the profile of the roads. It gave a literal edge to our travels.

The composition of our teams changed over the Christmas holidays too. New volunteers came in with positive attitudes, and it refreshed and relieved us. Bart and I found more quality time for each other, and we tried to get away in the late afternoons for an extended walk through the surrounding hills. Plowing through meters-thick snow, we witnessed the country take on a fresh look, and the blinding white seemed to wash away the horrible sight of burned debris and constant reminders of war. It also concealed the warning signs of hidden land and antipersonnel mines. As we walked the parklands on the edge of the city, we unknowingly had walked over mines!

As we relaxed a bit and spent more time together in the house, I started to feel exhausted and unwell. Before Christmas, I caught a cold while working at the distribution yards during the rainy days of late autumn. I had been in bed with a horrible throat infection and on heavy antibiotics. These always caused me pain in my stomach, and the nausea did not let up after the course. I was so tired; each day was a dread to get up. That penetrating smell of wet burned wood, the overpowering odor of dead animals, and the uncollected household trash affected my nerves and stomach. I started to miss my periods or had extended periods of heavy bleeding, and I experienced significant pain. I did the work in the office and kept feeding all the accumulated paperwork from the distributions into the database, but my heart was not in it.

Due to the limited power supply, electricity was scarce in the city, and the available power was shared among several districts. The power supply was rotated through all sectors, which meant that businesses, including the hospital, only received a few hours of electricity each day.

As I got sicker, one of our translators introduced us to a local doctor who checked me out and sent me for an ultrasound in the barely functioning hospital.

During the few hours of electricity allocated to the hospital, I sat in the waiting room as the equipment for scans or X-rays was being powered up. Nurses hurried the queue of referred patients through and finally I could go in for an ultrasound, just in time before the power supply was cut off again.

The hospital was terribly cold; the heating system was not working. I lay on the narrow bed, shaking and feeling nauseous. While the doctor scanned my tummy, I tried to imagine how the hospital must have looked when it was fully functional. But now, it had the atmosphere of an empty and desolate building—cold, unwelcoming, and well past its prime. The loud hum of the outdated electrical equipment filled the room, the power supply stuttered irregularly, and lights flickered on and off. I was waiting for the scanner to stop working, but the grainy screen continued to send images to the doctor, who mumbled to himself.

To prevent any personal information from being leaked or shared among the staff, we requested a hospital translator instead of using our own team's translator. However, we were unaware that the translator standing next to the doctor was a cousin of one of our local staff members. It did not take long for us to discover how well the local news delivery system worked.

Worried, I lay there, expecting him to tell me that I had a tumor or a spreading infection that was causing all my physical symptoms. When the doctor finally looked up from the computer screen, he said in broken English, "You! Pregnant five-week," holding up five spread-out fingers. I was totally confused as I looked at his beaming face. Pregnant? Dazed and uncertain about how to feel after that announcement, we left the hospital. We were so cold and shaky that we decided to take a break at a small Italian coffee house to let the news sink in.

I got a prescription for extra hormones because of the excessive bleeding, to be administered by injection. I had to find a pharmacy somewhere in town that was supplied by *Médecins Sans Frontières* and find a Red Crescent Clinic in the district where we could get the injections administered.

As I put the ampules in my pocket and searched for a clinic, I prayed that if this baby were meant to be, I would be able to accept this unexpected change in my life. However, I was not convinced it would stay, given how unwell I felt. I was mentally unprepared, physically exhausted, and in a lot of pain. Psychologically, I felt like I did not have enough mothering in me to be a mum.

Amidst the rubble, I spotted a white tent with the Red Crescent painted on it next to a partially destroyed brick building. The building had one room that remained intact and functioned as a nursing post. As Kosovo is predominantly a Muslim country, the International Committee of the Red Cross was replaced by the Red Crescent, and many of the nurses were male.

I entered the building, which was freezing cold and looked so empty and forlorn. I saw only a narrow wooden bench that was used as a treatment bed. From behind a curtain, a male nurse appeared, wearing a white coat tightly pulled over many layers of thick clothing. I explained what I needed, and a broad smile spread across his face. Holding out his hands for the ampule I had brought with me, he patted his back pocket and produced a glove. He continued to search his breast pocket and found a needle. His other breast pocket produced a syringe. I wondered what was next; he then pointed to the wooden bench and indicated that I bare my backside for him to administer the medicine. I had to peel off layer after layer of my thick winter clothes in front of him.

Walking back to the car, I decided that if this baby was meant to be, I would go through the pregnancy just fine without the ritual of finding ampules, going to a freezing building, undressing myself before a male nurse, and then having to stretch out on a dirty wooden bench.

Soon after, the bleeding stopped, and three weeks later, we were back in the hospital for a check-up. On the grainy screen, I saw a rapidly beating heart, still bigger than the little body forming around it. Life was happening right there under my heart. I marveled at the circle of life here in Kosovo. Lives had been taken throughout the country, and injustice was done from the city to the mountains. Still, here I was, growing a baby amid this traumatized community.

In the office after our hospital visit, I received hidden glances and knowing smiles from our local female staff. The cook gave me an extra portion of meat and laughed as I explained that I wasn't hungry. Then she pointed to my stomach and gestured that I was getting fat! I suspected there was talk about me, and I wondered if they knew I was pregnant. We decided to inform the whole team and staff during the weekly meeting. The local staff's merriment was great as they explained that they had known it from day one when we returned from the first hospital visit. The translator had informed her cousin, who worked with us as a translator. So much for trying to be inconspicuous and private about it!

Soon little presents were handed to me, and I was invited to the staff's family members who had just had their baby. They showed me how to feed, swaddle a baby, and how to mix a bottle. They were all guessing what it would be. History had proven to the people in this region that if there was a year in which many male babies were born, it guaranteed there would be a war in the next ten to twenty years because by then the army needed soldiers.

I was touched by how caring they were and how much attention they paid to me. They gave me the place closest to the fire to keep warm and offered me green tea to help with my nausea. They told me what to eat, how to sleep better, and which side to sleep on during my pregnancy. Over the next few months, they even gave me new clothes that I would still need to grow into.

Coming to the End of a Millennium

We planned to finish the emergency aid phase by February 2000. I informed HQ of my pregnancy, and we discussed the implications for my involvement in the projects and where I could get adequate medical care in the months ahead. We decided it was best to leave Kosovo earlier than our contract indicated. Medair HQ advised us to go back home to recuperate and prepare for the arrival of our baby.

This meant a total change of direction in our thinking about our future. Suddenly, aid work might not be the way forward for our immediate future. Questions piled up as the year 2000 approached. Bart and I tossed up various options, such as attending Bible school, doing a discipleship training school (DTS) with YWAM, switching to development work, or getting a regular job. Where would we live? Where should I have the baby? The millennium would be introduced with an explosion of change.

Locals were organizing New Year's parties ahead of the turn of the millennium. For many years, the Serbians had prohibited any celebrations by the Albanians. The girls were getting dresses from Turkey straight from displays. After the party, the dresses would be returned and put back onto the plastic mannequins that decorated the shopfronts in Turkey.

I did not have a party dress, so the girls organized one for me. I was invited to be pampered, and an extended session for applying makeup followed, and a hairdresser turned me into a model.

On December 30, 1999, we walked through the streets and joined the large party that headed toward an empty auction hall. I shivered uncontrollably as the temperatures plummeted far below zero degrees, and the dress was designed for warmer environments. The hall was unheated, and the few available hours of electricity had to be used for cooking.

Dinner was served in parts, as the prepared chicken had to be transported from other districts where power was available to operate kitchen equipment. Soon, everyone was hungry and cold.

Nobody ever saw my lovely dress—I never took off my padded jacket. Or the makeup because the tables were lit with weak, flickering tea lights that were good for a few hours and then slowly died. The cold was intense. Some people got their dynamo torches or battery-operated lights out to illuminate the huge hall. Once the music stopped because the petrol for the generator had run out, we engaged in the conversations that went on around us. Nobody complained about a lack of food, warmth, or light.

Soon people got up and started singing and dancing. Bart and I were pulled into the circle, and white handkerchiefs were twirling in the hands of the ladies as they taught us their traditional dances. The happiness and exhilaration of the people were contagious; they partied as if there would be no tomorrow.

The next day was the last day of the year 1999. We were entering a new millennium while living among the rubble of a destroyed country, but with a rejuvenated and exuberant nation as they celebrated new freedoms. We expected the people to become quite rowdy, so the team decided it was better to stay home this night as we breathlessly watched the hands of the clock creep toward midnight.

The year 2000 arrived with an explosion of fireworks, tracer bullets, and real bullets. Two neighbors across the street stood on their balcony, aiming AK-47s into the sky. Simultaneously, they sent streaks of tracer bullets that illuminated the entire area, just like real fireworks.

Next door, a drunken man ran outside and emptied a revolver below our bedroom window. We peeked out the window and saw many cars inching along the streets. Sometimes someone would jump out of the car, race to the trunk, lift a heavy rifle, and pull the trigger. Although disarmament was a continued project by the UN, many weapons were still present. We would dive back into the room as our theory was that every bullet that went up would also have to come down, potentially hitting a target.

I sat at the dining table and reflected on the past year. It had been full of adventures. I looked around at the team. Some quietly played a board game. Others were knitting away as they had just learned this skill from women in our area. Inside, I felt a little deflated; everything was so unusual and strange. Then a reverent silence flooded my soul as—in this new era, I would become a mother.

January turned bitter cold. Soon it was freezing, -20C, and the diesel vehicles could not start as the fuel had frozen over. A logistician brought out a hairdryer and lay under a car on the wet snow, blow-drying the tank so we could at least get to the city center where we would search for antifreeze to de-ice the other car engines.

Our lives were still overwhelmingly busy. For weeks, queues formed in front of our entrance every morning. Each person gave us a list of required building materials to insulate their houses against the terrible cold. We tried to procure the materials that now sporadically came in across the borders. At the end of the month, we would hand over all the projects to the newly appointed team leaders. They would prepare for the project's second phase, which we would no longer be part of.

We rented a small holiday home in Macedonia to build team spirit and get to know the new leaders. It was a safe place to walk around and have a break from the continuous requests that came from the Kosovars. During this brief break, those who stayed for the next phase could adjust to new team dynamics. Many of the initial team members had moved on or gone home for a lengthy recovery period.

It snowed most of the time, and we played around in the meters-high snow that had accumulated against our cottage. Like little children, we held a snowball fight and jumped into snow piles. We searched the snow mounds to identify our cars, which were totally hidden.

As we drove back into Kosovo, I felt we were at the end of a significant time of our lives; we were saying good-bye to our involvement in international aid work. After experiencing difficulties and gaining some painful memories regarding teamwork, I was grateful that we would end on a high note.

The only way to leave Kosovo was by a military charter plane. We were driven to the only functioning military airport nearby in Skopje, Macedonia. We joined the uniformed troops of the Swiss army who were also going for their R&R. This was the only time ever that we had Sten guns on a civilian aircraft.

The trip to Basel in Switzerland was long, tiresome, and surreal. Our minds were in disarray as we left an intense time behind and were thrown into a new chapter of our lives. I bought several CDs from my favorite singer, Céline Dion, and her beautiful voice overrode the drone of the heavy aircraft engines. Whenever I hear her songs now, I am transported back to that plane trip. We had no idea where we would live after the holiday in Switzerland we had arranged, and we had yet to determine where we would have the baby.

My parents were on holiday in Switzerland, and they allowed us to stay a little longer in their rented cottage, since we would also visit HQ in Lausanne to be debriefed.

A few weeks to recuperate did wonders for our spirits, walking for hours through the idyllic villages and enjoying the hills with thick layers of snow. We enjoyed cross-country skiing for the first time in our lives. In the first week, we fought trepidation to step off the pavement and enjoy freedom in the parks without fear of booby traps or hidden mines. But soon we did little dances on the grassy terraces bordering a road that drew curious glances from a passerby.

Our personnel officer arranged a visit to an obstetrician to check my condition. What a pleasant surprise when the specialist announced that I was much further along in the pregnancy than was diagnosed in Kosovo. I was seventeen weeks pregnant. On the following Sunday morning, as I woke up in the attic of the cottage, I felt the first stirrings of my baby. My spirit lifted, and suddenly I was able to think a little further than one day at a time. I wanted to start preparing and getting ready to receive this little life. We left Switzerland and entered the Netherlands, officially our home country as our passport stated. Inside, it just felt like an intermediate station. The next destination was still to be decided.

Part 9

Becoming Parents

The Year 2000

Initially, we rented a small farmhouse in the middle of the country. We knew from experience that returning to the Netherlands was not a straightforward process. We were apprehensive about all the official paperwork, especially if we needed to register the baby. Bart and I soon found temporary jobs, although I knew I would only be working for a few months before the baby was born. Unexpectedly, unlike the last time we returned to the Netherlands, we were allocated a flat that belonged to the Department of Housing. With the rental subsidy, we were able to live on Bart's salary, and I started to buy the first baby outfits and some furniture. We were warned about the area we lived in, as it was a low socioeconomic area with many refugees and asylum seekers. This only made us feel more at home, as we had lived in so many impoverished areas among so many deprived individuals who lived with traumas from the past.

We became good friends with our neighbors, some of whom could not yet speak Dutch. Early one morning, I received a knock on my door from a young Turkish girl who had just gotten married, asking if I could help them with some official papers that had come in the mail. She was wearing a hijab and traditional clothing. I ended up translating and explaining difficult governmental letters regarding visas and settlement issues.

One day, as I climbed the stairs carrying my shopping, loud wailing came from the corner apartment. A large traditional Turkish family lived there who made the most delicious fresh Turkish bread and always shared it with those living in the same corridor. I knocked on the door to ask if everything was fine and was invited to join a traditional wake as one of the elders of the Turkish community had passed away. I removed my shoes and sat with the many crying women on the thick Turkish carpet with our legs folded under us.

We became friends with a couple who had fled Afghanistan. They were highly educated doctors who had to go through the full six years of study again in order to be recognized by the Dutch Medical Board.

An Iraqi Christian neighbor took us to a local mosque where fresh local vegetables were sold. He told us how he organized Christian conferences for Muslims who had become Christians and how they were persecuted in the Netherlands by their own countrymen.

On a sunny afternoon, all the ladies on my corridor would get together to wash their adjacent windows. If only one person did their window, all the other windows would become wet, so we organized a communal window cleaning. Our level was always squeaky clean, and for days afterward, the hallway smelled of proper old-fashioned soap.

We would drink sweet, dark tea, often sitting on the carpet in the middle of the living room. Quantities of flatbread were made in the kitchen, using the floor as a large, floured board to roll out the sour-smelling dough. As always, the bread was shared with many others. Although our neighbors' home countries might have been at war, here in this little area, in the middle of Holland, there was peace and unity.

Bart and I could not have hoped for a better place to return to in our homeland and bring our first baby into this world. All of our neighbors had lived through their own horror experiences, and all of them lived with the hope of starting a new life in the Netherlands. We felt privileged to be part of this small community, and I did not even feel like I had re-entered my own country.

August came hot and humid. Often, thunder rumbled on the horizon, and I was heavy with our child. I had no clue what to expect when labor started, but the ladies in the apartment block tried to explain how things would progress and how they would be there for me, all expecting to hear me go into labor soon. On the evening of the fourth of August 2000, Bart and I walked for three hours; I had heard this would set the birth into motion. I still had ten days to go according to the official calculations, but no one was sure about the exact date. And sure enough, at noon the next day, labor started.

We still had a full agenda for that day as we had scheduled an introductory meeting with a potential Medair recruit. By 4 p.m., I told Bart that the pain was quite intense and asked if he could send the lady home while I went upstairs to begin the serious part of the birthing process. Soon after, my mother arrived, and I felt privileged to have her by my side. In the Netherlands, it is customary to have home births with a general practitioner attending, unless there had been complications during the pregnancy, which I did not have. So, I labored for another four hours with the windows open to allow a little breeze in. As soon as our GP's car was spotted, all the neighbors opened their windows, expecting to hear a lot of noise coming from our apartment.

At 8 p.m., our firstborn son entered the world. Holding him in my arms was a moment of pure beauty and joy after an exhausting labor. Later that night, our neighbors knocked on our door, asking if the baby had died since they never heard any screams, groans, or yelling! In many cultures, women scream during childbirth to help with the labor. The doctor smiled as she explained to me that making sounds really did help instead of suppressing the pain. Still smiling, she held up a mirror to show me my bloodshot eyes.

Having my mother by my side during and after the birth was a blessing. She came in with a hot cup of tea and toast, and I felt completely satisfied as I looked at our little boy. We named him Danny, which means "God is my judge," as he was conceived in a war-torn country where injustice had caused so much suffering. We knew that only God could alleviate any suffering from injustice, and we prayed Danny would become a peacemaker.

The days after the birth were a bit surreal as people came and went, and our hallway was filled with gifts from the residents of our apartment building. The family came to visit and admire Danny. While watching my child sleep peacefully one morning—and making sweet baby noises—I was suddenly filled with panic. Tears flooded my eyes, and I sobbed as the enormous responsibility settled on me like a heavy weight. How would I be able to raise this boy? How could I provide a safe and solid environment for him and help him become a well-balanced person in a world with so much injustice? Bart had to go back to work, and I lay there wondering what life would bring us next.

Suddenly, I became aware of a white figure standing beside the bedroom door. Silently, He held out His hands toward Danny, and I felt a rising joy as I figuratively laid Danny into His arms. He held the baby tenderly and close to His chest and asked in an unspoken voice, "Do you want to give him to me to care for?" I just nodded and silently prayed that Danny might always feel God close to him, whatever life would present.

That first year as a mother seemed as if another page had turned in my life. I did not have close friends with whom I could relate stories or confide in about my insecurities as a new mum. The ladies in the apartment were from diverse cultural backgrounds, and they dealt so differently with their children than what I had seen in my own culture. I had no idea how to be a mother. I had this image that to be a mum, you went for a walk with a stroller, had picnics in the city park, and drank lots of coffee with girlfriends. I never thought I would be so tired from lack of sleep and so unsatisfied with my sluggish brain and body that all I wanted to do was lay down and pass out!

And the worst thing was that I was not used to having to pause in the middle of an activity. I found myself frustrated with the disruptions as I sewed new curtains for the baby room. Danny would wake up and demand attention, and I had to stop halfway through a seam. I couldn't get into a book because Danny would want to be fed, cried, or threw a tantrum when he had had enough of being in the playpen. I felt unprepared for motherhood.

Suddenly, life was not about me, Bart, saving the world, or being purposefully driven. I felt lost in this new task and lifestyle, and doubts started to form in my mind that I might not be the mum Danny needed. I felt exhausted playing silly games on the floor, doing peekaboo, and rattling toys. It did not occupy my mind, and I was not interested in the music playgroup with toddlers that the ladies of our church organized. I tried harder and harder to become the happy and shallow person who played the role of a mother in the theater of life. I was only lifted from this darkening mood when we were able to travel again. Fortunately, that was possible during the one year we lived in the Netherlands.

Medair organized a reunion that we attended in Switzerland. Soon after, we visited London with Bart's sister and cousin and reconnected with some of our field workers from Sudan. One nurse who was present when we tended to a birth in Yirol had decided to do more study as a midwife after her experiences in Sudan. We decided to seek out more ex-field workers and visited a woman in Norway who had to stop working for Medair because she had cancer. She later died of the disease.

We were asked to assist at the Medair recruitment camp in which we trained new field workers and set up simulations to expose them to the challenges they would encounter in the field. We remembered our own time in France before we left for Sudan and loved seeing the next group of volunteers being prepared to go. Life felt much better, and we became volunteers for the new Dutch branch of Medair that focused on the promotion of the organization.

Wherever our activities led us, Danny came with us: sleeping in strollers, curled up on bus seats, hanging sleepily from a backpack, or sprawled out on blankets whenever he needed sleep. It was a glorious start for such a small boy as we traveled through at least six countries in his first year of life. He still regrets not remembering any of his early life adventures.

Back in Africa: Uganda

It became clear that we were not interested in settling in the Netherlands, so we began searching for organizations that could use us as a family in field positions. We were thrilled when Medair approached us with an offer for another position within the organization. Bart would be the country director for several projects in Uganda, while I initially had no appointed duties as Danny was still very young, and I needed time to settle in. After only a short time of thinking it over, we agreed to the position. When Danny turned one year old and started taking his first steps, I found myself packing boxes again. We would be taking over leadership in Kampala from Stuart and Rachel, the couple with whom we had previously worked in Sudan.

Of all the dates that we could have chosen to leave the Netherlands, we bought tickets for the eleventh of September 2001. While we were flying to our new destination, America experienced the historic terror attack on the Twin Towers of the World Trade Center in New York.

The moment we cleared customs in Entebbe, Uganda, we felt something was wrong. People were all intently looking at the TV monitors that hung in the arrival hall. The interim Medair country director greeted us with a pale face. Pushing us through the crowds, he pointed to the monitors as they replayed over and over again the moment the plane hit the Twin Towers and collapsed shortly after. Then we understood why everyone was so solemn.

Of course, I couldn't visualize what my life would look like in this new setting. As Bart was appointed country director and thrown into the handover from the interim country director, I found myself mostly tending to Danny. We were staying in the central office building from which Medair operated, which was a large house with many rooms that also functioned as a hospitality base for all field workers that came in for an R&R.

One large room was appointed to us with an ensuite and a walk-in wardrobe, which functioned as our baby room. Within days, I was bored and felt useless. I needed to be active, so I ventured into the offices and asked if I could be useful to someone. Soon, I got involved in administrative tasks and was later appointed as personnel officer and hospitality coordinator.

This proved to be a challenge as I carried Danny on one hip or tried to work on the computer with him on my lap. The moment I set him on the floor, he would start playing with the computer cords at my feet, pulling them out of the socket, or try to grab a phone from the hook and dial random numbers, imitating us having a conversation. Soon, I realized I needed someone to look after him while I did my work. I had heard that it was totally acceptable to have a nanny for your children as an expatriate, so I asked our cook Eva to inquire around for me.

Eva was an excellent cook and had learned baking skills from our former country director's wife. She had a sister who had just come from their village to live in the city. Although Medair did not officially employ her, she assisted her sister by sweeping and doing housework. As Danny was puttering around, this young lady would sit and play with him, and they bonded as if they were naturally chosen to be together. This is how our nanny, Belinda Kyalisiima, came into our lives. I employed her as my nanny, and she became part of our family in the years to come. Up to this day, we are still connected to her and her children.

We rented a lovely house with a large leafy garden in Muyenga, which was in the Tank Hill area of Kampala. Although we had local staff working with us before, I still had to get accustomed to employing domestic workers for personal convenience. This was something I was never exposed to in my own culture. We were brought up with the principle of being diligent and clean, and doing all the hard, tedious work ourselves. A good housewife prided herself on showing off white curtains, clean patios, and well-tended gardens.

The benefits for the local community outweighed the argument for me to conform to the traditional Dutch role of an independent, hardworking housewife, as modeled in my own culture.

The salaries they were receiving would go toward the education of their children or other needs. Soon, I had day and night guards at the gate, a gardener who kept the lawns impeccably green and clean, and our nanny and house girl who also served as our cook. All of these workers had their own stories, and soon I was their employer, mentor, provider, teacher, and a doorway to a better future for them! The house girl learned to sew, so she could design clothes to sell in the market. The nanny, gardener, and guards were sent to English classes to improve their communication skills.

Belinda played for hours with Danny in the garden, loudly singing praise songs while she pushed the swing higher and higher. Danny enjoyed every moment and soaked up the reverent joy she poured over him. I loved to watch her sit on our veranda behind a small blackboard, teaching Danny numbers and letters. He was spellbound as she read stories from the hardcover booklet or set up villages with the Duplo.

Danny raked the leaves together with our gardener Jonathan or helped him mow the lawns. They splashed in the rain and collected eggs from our chickens.

One guard, we'll call him Elias, came to us after he had escaped from the clutches of the feared rebel movement of The Lord's Resistance Army. He had been kidnapped as a child and had seen unspeakable horrors in his childhood. After years in the training camp of Joseph Kony, he escaped and ended up hiding in the big city of Kampala. He got employment in a security company and was assigned to our compound. In the long hours sitting at our gate, in a small lean-to hut, he mostly just listened to his radio.

One morning, I found him working on something foreign to me. He had a roll of wire which he bent and manipulated into a jeep. He attached a long shaft to the front wheels, and at the other end, he fastened the steering wheel. He came and offered it to Danny to play with in the compound. It was a unique and fantastic toy. "Elias" had great practical and artistic skills to create such an integrated gadget from scratch, without even a model to copy from. I asked if he was interested in learning other crafts. He beamed at me when I gave him a thick book full of craft ideas. He picked the page where weaving was explained, pointed to it, and asked if he could learn to weave. I had not done that myself, so we both tried to read the instructions and practiced on a piece of cardboard on which we had wound rows of yarn. He practiced at home, and when he came back, he was an expert! He brought sisal rope for his weaving projects and twisted it on his leg to create the right consistency or worked in colored yarn.

Within weeks, he created beautiful baskets and handbags and sold these in the market.

We were fully aware that, after being employed by us, our staff members might find themselves back on the streets, needing to gain the necessary skills to secure other jobs. That's why we aimed to provide them with a work environment that would facilitate their personal development and lift them out of the poverty existence they had known all their lives. We continued offering them courses to assist in their growth process.

Ordeal in the Forest

One day, I asked "Elias" if he would like to write down his story. It would give the reader an insight into the challenges that these young men had to overcome. I did not change his English much.
Written by "Elias":

> The difficulties I faced, caused by the Lord's Resistance Army (LRA) under the rank leader Joseph Kony in Sudan.
>
> I was abducted by two LRA rebels when I was still very young They traveled with me toward the forest in a single close line. I was tied up with a rope around my waist to the others. I was abducted to carry a bucket of millet, heading toward Sudan. It took us four days to reach Sudan, several kilometers upon kilometers of barefoot walking through the jungle. When I was limping badly, a vehicle carried us from the border to the base camp.
>
> It was a big camp. There were restrictions never to move around without permission from the 'askari' soldiers or only if being escorted. A few months later, I was no longer being escorted within the camp, and after I had been trained with a gun, I was given an AK rifle and selected among others to 'stand by' as there were more to come who were abducted during the food raids in Uganda. It was exceedingly difficult to escape from Sudan. Soon I would be deployed to Uganda, and I thought it was going to be the right time to escape. Many people were killed when they tried to escape. The only punishment for escaping was death when caught.

Ordeal in the Forest

Unfortunately, I was not chosen to go and reach Uganda for the raid operation. Some of us had to remain at the border. The operation was commanded by Chief Leader Joseph Kony himself, and I was in the battalion guarding him. Though we were close to the border and could move freely, I was not strong enough to push aside large bushes. We had to wait for others who returned from the raid across the border. To my disappointment, after they had come back, we moved back to the base in the middle of Sudan.

In November, early in the morning, at around 6:30 a.m., we were attacked by troops from Uganda. First, I heard a bombshell going off in the camp, and then the Sudanese troops fired their tanks. Kony was operating beside them, and our base camp was next. Shortly, the whole place around us was exploding. This was my first time engaging in the battle of the war; there were constant bombing attacks followed by hand-to-hand combat in the forest. I felt like a coward, panicking and fearing that I was not going to survive. Many were killed, and I heard some wounded crying for help. I asked myself, 'Is this the way I shall leave the soil of my forefathers, not even saying good-by to my people?' I witnessed the death of my comrades each time, and I was waiting for a bullet to tear into my flesh.

After the bombing stopped, my company withdrew, running toward the road where we were met by an enemy tank coming toward us. So, we ran back into the bush. Suddenly, our small group was separated from the others, we had to clear the way with a stick as we had no panga (machete). It required a continuous extraordinary effort to break through while the commando shouted to hurry up. When I was too tired, the commander ordered my gun to be taken away, and he left me behind. This meant that I would be killed. I begged the 'effendi' to forgive me, but he beat me with the rifle butt. I struggled up and walked swiftly to continue to clear the path with the stick. My mates encouraged me not to stop. Otherwise, I would have been killed.

We walked until late into the night when we were told to stop and take positions to sleep. Immediately, everyone fell on the ground. It started to rain heavily during the night, and I became icy cold. At 5 a.m., the order was given to move, and it was still dark. I followed in the middle as we walked for kilometers and came across the road from Juba, Sudan.

We continued following this road as we were now far from the enemies.

The following day, I was chosen to carry the wounded on stretchers. This was the third day without proper treatment, and the injured had a terrible smell. However, we continued until the evening and rested for the following day. Kony came into his Land Rover and carried them on toward Juba for treatment. Some of them had already died from lack of treatment, and no other medical facilities were available besides a first aid kit.

After the wounded were taken, we had to go back to engage in the fighting. Suffering was now a part of life, and I had no hope. The food needed to be more; three cups of posho (maize flour or cornmeal cooked with water to a thick porridge) and one cup with beans were for ten soldiers. I was very weak and could barely carry my gun, and I ate whatever was edible in the forest to survive.

After two months of the war, one of my mates told me their plan was to escape with a group of six soldiers while they were getting water. He said, 'Do not remain when you see us go!' A few days later, around 3 p.m., I saw them preparing their equipment to go as they had planned. I also took my gun and ammunition. The other five of the six never knew that I had known about their plan, and they refused me to follow them. My mate told them to let me join because he was the one who had told me their plan.

We walked from the camp into three groups to avoid suspicion. When we reached the water well, we drank water and then all of us started running until late at night. We had to sleep with our heads in the direction of where we were fleeing so as not to get lost. Early in the morning before we moved, we said a short prayer to God to lead and protect us through our journey. We were being pursued, so we kept on running and walking swiftly. We rested overnight and walked by daylight, living on water only.

On the third day of our journey, we entered an ambush. I heard gunshots and bullets slamming around our defenseless bodies. Although we had a gun, none of us dared to fire back. We were too afraid to use it now. Four others from our group ran into the forest and left the two of us alone. We kept running through the woods and lost our pursuers. Luckily, we recognized the place where we were. I had been here before the war, and locating our position was a bit easier.

By now, I no longer had any fear. We continued the journey for another four days and entered northern Uganda. In the village, we found the other four who had run away during the firing in the forest. We assembled together again. We were incredibly happy to see each other alive without further injuries. I lost my gun during the ambush.

Here in this village, we reported it to the authorities and handed in the rest of the guns. I stayed in the hands of the authorities for four months and was sent back home.

I vividly recall my experiences, both the physical pain and the mental anguish. It brings me to tears to write it all down, but I want you to understand the extent of my suffering so that you can share it.

Now, I am a free person living with my mother, as my father passed away when I was young. I am also caring for my older brother's two children, as he was killed by the rebels.

Brother Bart and Sister Maria, I need help from them to continue education and cover living expenses. Despite everything, I am grateful for God's protection and that I am still alive. My survival feels like the story of Daniel in the lions' den, where God intervened and saved him. As for Joseph Kony, based on what I witnessed, he is a lost soul who needs forgiveness and guidance. We are all part of a confused generation, living in a time of great confusion."

- "Elias"

Career Change: Adjusting to Motherhood

The initial reason for Medair's presence in Uganda was to implement hygiene programs among the Karamojong tribe in northeast Uganda. The Karamojong were cattle-raiding tribes who had set up semi-permanent villages around water holes. These water holes were used by both humans and cattle, resulting in the spread of waterborne diseases. Medair's team had established a camp in Kotido, the economic center of the area, and conducted surveys to identify the most pressing needs. Hygiene programs were implemented in the surrounding areas, educational materials were distributed to schools, and latrines were constructed in the town center. The area was relatively safe as long as we did not travel at night or during a cattle raid.

The Karamojong are fierce warriors, and their scarred incisions indicate the number of individuals they have killed using either spears or guns. They kept to themselves, making it a challenge to establish trust within their community. They lived in low huts constructed of sticks and dirt, referred to as "manyattas." Their compound was entirely closed off by a thick wall of woven bushes and twine, with only a small crawl-through opening.

The projects in northern Uganda were implemented by ever-changing field workers, which kept us on our toes at the Personnel Department in Kampala. The projects and their delivery could also be altered based on the situation in Uganda as a country, including political unrest, rebel attacks, and cattle raids around our field positions, all of which had an impact on our ability to work.

Additionally, we served as a logistical base for Medair's medical projects in the neighboring country of Congo.

Life for me in Kampala was quiet compared to the action we had experienced in Sudan and Kosovo. Or perhaps, I had grown accustomed to being exposed to high-stress situations and missed the excitement. We needed that resilience in the field as we had to operate in insecure regions while implementing the projects and delivering time-sensitive programs. Emergency aid workers commonly experience prolonged periods of elevated stress levels, and many become addicted to the adrenaline rush.

There were days when I felt so tired and just spent my time playing with Danny or doing mundane administrative tasks for Medair. I did the housework, tended to the garden, and cooked meals, but I couldn't shake the feeling of being unimportant. Even Danny seemed to have more enjoyable activities than I did.

I struggled to find a rhythm in my new role and felt sidelined, unable to feel significant. Looking back, I realize that this feeling was rooted in deep-seated insecurities that I had never properly addressed. Though I made a difference in the lives of our local staff, I held onto the belief that I wasn't important enough for leadership and needed more education and training to mentor national or international staff.

I became a little bitter that Bart was progressing in his career while I felt stagnant. He was engaging in essential matters and meeting influential officials, while I was just working with our household staff. Bart's English improved as he wrote many official reports, conducted donor meetings, and filed significant funding proposals, while I only spoke basic English with those around me, including our toddler.

There were days when Bart walked in the door late, after 7 p.m., and I had been looking forward to having an adult conversation all day, only to have a husband come home exhausted. Danny had already gone to bed, and when dusk settled over our compound, I closed the curtains, trying to show Bart my displeasure with his tardiness. However, my attitude was accusing and nagging. And I was upset, feeling deeply sorry for myself. My negative thinking fueled my sense of being left behind, and instead of discussing it, I sulked. Our relationship grew

Reflection:

Many couples experience difficulties in their relationship, and women often struggle with the changes that motherhood brings to their daily routines. However, I believe that in this moment in time, I entertained unconscious core beliefs and negative thinking patterns because I didn't feel secure in my identity, safe in my relationships, or significant in my role. I had yet to embrace my identity in God's eyes, and instead of relying on Him, I attempted to fulfill my needs using my own resources.

tense and superficial, and Bart stopped sharing his struggles with me as I was too focused on my own discontent.

In my journal, I analyzed my unease about myself and my battle with feelings of insignificance. I discovered that my driving force in life had been the need to be needed. I believed that I would only be worth something if I was fulfilling someone else's needs. It would take many years before I realized that these negative thoughts were defiling my thinking, attitude, and behavior. Through Christian counseling, I learned how to deal with the source of my brokenness.

One significant consequence of my brokenness was my inability to trust others and form long-lasting and positive relationships. Although there were plenty of women to befriend, I expected that nobody would like me, and I believed that I was not worth being taken seriously. I reinforced these negative expectations with seemingly good self-talk like, "I do not need anyone; I am strong enough to do life on my own."

This created a stronghold in my mind, and I kept others at bay. I was continually afraid of being rejected and feared making mistakes or being vulnerable in a relationship. I transferred these insecurities to others, which may have caused them to perceive me as unapproachable, too needy, oversensitive, or even judgmental. When others kept their distance from me, it fulfilled my expectations that others were not interested in me, and it fueled my insecurity. These root issues were silenced during the years of frantic, purpose-driven activities and motherhood. Although they kept coming to the surface, I pushed them away.

I observed how other expatriate moms did life with their toddlers, and I tried to be an engaged mom. I made play dough from scratch using shared recipes and learned English nursery rhymes. I even bought CDs and practiced singing the songs so I could join in during baby group and not feel like an outsider. It was great to have fellowship with other moms, but I never felt part of it. Despite all my efforts to fit in, I felt like the odd one out.

I found myself comparing my husband to other husbands as their wives spoke about their essential roles in the community. Unlike these couples, my husband didn't have a high-status position in the government or the UN, we weren't famous missionaries, and we didn't work for a well-known international organization that had a significant impact on poor widows by setting up micro-businesses.

We also weren't affiliated with an embassy, so I couldn't talk about embassy parties. Furthermore, I wasn't involved in running an orphanage, and I didn't have sensational stories of finding abandoned babies and arranging adoptions. As a result, I felt like their social standing was far above mine, and I often felt like an outsider just observing and tagging along.

Some expatriate families had vast amounts of experience in other African countries, and they moved through the ranks of the expatriate communities. They always knew someone and were busy networking. They would set up important humanitarian para-church organizations and play significant roles in developing the local economy and social clubs. They were part of the theater group and a book club. Their energy seemed to have no bounds. How did they do it all?

One of the women in the expatriate community had the idea to create a play center for toddlers called "Wacky Woodhouse." The center offered a music hour where moms could bring their babies and toddlers to enjoy English nursery rhymes and poetry, which introduced me to English literature and fantasy stories for the first time. I read books written by C.S. Lewis and J.R.R. Tolkien, which allowed me to explore the use of fantasy and biblical principles in literature. Some ladies would exclaim, "Why! You never read any of these? They are classic literature for every high schooler!" I felt dumb and undereducated, although I realized it was because of my different cultural background that I had missed out on such important educational input.

Over time, Wacky Woodhouse expanded its activities to offer unique children's programs, and I became more integrated into the expatriate community. We organized various social activities such as picnics by Lake Victoria, visits to a nearby stable with horses and ponies, and enjoyed a newly opened resort with a swimming pool and restaurant where we could drink cocktails and eat dinner while overlooking the lake. As I became one of the long-term expatriates, I began to feel more comfortable and secure in my positions.

Changes Within Medair

Our second year in Uganda. Medair was dedicated to fulfilling its mandate of caring for its volunteers. HR and program directors visited us regularly in Kampala and professional development programs were offered to team members on all levels, including local and overseas workshops and information evenings. Medair also invested significantly in our spiritual and mental well-being, sending us pastorally minded staff members from Switzerland.

During our stay in Uganda, Medair went through significant changes. After many years of directing Medair, Erik decided to hand over operations, Josiane had already retired from her HR director position in 2000. Erik left his CEO position to the next generation of highly trained managers, and a new CEO was appointed. Although we had not yet met him, all country directors and top-level managers were invited to Switzerland to attend a conference and be introduced to the new CEO. We held Erik and Josiane Volkmar in high regard, as they regularly visited all projects and guided us through the initial process of becoming aid workers. This would be a farewell to our mentors.

Coming from the African continent and flying over the majestic Alps set the stage for an impressive break. While driving to our location, we felt the peace surrounding the beauty of the rolling hills with white-capped mountains in the distance. As usual, Medair had booked an idyllic venue in the Jura. I didn't need to attend the official parts of the conference, which Bart was required to participate in as country director. We took Danny with us on this trip, and I organized someone to look after him because I wanted some time alone. I soaked in the countryside as I walked some trails in the mountains.

A well-thought-through program was offered, which included: briefings on new developments; training in people management skills to sharpen our skills to deal with the dynamics within the international teams we directed; and engaging workshops on program management principles.

An international speaker was invited to give us spiritual input with thought-provoking devotions. During this specific visit to Switzerland, we had an overall theme in which we studied the book of Revelation. The speaker ran parallel and analogous points with the movie series of *The Lord of the Rings* that had just been released. Spread over two nights, we looked through the entire sequence of the trilogy, which totaled eleven hours. We savored the experience with excellent French wine.

Josiane and Erik were not attending the conference, but they usually sent send greetings or briefly stopped by if they could. Unbeknownst to us, something else was going on in the background. Instead of the Volkmars stopping by or sending a greeting, we were honored this time by a visit from the board of Medair, which was highly unusual, and all of us suspected something was amiss. During one of the meetings, we were called together and a communication from Erik was read. In a soft, sometimes broken voice, the board member started to read the letter.

Erik had been dealing with a lifelong struggle and was ultimately diagnosed with gender dysphoria. After undergoing treatment for some time, Erik felt it was time to inform his wife and Medair of his decision to change gender. In the letter that was read by the board member, Erik introduced himself as Erika, the name she would be known by, from then on.

After receiving the news, a stunned silence fell among us. We struggled to comprehend this development and tried to come to grips with the possibility that this was happening to our former CEO, leader, and mentor. None of us had seen this coming. I decided to drive to Josiane and Erika's to speak to them and try to fathom this significant change in a person. I was able to talk to Josiane and hear a little about how she was dealing with this in her life.

As we traveled back to the Netherlands before returning to Uganda, Bart and I couldn't stop discussing Erika's letter, which had become the dominant topic of our conversations. Many of Medair's staff and volunteers came from inter-denominational backgrounds, and we learned to accept many different views on theological topics. But this news shook us to the core. We decided not to judge in our hearts and wrote a letter acknowledging the announcement. We realized that we could never understand what really goes on in someone's mind, and that the impact of this world's brokenness, which we experienced wherever we went with Medair, was also within us. We were always asked to embrace each worldview and its cultural expressions and adjust to the locally acceptable behaviors in different countries. We were admonished not to make a judgment regarding the conflict if our work took us to war-torn countries. We decided to apply the same attitude toward someone from our culture who grew up within our worldview and background. Maybe we would never understand the pathway that Erika chose to resolve her inner conflicts, and we didn't want to make theological statements or utter uninformed opinions toward this decision.

This incident deeply impacted us, and it sparked a conversation between us. We needed to delve into ourselves and confront our own struggles in life. Additionally, we needed to think about our future, how to raise our children, and prepare them and ourselves for growing up in a changing world.

The pastoral character of Medair didn't change. Every year, Medair provides its staff with six weeks of leave to rest from the demanding work. Bart and I saved some of our allowances to travel during this time. Our conversations inevitably revolved around where we would make a home for our family when we could no longer continue working with Medair. We discussed various scenarios, including staying in the so-called expatriate community and finding employment in development agencies. We discussed schooling options for our kids, including local schools, international schools, and boarding schools in neighboring Kenya. However, none of these options seemed to be the right choice. Returning back to the Netherlands didn't seem like an option, as we felt we had outgrown our own culture.

During our long breaks, we visited different countries, including South Africa, New Zealand, Canada, America, and southern Europe, to explore possible immigration options. However, none of these places felt like the right choice for us at the time. As we thought about settling down and having another child, we prayed for a sibling for Danny, and I became pregnant again.

As our next annual leave approached, Bart suggested that we visit New Zealand to investigate whether it was a suitable option for immigration. I agreed, and we booked a trip during my second trimester in a camper van to travel through the two islands. While I looked forward to showing Bart the diverse natural beauty of the country where I had lived a decade ago, the three weeks of travel proved to be tiresome. We camped on roadsides, beaches, deep gullies, and under the vast starry sky in many meadows. Unfortunately, Danny did not enjoy the trip as much as we did, and he cried a lot as he only saw the passing gray rock formations or the dense, dripping forests, as it rained a lot in November. Although I could see the potential of living in New Zealand when the sun shone in sporadic moments, Bart was not impressed.

During our trip, we visited my auntie and cousins who still lived in New Zealand. Being back in the country also triggered memories of my time there with my ex-fiancé from 1987 to 1991. The dreams at night and the dark clouds of depression in my mind made it difficult for me to appreciate the rugged beauty of the sculptured landscapes while we drove through the South Island. In the ten years since my last visit, I had changed, seen other lands, and traveled to different parts of the world that captivated me with their beauty. New Zealand had become a memory, and the present reality of the country did not appeal to us.

A Growing Family

When we returned to Kampala, we removed New Zealand from our list of potential immigration destinations. All our attention was focused on work and the arrival of another baby in our family. As the end of 2002 approached, Bart's workload grew even heavier. In addition to his existing programs, he oversaw logistics for Medair's Congo operations, shipping medical equipment and supplies to hospitals and clinics. He traveled regularly to Kotido in northern Uganda and coached the team that worked with the Karamojong tribe.

Another conference for Medair's country directors was scheduled in Switzerland to discuss new policies and management changes, as well as to provide support and training for the often-overworked staff. This time, Bart traveled alone, as I was in my final trimester of pregnancy.

At seven months pregnant, I struggled with feelings of depression, possibly due to the many changes we had experienced, our uncertain future, or the hormonal fluctuations caused by the pregnancy. To support me, my mother came and stayed with me while Bart was away. She was a great support as I struggled through the last few months of 2002.

My parents were also in the process of moving to Uganda, settling in the small village of Busia near the Kenyan border after the birth of our second child. They were setting up another branch of their pastoral work among local churches in Africa. My father also offered introductory counseling courses to universities, police academies, army barracks, remote villages, and refugee camps. Eventually, he expanded these activities to Rwanda, Burundi, and Kenya.

In December, all international staff were pulled out of their field positions to rest and enjoy Christmas. I organized their rooms, set up Christmas decorations, and planned a Christmas BBQ. We played games and enjoyed this fun and recreational time, and I used the time together to debrief our staff members.

The baby was due in late January, but just after the New Year, I went into early labor. The regular doctors were on leave, and I didn't want to give birth in the local hospitals, because I had heard horrendous stories from my local staff. There were two midwives who had been trained in home births, and one of these ladies was available on the night I knew the baby would come. Early on the morning of the third of January 2003, after only four hours of labor, our daughter was born. We named her Jodie, which means "grace."

It was a unique birth experience as Debbie, the midwife, started to pray over the baby the moment her head was born, and she dedicated Jodie to God in a heartfelt prayer. I have never forgotten how reverent I felt when she held up this baby girl, set apart to God from birth.

We buried the placenta under the bushes beneath our bedroom, as our local staff told us to do, "Where you are born, there your heart will be forever." We vowed that Jodie would return to her birth country one day. Uganda had become home to us, and part of our hearts would always feel attached to this place. As the only family member with a Ugandan birth certificate, Jodie has the right to buy land in Uganda.

We did visit Uganda again in January 2024 when Jodie turned 21 and visited the house where she was born. In the 18 years of our absence, the compound had undergone massive changes and had become a Gym. But the back balcony was still the same and Jodie did experience a small feeling of familiarity when I pointed out the place where we buried her placenta.

I enjoyed the quiet days of recovery after giving birth. The international staff members returned to their respective countries, and I absorbed this new dynamic within our family. Again, I sought a word from the Lord for Jodie as I had for Danny. I recalled that Jodie was also born at a challenging time. As I opened my Bible, God drew my attention toward the verse in Revelation 1 where God says, "'I am the Alpha and the Omega,' says the Lord God, 'who is, and who was, and who is to come, the Almighty'" (Revelation 1:8 NIV). We designed the birth notices for our family and friends and wrote this verse in them. God had overseen our lives, and Jodie had been dedicated from birth to His care. He is truly the beginning and the end. She was safe, and our future would be in His hands.

A few days later, as I rested and read my Bible, another verse sprang to life. I felt God was speaking to me as I meditated on Isaiah 44. I asked the Lord why this specific verse made my heart pound, and a very straight answer came back: "You will have yet another child who will be Mine."

The verses that caught my attention read, "For I will pour water on the thirsty land and streams on the dry ground; I will pour out My Spirit on your descendants and My blessing on your offspring. They will sprout among the grass like poplars by flowing streams. This one will say, 'I am the Lord's'; another will call himself by the name of Jacob; still another will write on his hand, 'The Lord's,' and name himself by the name of Israel" (Isaiah 44:3-5 HCSB).

I just wrote it down in my journal, not thinking about yet another child as I was enjoying my second newborn. I did not know what the future held, but the above verses from Isaiah were about to become a reality—even the surroundings of a dry ground described in those chapters. We still had more adventures to come.

Jodie grew into a graceful lady with a perceptive heart for God, her peers, nature, especially animals. In 2022, she began studying Wildlife Conservation and even started training for her pilot's license to one day fly over the plains of Africa, the continent where she was born.

Life in an International Community

I worked part-time in the Medair office, where I oversaw hospitality and enjoyed decorating rooms for the international staff. Whenever they returned from the field for R&R, I would prepare their rooms with a welcome package. I also loved roaming the local marketplace, Owino Market, and haggling over prices. As I got to know the local shop owners and the back roads, I became more confident navigating through the chaotic traffic. In a nutshell, Kampala became home.

My mornings usually started with a jog through the outskirts of Muyenga, often passing through the local slums where children would briefly join me for a short distance. Alternatively, I would go for a swim at a local resort where the small swimming pool was open to city residents. Afterward, I would order a sweet chai and then open my Bible to immerse myself in Bible studies.

For our spiritual well-being, we joined a small group of expatriates that met in a garden on Sundays. Within a year, the group became officially "Kampala International Church" (KIC), and we moved to a larger assembly hall at an international Christian school that was still under construction. At the end of our stay, I became part of the leadership team and led a women's Bible study group, which I loved preparing for.

I also attended other Bible studies with expatriate ladies. One of these studies paved the way for significant healing of my soul wounds. A study based on Isaiah 61, called *Breaking Free* by Beth Moore, spoke clearly about how our brokenness can be healed through Christ's brokenness and His resurrection power. As I allowed Christ to go into those areas that needed healing, I felt myself slowly coming to life. It was the start of an awareness of what God had in store for me as I surrendered more to His transforming power. Then, God spoke to me, again, unexpectedly.

We were meeting in one of the ladies' homes in town. Although I was usually very careful with sharing anything about myself, I had

Life in an International Community

grown comfortable in this group—as long as there were no changes or new members joining the group, which would make me feel insecure again.

One morning, one of the ladies brought a friend from Kenya. I felt the familiar feeling of wanting to pull out of the fellowship as we listened to the video tape and I watched Beth Moore speaking and teaching the Word. Suddenly, I heard a loud voice in my head say, "This is what I have called you to do." Immediately, I dismissed it and argued with the voice, "*Go away voice. It couldn't possibly be God speaking to me because I am just a woman, public speaking is not allowed, and I have no platform to work from.*" However, throughout the hour, it kept gently repeating, "This is to which I called you."

I got nervous and very uncomfortable. I was still breastfeeding Jodie (our daughter born in Uganda), and I was relieved she woke up and asked for attention. I went to another room to feed her. Once I was back, the session was closing, and people were leaving, except the lady who had brought her friend with her. The moment I walked back in, she beelined for me and announced, "The Holy Spirit spoke to me the moment I entered this room. He pointed you out to me and announced: 'She is the one I have called and anointed.'"

Nothing like that had ever happened to me before. Taken aback, I stuttered and fumbled and finally was able to say, "Thank you." I was also not used to people speaking about the Holy Spirit like it was a Person in the way we address God as Father or Jesus as our Savior. And I had not been exposed to words of knowledge or the use of prophecy in any denomination I had been to.

Quickly, I gathered my things and prepared to leave. From the corner of my eye, I saw the lady leave as well, and I sighed a sigh of relief. *Whatever that was all about, she is leaving now!*

But not so in God's plan. Just as the lady stepped through the door, she bounced back into the room and talked to me again, "The Holy Spirit just told me that He is not finished with you yet and has more to say and He wants me to anoint you with oil."

I had no idea how to react to this sudden intrusion, and the idea of being anointed with oil made me even more uncomfortable. Especially after I still struggled to identify that voice in my head from earlier on during the study. If I was totally honest, I had recognized that voice as the voice of God whom I had heard when I was a young child and later as a young adult while sitting at a graveyard during my depression. Now this lady insisted that the Holy Spirit wanted to reveal more to me, and she invited me to the place where she stayed.

I followed their car to the house and once there, she immediately asked her host if they had olive oil. While the host searched for the oil in the kitchen, I interrogated the lady about the authority behind her prophetic words. I was still very suspicious, but she calmly spoke of her prophetic ministry in Kenya and remarked that she had never encountered such a reluctant hearer as myself.

Both ladies knelt and began to pray for words of wisdom and knowledge of God. The lady then stood up and asked if she could anoint my head. Tentatively, I allowed her to speak her words, which were straight from the calling of the prophet Jeremiah. Then she poured some oil over my head. After pausing and praying some more, she said, "The Holy Spirit prompts me to anoint your feet also as you will travel to the ends of the world to speak the Gospel." I derided inside, thinking, *Where would the end of the world be?* and shrugged off any significance to her words. She continued, "I even see you speaking in our church in Kenya."

Kneeling in front of me, she asked if I had ever heard God speak to me or received a calling from Him. She reiterated that everything she said should be tested and confirmed by God Himself. I acknowledged that God had been calling me before and I did recognize His voice, which I also had heard that morning during the Bible study. The lady nodded and said softly that God would bring to pass what He had promised and that I should wait patiently on the Lord.

In the days following that incident, I kept praying to God to confirm the words she had spoken over me. Although I was willing to travel around the world, I had reservations about public speaking because of my conviction at that time, that women should remain silent in the Church. I asked God to bring about this charge and give me peace about it.

Then, a few days later, I woke up with the now-familiar voice in my head. I lay very still as the voice became clearer, and I was able to discern words. It became a repeated sentence, like I had experienced before as a child. I heard three times with emphasis, "*SPEAK* words of life to the Church...Speak words *OF LIFE* to the Church...Speak words of life *TO THE CHURCH.*"

Silently, I got up so as not to wake Bart or the kids and grabbed my journal. I dated it and wrote down all the events. I didn't yet know where this would lead me, but I was aware that God was preparing the way for whatever He had in mind for me.

Reflection:

Has it all come to pass? No, not yet. There was still so much work to be done in me, and I wasn't ready to carry His mantle. Nevertheless, I have traveled the world, led Bible studies, and eventually ended up living in Australia, the ends of the world according to me.

Much later, in 2017, I wanted to pick up a study and get a diploma in something, as I never was able to further my education. I had gone through a significant time of healing, and as I picked up a daily devotional one day, my eye caught an advert in the middle of the booklet. It said: "Speak words of life to people, come and study Christian Counseling at AIFC," which consequently I did. My private counseling practice carries the tagline: "Speaking Words of Life."

Our Nanny Belinda

Our nanny Belinda had her own unique story. She came to us through her sister Eva, who worked in the kitchen as well as the household manager of the Medair office. I first saw Belinda sweeping the floors while assisting her sister in the early days when we arrived in Kampala. She looked like a beautiful young teenager, but little did we know that she was already the mother of two. When we asked her to become Danny's nanny, she readily accepted.

Belinda came from a small village close to Lake Albert and the Congo border, near Murchison Falls Park. She was raised by her mother, with whom she had a close relationship. Being the youngest daughter, she stayed with her mother until her father passed away.

In their culture, marrying young was totally accepted and as she couldn't pay the school fees after their father's death she married at just seventeen. She was brought to her mother-in-law's hut and soon she became pregnant and gave birth to her firstborn, Jovia. The entire experience traumatized her, and her mother-in-law treated her unkindly and made her do all the domestic duties.

Belinda's husband went on long journeys away from home and she knew he had other wives in other places. During one of his long absences, she ran away, back to her mother. When her husband returned, she had to go with him since she was pledged to him. She became pregnant with Youngeston, now called Anderson, who was just a little older than Danny. They played together and even now they still keep in touch.

Soon after Belinda's husband found out she was pregnant again, he left her for good, and she went back to live with her mother, who also looked after her children. She found a job with a local missionary and had a much better time there. When they finished their mission and left Uganda, she decided to leave her village and move to the city. Her two children stayed in the village with her mother. She had become a devout Christian and visited a local Pentecostal church. Belinda practiced the newly learned songs on our children as she pushed the handmade swing hanging in the avocado tree in our tropical garden in Muyenga, Kampala.

Old-fashioned evangelistic outreaches were conducted throughout Kampala, and she would listen to the preaching for days. One day she declared that she was going to be baptized and asked me if I could attend to witness this event. On a sunny morning, I dropped Danny at a daycare center, packed Jodie in the four-by-four, and drove to the shore of the ancient river Nile.

When I arrived, the grassy banks of the Nile were flooded with people getting baptized. Long lines of people waded deeper into the river and were submerged by church volunteers. When they rose from the water, they burst into spontaneous songs, then waded back to the riverbanks, where they fell to their knees. Hands were thrown into the air as voices rose with cries of joy and praise. Many started to speak in tongues, and ululations rose as an offering to God.

An elderly lady walked up to me, picked up Jodie from her stroller, and prayed over her, holding her close to herself. I never knew what she whispered to Jodie, but her face was radiant and peaceful. I gave my Bible to a lady who sat sobbing under a tree, worried about what her Muslim family would do to her if they ever found out that she got baptized that day. What a privilege it was to share these moments in Belinda's life.

However, tragedy struck when Belinda's mother passed away, leaving Belinda devastated. Her grief was so deep and traumatic that she became ill. We cared for her in the staff quarters and called her pastor to minister to her. I felt her pain as I watched her lose weight.

She refused food and lost the will to live. It was only at this moment in time that we discovered she had two children in her village who depended solely on her now deceased mother. We had to nurse her back to health and pray for her spirit to be restored. Eventually, we sent her back to the village to see her children and encouraged her to look forward to the future.

When Belinda returned to the city, she needed a larger place to live with her children, so we offered to pay rent when she found a suitable house. Soon, she settled into a new home and into a routine, but I was concerned about how she managed as she came to our house every day to care for Danny and Jodie. She never said much about her children. When I wanted to visit her, she refused to let me come to her house, fearing her landlord would increase her rent if he knew she worked for white people.

One evening, just before dark, I decided to take her home for safety's sake. She suggested I drop her off on the street corner because the access to her house wasn't suitable for our car. This made me even more doubtful about her circumstances. I parked the car, prayed for protection, and got out to have a look around. There were no streetlights in that area of the city, and in the last light of the day, I saw that the house she rented was still being built. As I stepped closer, a little girl, maybe five or six years old, carrying a bucket on her head, came around the corner of the house. Politely, she greeted me and introduced herself as Belinda's daughter, Jovia.

Gingerly finding my way through the mud to their front door, I saw that the house was being constructed from concrete block walls and a leaky corrugated iron roof, with no toilet or running water. There was no furniture, no place to store their belongings, and all three of them slept on one thin mattress on the floor against the wall. The house was surrounded by muddy mounds of upturned earth, which were smelly and slippery. Scruffy, half-mad dogs came yelping and barking after us when we walked around the house.

Unbeknownst to me at the time, Belinda did not have the means to send Jovia to a good school in the city. While Belinda worked as our nanny, Jovia stayed home to take care of her younger brother and do most of the housework. My heart filled with deep compassion, and I questioned myself: How could I take a mother away from her children? Belinda needed to work to support her family, but at the same time, she needed to be there for her children. What could we do to improve her situation? Bart and I decided to start paying for Jovia's school fees, and later for Anderson's too. We invited Anderson to play with Danny until it was time for him to start school. We also encouraged Belinda to find a better place to live, and after moving several times, she finally found a home that was large enough for her family. This was a much better solution!

When we left Uganda, we helped Belinda find a new job as a childcare manager for the nursing staff in a mission hospital. We also pledged to pay her rent and assist her financially in getting both her children through school until they finished high school. In 2012, we planned to visit Uganda but had to cancel due to an outbreak of Ebola in the region. The money we received as a refund from the airline was given to Belinda, who used it to buy a plot and start saving money to build her own home.

After some years, she left the International Hospital and set up a creche for the children of members of Parliament. During our visit in 2024, we were invited to admire the well-run facilities and even were able to sit in a Parliament session. Belinda is a well-respected nanny to many children of members of the Police Force and Members of the Parliament of Uganda.

In 2018, she finally moved into her own house. Jovia completed university, got married in 2019, and had a baby soon after. Anderson finished high school and completed his social studies at Kampala's Makerere University in 2023 and continued his studies in Canada. He is also a skilled music composer and DJ.

Local Experiences

Uganda is a country with a mix of religions, including animism, which was practiced all around us when we lived there. One night, we woke up to horrifying animal-like noises, including grunts, screams, and gurgling sounds that made it difficult for us to sleep. With the hair rising at the base of my neck, I walked into the pitch-black night through the back of our garden to peek over the fence into the neighborhood. There, directly behind our property, a local witch doctor was performing an exorcism. We prayed and loudly proclaimed the Name of Jesus over our property, the air, and our children.

Early the next day, our gardener woke us up. Jonathan always started before sunrise to sweep the leaves and flowers that had dropped during the night before the kids started playing on the grass. The collected garden refuse was dumped onto a compost heap on the other side of our fence. Occasionally, he would burn the pile to a low mound, after which it would slowly build up again.

That morning, as he shoveled into the heap and dumped more cuttings and clippings, he found two shallowly buried white bundles of cloth. In a panic, he ran to us and pounded on the door, asking us to come with him to check these small, swaddled packages. He had already heard from neighbors that there had been an exorcism the previous night, and he also knew that after a witch doctor had been summoned, he would have asked for a sacrifice. Depending on the ritual, a newborn baby was usually salted and buried alive. He was sickeningly pale as he told us how he had found these two bundles in the garden waste.

As outsiders and strangers to their culture, we couldn't do much, so we asked him to inform the police. Shortly after the call, two very reluctant policemen turned up and carefully unwrapped the bundles, only to find small piglets, instead of babies as Jonathan had feared. Long after the event, we still felt the air filled with the dark forces that were provoked during that night. From that moment on, we dug a deep hole in the corners of the garden within our compound walls to bury our garden refuse and started a compost heap to be used as fertilizer on our garden beds.

Another practice that stirred us deeply was the administration of mob justice instead of relying on the corrupt police system in Uganda. Early one morning, as the traffic in front of our house was getting busy, I heard an unearthly scream and yelling for help. It continued until I realized something was horribly wrong just outside our gates. I called our security guard to tell me what was happening, and he went outside to check it out. He came running back shouting, "People next door just caught a thief! They are killing him!"

A little house was being built on the empty plot next to ours, and the windows were not yet installed. The owner slept in it for security reasons. He only had a mattress in one of the half-finished rooms of the house. After leaving the place to go to work, the owner saw someone tumbling out of the window and caught him red-handed. He was livid and started to beat the thief, which attracted a crowd who incited the owner even more. An *unofficial court* was formed, and the man was found guilty of stealing.

When I looked over our compound wall, the man had just been secured with a car tire around his upper body. People kicked him in his stomach, dumped him on the ground, rolled him around, and stomped on his hands and feet. Someone climbed on a heap of rubble and jumped onto his writhing body. A boot plunged into the man's face, and I heard his head crack. A few men collected gasoline from their car and prepared for the next stage: burning him alive. Frantically, I dialed the police while the guard tried to talk me out of it. Apparently when a white person interfered with mob justice, it could turn against me.

The endless beep at the emergency department made it clear that the police would not answer the phone soon. I called the fire department to see if they could assist or get through to the police, but no one answered the phone.

Suddenly, I heard police sirens, then an open ute skidded to a halt, and a few police officers jumped out. As they approached the scene, they stopped, watched for a while, and asked a bystander what had happened. Meanwhile, a crazed crowd was stomping upon the now-silent body of the offender. Finally, the police took some action, and the man was freed from the pack and lifted into the back of the

Local Experiences

ute. I never knew if the man lived or was already kicked to death. I just saw that, even if the police turned up, they left justice to the crowd.

Danny had grown into an inquisitive three-year-old toddler who went to a local kindergarten. Early in the morning, Bart would wave down a "*boda-boda*," a small motorcycle, and paid the driver a few shillings to drop Bart at work and Danny at kindergarten. The three figures sat tightly behind each other. Danny still recalls the strong body odor of the drivers as they drove through the early morning air.

On one of these morning rides, Bart recalls that the driver slammed on the brakes near the gate of Medair's office. A school bus had also stopped on the side, and children were piling out to see something lying at the intersection. A stiffened and blackened form lay on the tarmac. A blistered arm grotesquely pointed into the air as if it were warding off an oncoming disaster. A strong smell of burned flesh permeated the whole scene. People stood around gaping at the charred remains while Bart quickly shielded Danny from the sight. He called me to come and arrange sheets from the office to cover the body, giving the man some dignity and protecting the public from the horrible sight.

Overnight, he had stolen vegetables from a small marketplace on the corner of the street. He was caught by locals and subjected to mob justice, and they burned him alive. When the police arrived to investigate the incident, our office staff had to give them masks and gloves because they had no protective gear to deal with the body. This was Uganda, the legal system was insufficient and corrupt, making it difficult to deal with individuals who violated the law.

Part 10

Immigration

Leaving Uganda

A slightly more uplifting experience was when we were asked to be extras in a major box office film. For this film, they needed white faces and asked Kampala International Church for expatriates to volunteer. The story itself was still very sobering since the film was based on the novel *The Last King of Scotland* by Giles Foden and depicted the historical drama of the dictatorship of Idi Amin. We all dressed appropriately in '70s attire for the movie. Forest Whitaker played the role of Idi Amin and won the Oscar for Best Actor that year. In the film, Danny and Jodie both briefly appeared, and the sound of a crying baby in the background was Jodie, who had woken up during one of the many retakes of the airport scene "Operation Entebbe."

Our time in Uganda was significant in many ways. We grew up and matured in various areas, established a family, became part of a growing church, and developed as much as we allowed God to work within us. After four years, we felt it was time to leave. We sought advice from Medair, who fully supported our decision to begin looking for other possible long-term and sustainable employment while raising our children.

As part of Medair's exit strategy and debriefing process for their staff, volunteers were referred to a resident psychologist, Vicki Owens, who lectured at Makerere University in Kampala. This reentry program was the first implemented by an international organization to assist its staff in reintegrating into a "normal" lifestyle.

Vicki listened carefully to our stories. As we prayed together at the end of our session, she left us with a significant challenge: "Would you consider taking a sabbatical and not making a hasty decision about the future?" She counseled us to think about it before deciding to stay in this kind of work, becoming permanent expatriates, and not having a home country for our kids.

"Explore the impact it can have on your children. You have been children of missionaries, and you have become what we refer to as third-culture children and adults." She continued, "The background you have come from, and your lifestyle left lasting impressions and have formed your identity. Think ahead and see if you want this for your children. Do you want to raise them in the same travel lifestyle and not have roots in a culture or home country?" Her counsel stayed with us as we explored our options.

Back home in Muyenga, we placed a rotating world globe on the table and spun it around. The world lay open before us, but the way forward was not yet clear. Nevertheless, the excitement of new possibilities surged through us as we pointed out countries of interest, reminiscing about how we had lived on various continents already. Passing through our mind's eye, we revisited the countries we had lived in or visited in the past. We played around with the idea of returning to each of these and imagining what it would be like living there as a family. It dawned on us that we had plenty of opportunities to explore the rest of the world, and nothing was impossible. We prayed for guidance, asking God to show us where our next steps should be directed, which country we should live in, and what type of work we should do after leaving the international aid workers scene.

As exciting as it was, a different idea began to take shape. What if we took a year off and devoted ourselves to studying God's Word? We redirected our search and dove into investigating different Bible schools in different countries, with one priority being that the school could host and accommodate a family at an affordable cost. We sent several requests to various schools worldwide, but many were not suitable for housing families or were too expensive. Additionally, most schools only offered courses extended over several years, whereas we only considered a one-year sabbatical.

Being part of an international church and a large expatriate community had many advantages. One of our best friends was the director of Veritas International, and they told us that their curriculum was being introduced to a Bible school in Australia. We loved how Veritas International equipped local leaders and pastors to interpret the Bible with the Bible itself. By applying these interpretation principles, leaders from the most remote villages didn't need to attend expensive Bible schools or invest in thick theological books or have access to a vast library of Bible commentators.

Then came the e-mail in which we were introduced to Perth Bible College in Western Australia, which ran a one-year trial course called *Cert IV in Biblical Ministries*. It included a component run by Veritas International covering the interesting unit *How to Interpret your Bible*. This was the same course that our friends distributed throughout Uganda! It was also the only school offering accommodations for families on campus. They hosted a diverse international student body with students from many countries in which we had worked previously.

Because we had traveled so much and were uprooted from our home churches, we now only had a handful of supporters overseas who could help us financially. It would require faith to be able to go to Bible school.

We took a step forward in faith and started to prepare for our departure, beginning the process of getting the required student visas for Australia. We wrote letters to our remaining supporters and explained our motivation for taking a year off before making significant changes to our family and lifestyle. The missionary board of our former church, which supported missionaries like our parents, offered financial support. This was another confirmation that our plans were moving in the right direction.

Medair sent a replacement for Bart as country director, and we began packing. Not much filled the boxes as most of our personal items were toys for the children and artifacts to remember Uganda by. We looked around the house, which had become our home, and I felt sad. We said good-bye to our staff and made arrangements for Belinda so her children could finish school.

Close friends prayed over us, and words of knowledge were shared. We wrote them down so we could read them when we felt discouraged. We entered a very vulnerable time in our lives. Uprooting our children, although still young enough to adapt, was heavy on our hearts. Leaving friends behind, knowing that in the expatriate community, loyalties change quickly, and although not forgotten, life would go on and we would slip away from their lives. We had done this before, but it became more difficult as we established deep relationships.

As the new country director and his family moved into our house and painted it in unusual colors, I grieved. All the familiarity disappeared before me, and I fled into the garden. Even there, I felt the emptiness; the chickens had been given away, the kids' swing was gone, and the BBQ was swept clean. Jonathan had plans to pursue his desire to go to Canada, and "Elias" had applied to become a chauffeur in pursuit of a long-term career change. We had invested in them; they were now following their paths, and I felt fulfilled. We knew we had been instrumental in their personal growth.

It was December, and the frangipani was flowering, its scent permeating the garden around me. It will forever stay with me as a part of my life in Uganda. And now it was time to leave it all behind. The last day approached; we stepped onto the tarmac of Entebbe's International Airport for the last time and flew toward a new future.

2005: Applying for an Entry Visa

I looked down through the plane's small window. The Sahara Desert lay simmering below us. The monotonous yellow color and shifting shades seemed to encircle us. It looked so vast and empty. We hung suspended in the immensity of the expanse, leaving behind one life and not yet starting another. Danny played at our feet while the hum of the engines lulled Jodie to sleep. I loved those moments when I traveled back and forth through space, a lull in time, nothing behind me and nothing before me. No responsibilities or demands, just being and reflecting. No book was needed; no movie to indulge in...my life played out on the screen of my mind.

I remembered a verse that spoke to me years ago, "I make known the end from the beginning, from ancient times, what is still to come. I say, 'My purpose will stand, and I will do all that I please.' From the east I summon a bird of prey; from a far-off land, a man to fulfill my purpose. What I have said, that will I bring about; what I have planned, that I will do" (Isaiah 46:10-11 NIV). Wherever our path would go, I knew that God had it under control, even if I didn't feel anything was straightforward.

I shivered when we exited the plane and entered a misty, cloudy Netherlands. We had flown into the thick soup of gray clouds and could not even see the outline of the well-measured and straight lines of the fields below. I knew we had returned to our roots when we heard the guttural expressions of the Dutch language as we waited for our luggage at the conveyor belt. It was strange to listen to the familiar language spoken all around us. We understood the words but did not get the meaning. They talked about things that had not been part of our lives for many years.

I remember when we returned from the Caribbean, trying to get settled into a culture from which we were estranged. Somewhere in my mind, I felt relief that we would only be here temporarily. We didn't need to go through the tiring treadmill of proving ourselves worthy of our citizenship or making our stamp on a society with which we no longer felt a connection.

We had rented a cabin in eastern Holland. During the summer holidays, the resort would have been booked up, but in winter, the management made it available for short-term rentals to people who needed temporary accommodations. The park around our cabin was lovely, with mature oak trees and small lakes. The trees were now bare, and the lake had frozen over. Danny and Jodie excitedly jumped around in the soft snow and played on the lake's frozen surface. They tried out everything with their bare hands only to discover how the pieces of ice and snowballs hurt their little hands. The solidity of ice and the softness of snow were all so new to them. As Christmas approached, a fresh blanket of snow covered the gardens and pathways. Early in the morning, we saw the many trails of birds and animals pressed into the soft whiteness. We all dressed up and had a snow fight.

We heated the cottage, turning up the temperatures, while we adjusted to the colder climate, and I shopped for winter clothes for the children in the cozy streets of the city. Christmas lights were everywhere, and hot chocolate was served in stalls. Christmas songs filled the air in the city center over the installed loudspeakers. Round ice-skating rinks were set up in the city square; the twinkling lights threw moving shadows on the gliding figures in the late winter afternoon. Darkness came early, and we would huddle up, watch Dutch TV programs, and complete puzzles on the floor. We sprayed Christmas trees, stars, and church bells on the window from a spray can with white fluffy fake snow. During business hours, we filled out piles of forms to start the lengthy process of getting student visas for Australia.

Our visit to Amsterdam to pick up official papers made us feel like tourists as we walked the ancient, cobblestones beside the canals. Input from doctors and specialists ensured our physical well-being before we could enter Australia; X-rays of our lungs to exclude TB, and blood tests to confirm our exposure to leprosy, dengue fever, malaria, bilharzia, and other tropical diseases. None of these had left any detrimental marks over time. Our blood, except maybe for plasma, would never be used again for blood bank collection. It didn't bother us; we were declared healthy to continue the process of immigration.

Still, Another Will Write on His Hand: "I Belong to the Lord"

What was not apparent was that our marriage was under stress. Uprooting our lives once again was reflected in our relationship. We felt alone and were searching for each other. Trying to rediscover our intimacy made us aware that somehow, we had lost the touch of friendship within our relationship. Not being busy or weighed down by heavy responsibility and not having a daily structure fed our dissatisfaction with each other at that moment in time.

Arguments became sharper and more personal, and we hurt each other with our words. Disagreements that had popped up briefly during our life together in Uganda were now coming back to the surface. We revisited painful situations that had accumulated over the years but never talked through. Having lived a public life with so many visitors and always surrounded by local staff, did not give us enough opportunities to create learning pathways to deal with conflict. We hadn't been able to find a compromise yet between our different perspectives or opinions.

Bart suddenly didn't need to focus on the pressures of work, and my old search for significance became a vacuum in which we discussed our future. It did not seem like a good place to start discussing a new life and deciding on our immediate future. Bart struggled with personal issues, and our arguments were loud as we thought nobody would hear us in the forest anyway.

I took long walks on my own, following outstretched country lanes and wondered if we had done the right thing by uprooting our family and leaving behind a lifestyle we had grown used to. It would have been so much better to stay in the rhythm of the familiar. Nothing made sense anymore. My desires didn't seem important at this moment, and Bart's career was totally up in the air, which made him feel unsettled. Who could we turn to since we didn't have many friends in the area? Our relationships with some we still knew from years ago had become too distant over time, and we missed the deeper level of trust we had with our friends back in Uganda. Family members came to visit, and we visited them, but they were absorbed in their own lives. And their working hours restricted the opportunity to reconnect or visit during the day.

We decided to join a local church for the two months in the Netherlands and found at least spiritual food for our disturbed souls. The Netherlands in the winter was cold and dark, and we would spend a lot of time inside. We needed positive input and thought doing a Bible study together could help us. That way, we invested in both our relationship and with God. As we waited for the immigration application to be processed, we opened our Bible each morning and started the course, *Jesus the One and Only* by Beth Moore.

Christmas had just passed, and the New Year of 2006 had begun. The reading led us to the birth of Jesus, which marked the start of a new chapter for Israel and the entire world. What would this year bring for us? One day, I opened the Bible to Matthew and started reading about Jesus's birth. As I skimmed through the genealogy, my eyes suddenly fell upon verse twenty-one: "She will give birth to a son, and you are to give him the name Jesus, because he will save his people from their sins" (Matthew 1:21 NIV). It was a beautiful statement about Jesus's purpose, but something else stirred my spirit, and my heart began pounding. It was as if I had been struck by lightning. The words "She will give birth to a son..." seemed to be highlighted and raised from the page. I sat up straight and looked at Bart writing in his coursebook. Another verse came to my mind that I had received many years ago: "This one will say, 'I am the LORD's'; another will call himself by the name of Jacob; **still another** will write on his hand, 'The LORD's'" (Isaiah 44:5 HCSB, emphasis mine).

This was the verse that I had written down shortly after Jodie's birth, but at the time, I had dismissed it. This last week, Jodie had just turned three, and I had not thought back to the events of her birth for some years now.

I stood up and rummaged through my suitcase, found the diary in which I had recorded significant moments in the past, and searched for the entry of the week after Jodie's birth. And there I saw it. God still had another child in mind for us. I stood up and told Bart that I needed to go shopping without explaining myself. At the chemist, I bought a pregnancy test and went back home to wait for the results with a pounding heart.

I stood wide-eyed, staring into the mirror of the small bathroom in the cabin in the forest. I was pregnant. I should have known; God had said it before. Still, I was upset. I was entering a stage of life in which I wanted to be less absorbed by diapers and full-time childcare.

I had been looking forward to the fulfillment of a lifelong desire: to go to Bible school and learn more of the Word. My deepest longing was to become a preacher or a public speaker worldwide. Hadn't I received words of knowledge in the past, confirming that God would bring that to pass? Hadn't I had vivid dreams of standing on a platform, speaking to a foreign crowd when I was still a teenager? What about God's other personal promises of fulfilling His purposes in my life? All of these past visions were overshadowed in my mind by the knowledge that I was pregnant and would have to stay home for many more years. I was hanging in limbo, contemplating starting another life in a foreign country without history, friends, or support. How could I accept this change and know that God was still in control?

I would be a hands-on mom for at least another eighteen years until my youngest child became an adult and left the house for studies or to become independent. The upcoming school years for Danny and Jodie would give me more freedom to study and engage in ministry. They were out of diapers and would soon be going to kindy. Now, I saw myself doing another stint of being a preschooler mom, this time in a foreign country with unfamiliar cultural values and habits to which I would need to adapt.

I feared feeling insignificant, as I had in the beginning years in Uganda before I had established myself. I had just overcome those crippling feelings of trying to fit in and had found purpose and structure in my life over the years in Uganda. I was happy, and although initially thought I was unfit for friendships, I had made beautiful and meaningful relationships. But now, suddenly, I had this vision of myself kneading more play dough and buying more toys that would clutter the floor for another decade...

I sought the Lord day after day as I walked through the parklands in the Netherlands, and slowly arrived at a place of acceptance. Dissatisfaction, questioning God's sovereign plan, and self-pity can destroy a life of joy and peace. Once again, I surrendered to His will. God knew what He was doing; He knew about my doubts and questions. He also knew what still needed to be addressed in my soul and that my spirit needed to be in tune with His Spirit. He was the Potter who shaped and molded me into the person He had in mind and taught me to trust Him more.

Above all, He had my next son in mind, His child, chosen from before the foundation of the earth to exist and be part of God's Kingdom. I started to pray blessings over this child. God's appointment was already on his life.

We inquired whether being pregnant would influence the immigration or visa application process. Nothing seemed to be changing, and our visas to Australia were granted.

Funding for our living costs during our stay at Bible school came through the Nehemiah Foundation, which also funded our parents in the mission field. We corresponded with Medair, and Josiane Volkmar stepped in and pledged to support our Bible school fees for at least half a year, after which they would reevaluate and consider further funding.

All seemed ready, and once again, we packed our suitcases. We had bought one-way tickets to Australia and had yet to learn where this step would lead us. We only knew we had a visa and enough finances to live in Australia for a year.

Schiphol lay under a thick layer of fog as we ascended into the sky early in February 2006. Winter still had its grip on northern Europe. We left the Netherlands for the last time.

2006: Western Australia

I looked out through the plane's small oval window. The route ahead lay stretched over the entire globe. We could not go any farther than Australia. We had climbed mountains, walked plains, crossed oceans, tracked through jungles, lived in mud huts, and embraced people of all colors and creeds, but we were not yet finished adding more diversity to our lives. With two children by our side and another one on the way, we were now settling back into a Western society. I knew there would be enormous challenges to overcome, not only for us as a family but also in how we would adjust to a settled, regular life. We had traveled so much, seen so much, and stored away so many memories. We were entering yet another new chapter of our lives, and we had no idea what lay ahead.

We read a little about Australia and visited the Royal Museum in Amsterdam, which featured an Australasia theme at the time. It was apparent to us that it had a rich history, but we soon found out that it was not always presented well to the rest of the world. There were deep-rooted problems within this society that trailed and haunted this country as a penal colony. It saddened me to see the effects the English settlers had on the indigenous people who had lived on this vast continent for thousands of years. I wondered if it would impact our family as we contemplated immigrating and bringing up our children here.

For now, we entered the small world of the Bible school community at Perth Bible School in Karrinyup. As the pregnancy progressed, we started to experience again what it meant to come into a country with nearly no assets or family support. We didn't have a car and would walk toward the large shopping mall near the Bible school to get groceries. We tried to be as diligent with our budget as possible. I grew heavy, and often my back hurt as I walked long distances.

Although we had no idea how we would be able to fund it, I started to wish for a car. I saw it as necessary as the temperatures were soaring, radiating heat from the concrete and asphalt around. This dry desert heat was different from what we had experienced before.

We investigated buying a small car that came up for sale from departing students, but none seemed right. As I walked through the parking lot underneath the shopping mall, I saw a family entering a nice-looking van. The sliding door opened smoothly, I saw lots of room for several baby seats, and I heard a voice inside my head, "Why not ask God for a van?" I asked the Lord to provide.

On Sundays we arranged a lift to a delightful small church which we had decided to join. We connected with various families and became part of a small connect group that met during the week. One Sunday we came to church, and our pastor walked up to us and told us that a local Christian mechanic had a car available for us! This mechanic would buy older cars, fix them, and then give them to people needing transportation. The pastor thought of our situation, and the mechanic immediately said he would take care of it. When we came home that afternoon, we found a set of keys on our front doorstep. The mechanic had already parked the vehicle behind the apartments of the Bible school.

We stood in the sweltering heat in the middle of the parking lot and started searching for the car. We tried several, pushing the keys into the locks, but none fit. Then we went to look at the upper car park, reserved for students. There, shining white in the afternoon sun, stood a Toyota Lite Ace van. The keys easily fit in the locks, and I felt stunned as I had only tentatively prayed for a van earlier.

I smiled as the doors slid easily open, with enough room for baby seats. We would live, feed, and sleep in the van. It was once again the assurance that God would take care of us, whatever happened. And of course, our life story would not just be ordinary; many adventures lay ahead, lessons needed to be learned, hurts had to be dealt with, wounds needed healing, and attitudes changed. We drove our miracle van for many years around Australia.

In these last weeks before the semester ended, we heard that our financial support from Josiane Volkmar would cease, and Erika would go into her final transition phase of changing gender. It was like we had said good-bye to a significant chapter. Medair stopped playing an active role at this stage. We felt torn, and sad. Although God had proven faithful, we still had questions. How would we survive the next half-year? Could we even finish our studies, pay the bills, and, above all, where would we live after the course? How would our lives look from here? There was no money to go back anywhere. The tickets were one way; we had entered Australia with just a few suitcases.

Entering the Second Semester of Bible School

Perth, July 2006. Outside the college, the wind blew fiercely through the palm tree leaves. The temperatures had dropped, and instead of air-conditioning cooling the classrooms, we now huddled in front of heaters before lectures started. When we drove to church, the ever-blue sea was choppy and wild. This was winter in Perth, Australia. Although it was the driest winter of all time, we enjoyed the cool temperatures, which did not seem to drop far below 14 degrees. The nights were cold, but it was snug and warm in our apartment, where we had settled into a routine.

We ventured around Perth during the Easter holidays and saw our first emu and kangaroo. We earned some wages during the grape harvest and repotted a thousand young olive trees at a small farm a few hours north. We enjoyed the closeness of the sea, and on most weekends, we went for a long walk along the beaches, enjoying either the sun or the wind. Slowly our circle of friends extended a little outside the college.

We loved the fellowship at Vineyard Church and visited a connect group each Tuesday evening for Bible study. At college, we developed friendships too. During the week, after the lectures, the ladies of the compound met for tea or coffee. We chatted on the porches as we shared our life stories. We often ended up praying for each other. Bart found South African friends who were interested in starting some touch rugby, and on Thursdays, the sports enthusiasts of the college played themselves into a sweat trying to catch the oval ball!

Danny was enrolled in kindy at the local primary school and seemed to take to school as much as we enjoyed our studies. Jodie enjoyed every minute of her freedom within the safe compound where we lived with six other families with children. She could choose to play with fourteen kids aged one to eight years. Sometimes she came with us to our classroom as we were the only students for some lectures in which we had enrolled.

We were also auditing other subjects, initially, we would not get credit for these as we had only enrolled for the Cert IV in Biblical Ministries and weren't doing a theological degree. It gave us a theological basis for what we were covering in our course. In the end, the school accommodated us to sit the exams as well, and we did get credit for Effective Communication, Evangelism, Introduction To Theology, Old Testament, Psalms, and Introduction To Counseling. If we later decided to do a theology degree, these would count toward that degree. We also completed the first modules of Veritas (interpreting the Bible) in that half-year, which was part of our Cert IV in Biblical Ministries.

The weather had changed, and we watched the wild sea as storms raged along the coastline. The rain drenched the college grounds, and the kids mainly played inside. Our baby was due in September, and I tried to study as much as possible ahead of time. Soon, my life would change, and I might have to adjust the study load with a newborn. We were thinking about settling permanently in Australia after our studies. Bart had contacted Immigration Services to find out what was required to get a working visa. It meant that Bart would have to find a job in engineering or general management after our time at Bible school.

The school often invited guest speakers from mission organizations who presented their work to the students and encouraged them to join their missions. These were the times when we still felt the "pull" to get back into overseas work. However, with the baby on the way, we had to adjust to a different pathway for our immediate future.

On the last day of August, it was raining and cold, which felt strange after years of tropical weather and the summer heat of Perth during our first few months there. We had just celebrated Danny's sixth birthday, and we cheered Jodie on as she learned to ride her bike on the concrete pathway within the small compound where we all lived. That night, I had trouble falling asleep and felt very alert. At three in the morning, I suddenly woke up and told Bart that I thought the baby would arrive a few weeks earlier than expected. Birth pains began, and they were severe and regular. We woke up the lady we had lined up to help us out if the baby was born during the night, and she came and stayed with Danny and Jodie.

We stepped into our van, and in the pouring rain, we drove to Duncraig, the private hospital where our third child would be born. I hurried Bart on as I felt this birth could be much quicker than I expected. The wind tugged at the van, and rain drummed on the roof. We stopped for a traffic light at a busy intersection, and I doubled over from another contraction. At that moment, our miracle van decided to cut out. Frantically, Bart tried to restart it, but nothing happened. My contractions were now close together, and I urged Bart to find someone to help start the van! I heard Bart praying loudly for a miracle.

We looked around, and suddenly Bart pointed across the road. We had stalled the van right in front of our pastor's house! One last time, Bart turned the key...the motor coughed and finally caught. I felt relieved and grateful that we did not need to wake up the pastor to give us a hand. We praised and thanked God for His intervention.

I had felt so much older during this pregnancy. I was often exhausted, and I remember thinking during those two hours of intense labor, *"I don't want to do this anymore; I want to have this over with!"* Birthing is such a private experience; in those all-consuming moments, a lifetime can go through your mind, and I was unaware of my surroundings. Bart was trying to get my attention, and with his mouth close to my ear, he said, "Maria, stop kicking the doctor in his stomach; he cannot do his job like that!" At that moment, supernatural strength surged through me, and I breathed a prayer, "I want the baby to be born NOW!" And then there he was after only two hours of labor. My last-born, and of course, it was a boy, just as I knew he would be. They laid him on my stomach, and he looked up at me, surprised, his little nose wrinkled. He didn't cry those first moments, just breathed easily; he lay there, my son.

We named him Deron, an ancient Armenian name meaning "Belongs to God." This reflected the verse I received shortly after Jodie's birth, which returned to me when we arranged the visa to go to Australia.

Southwestern Australia

With our certificates in our pockets, we looked toward a new infilling of our lives. Bent over the local advertisement paper, we started searching for jobs that Bart could get with his limited experience in civil engineering. Two advertisements stood out, and Bart applied to both. Within a week, Opus International Consultants called Bart, and during the telephone interview, he was hired! It meant we would move south to a small town called Albany in Western Australia. We looked it up on the world map and saw it lying on a small outcrop of the land mass, far away from main cities, on the edge of several national parks.

The spring wind blew fiercely as we piled into the van and started our journey south in November 2006. Opus International Consultants had booked a motel for us for three weeks until we found a rental house for the longer term. As we traveled along the highway, the van shook with the gale-force wind. It was supposed to be spring and sunny, but our entry into the Great Southern greeted us with storms and rain.

After six long hours, we entered the town of Albany and drove along the scenic coastal roads toward our temporary residence. It took our breath away, deep blue waters now disturbed with white-capped waves and rugged escarpments that plunged deep into the ocean below. Then suddenly, the views changed, and white sandy beaches appeared, some with rock formations on which fishermen tried to catch their prize or food for the day. We had entered a taste of paradise!

Suddenly, another memory came back to me. When we left Uganda, I had contemplated what a good place would look like where we could bring up our kids and get them through their schooling. I was dreaming ahead of time of a beautiful spot where we could live a "normal" life. I remembered praying with a list of requests on my mind. My wishes consisted of having mountains with walking trails nearby, sandy beaches, and deep seas where we could walk, swim, and build sandcastles, a river so we could go on canoe trips, and endless blue skies. It was an impossible list, really, but God had prepared just that for us!

All of these natural features were present in the surroundings of our new home. We had access to world-renowned places, rivers that glowed at night during the summer, and seas where majestic whales breached during the winter months. We hiked the hills and mountains in the nature reserves surrounding Albany. Sometimes they were hidden in mist, while at other times, they glimmered beautifully in the morning sun, especially when the tops were covered in winter snow. This was a place where we could find peace and safety to raise our children.

The caring members of the local Anglican church were instrumental in helping us set up a house by assisting us in making the right choice of renting a house in the catchment area of good schools for our children. We started regularly attending this church which was known for its inclusiveness toward all who came through the door. Coming from Bible school and leading a highly active mission-focused life, we were immediately asked to connect with the church programs that were already up and running. The churches in Albany seemed to have a vision of unity among diversity and joined hands in many outreach activities in the region. It felt like this church could be our spiritual family, a promising start to our new chapter in life. We would need this support as there were challenging times ahead that I had not anticipated.

Part 11

Dealing with the Past

The Dark Night of the Soul

*There were challenging times ahead
that I had not anticipated.*

These written words ending the previous chapter are deeply engraved in my memory and heart. In the coming pages, I will share with you the internal battles that took place, which I gave God permission to use to reform and transform me from the inside out. The following chapters will not contain sensational, culturally diverse encounters or outrageous, exciting adventures from overseas. I will share how we tried very hard to become settled and live an everyday life of going to work and raising children, how I had to heal from the past, and I will share my learned lessons during the healing process.

Just like an athlete who is used to running the marathon and suddenly has to stop because of an injury, that's how I felt when I tried to live this regular and seemingly established family life. I was used to being on the move and living under stress; my body and spirit reared and protested, bucking against the restrictions I felt. Underlying hurts from the past came to the surface and would not be pushed back down again. I had to deal with them.

The first year in Albany was mostly taken up by this settling down and trying to belong. We explored the small city, settled the kids into a daily routine, and Bart got a handle on civil engineering again. I was mainly at home as Deron was only four months old when we arrived in Albany.

We found out how cold winter could be as the piercing wind blew in from the Southern Ocean with the smell of Antarctic ice. The temperature dropped and we needed wood for our wood burner. Farmers gave us access to their properties where trees had been uprooted by previous storms. We made it a family weekend event and rented a chainsaw and, with some axes, chopped the large branches into pieces. With the wood stove lit—which was conveniently placed in the middle of the house—we read many stories in front of the flickering flames. From the formal living room, we had a view of the ocean and saw freight ships coming and going from the harbor. Sometimes huge cruise ships came through the King George Sound, entering the harbor by sounding the horn and leaving again while shooting beautiful fireworks into the night sky. We loved the sea.

When the weather was nice, I walked to school, made new friends, or shared school rides with other moms as we all lived in the same school zone. I went to community parks and pushed the swing, sat on the short, perfectly mowed lawn, or let Deron play with sand on the beach. The days could be pleasant, even in winter, and I made coffee and sat in the low-hanging sun outside on the driveway, watching Deron play. He started to crawl, and soon after his first birthday, he stood up. Not long after that, he figured out how to guide himself along the walls. Then he started to walk, giving me a full-time job to keep up with him.

As I walked behind the stroller, smiling at other mothers, I felt distant and incredibly bored. A sense of emptiness crept inside me, but mostly, I felt tired. There was no structured program for the day besides caring for Deron and what the kids had organized after returning home from school.

I had no job or studies to keep me busy, no significant ministry, and I didn't know anyone who needed my help. At this point in my life, I didn't believe anyone needed me outside my small family. Needing to be needed had been my focus for many years and had become my identity. I felt worthless if no one needed me. Others' needs somehow gave me the affirmation I craved. It made me question if I had reached a dead-end as I didn't see any road signs telling me where to go from there. Becoming a stay-at-home mom felt disappointing as I spent my days doing mundane tasks such as dishes, cleaning, and feeding the family. I kept everyone running, except myself. My heart's flame flickered, despondency took over, and depression loomed around the corner.

I needed to be busy, so we started an introductory course for young believers. On another evening during the week, we opened our home to a connect group with other members of the church. We were asked to be on church rosters, and I even received invitations to preach in our church. We also got involved with children's ministry and Sunday school. However, despite all these activities,

The Dark Night of the Soul

dark thoughts stirred inside my heart, and I grew even more exhausted. I couldn't understand what was happening, or from where these feelings stemmed. New friends suggested postnatal depression, and others recommended a DVD on burnout. However, something much deeper was lurking inside, and I needed to address it. As we crept into the second year of living in this most idyllic small town in the southern parts of Western Australia, I entered one of the darkest hours of my adult life.

The priest of our church offered us their family cabin at Peaceful Bay, a famous camping spot for locals. The weather was dreary, and it rained on and off. The cottage was crowded with memorabilia from another family who had had great moments together. They'd spent time with each other, swimming in the blue waters and cooking freshly caught fish on the BBQ at night.

I did not experience peace, as the name of the place suggested. Rather the dull, dark, and cold weekend perfectly matched my state of mind. Between rain showers, we ran to the playground to let the kids get rid of their mounting energy. As I stood there pushing Deron on a swing, I lifted my head to see the thick clouds accumulating again, ready to dump another downpour. I looked at Bart, who was playing with Danny and Jodie a short distance away, and announced, "I cannot do this any longer. Please take the kids for a walk." Chilly rain poured over my face as I walked back to the cottage and dived into bed. I wanted to escape the overwhelming despair that clung to me like the gray clouds over Peaceful Bay, the idyllic place for quiet family holidays.

Sitting on that old, bumpy mattress, sleep would not come. Of course. My mind screamed for relief and an answer from God. A supernatural interference to calm my swirling thoughts that grew louder and louder. I felt like a volcano, ready to burst, and afraid of the intensity. I picked up an exercise book and began to write:

> October 2007
> I feel so tired of everything, especially Christianity. It seems like I have to strive to be a good Christian, while I feel like a failure. On my journal pages, I will rage, complain, and lament. At the same time, I know that God hates grumbling, and

might have to teach me to be grateful. I should be full of appreciation for His grace and thank Him in all circumstances. Instead, I have only questions. How will He deal with me in my faith struggle? Like with the Israelites in the Old Testament, He might send snakes that bite, a lesson of being thankful learned the hard way. I am no better than them as they walked through the wilderness. Is He truly the kind of God that deals harshly with His people when they do not please Him? Is He allowing such lessons to be learned because I have forgotten to be pleasing to Him? Have I forfeited His protection by doubting His goodness? Where did I lose my attitude of surrender to God's sovereignty? Did I sin in unbelief and rebellion? This is where I am now... God help me.

I started to doubt several pillars of my faith and wrote sixteen statements in which I expressed my deepest doubts and called God to account. Not only did I start to question my faith, but also God's faithfulness. I wrestled and spent days submerged in dark thoughts and negative beliefs about myself and God. It was a struggle to breathe every day, and all my energy was directed at surviving each minute. I wrote:

> My heart is so sad. I have this uprising cry from the depths of my soul: I want to know Christ! Who is He? God, show me who you are so I can get to know you. Show me what that cross meant for you because I do not feel any emotions toward the worth of your sacrifice for me. I know that it starts there, at the cross. Jesus, help me!

As the weeks passed, my despairing thoughts would abate for a moment and just hover in the background of my mind. I visited friends and prayed with those who were in need, saying all the right things. I was still able to encourage others, and life just got lived.

But then my thoughts would spiral out of control again, and

everything about Christianity seemed dreary. This mental suffering proved unbearable, and I longed for the moments when I felt like I had grasped Christ. I believed in Him and had proof of His existence and care for me in the past. His Word had spoken to me so clearly, and He had felt so close. I had not forgotten or doubted those moments, but I desperately wanted a fresh revelation of Him. I wondered if a deep relationship with Jesus only came about through suffering, from which I concluded that I had had enough. However, spiritual growth seemed to go hand in hand with suffering, which would lead to perseverance, character, and finally, hope (Romans 5:3-4). How could I welcome suffering or be thankful for it, if that was the only way to intimately get to know Christ? "God, Lord Jesus Christ, speak to me. I don't know if I want to take this road!"

I was rapidly losing sight of God's character, focusing on my performance, and living by rules instead of maintaining an intimate relationship with Him. Much later, I shared some of these deep struggles with others and heard the phrase "the dark night of the soul" for the first time in my life. Still, I was determined to pursue and allow God to come into the darkest corners of my heart. Through this process, I would come to know His heart.

The Slippery Slope

During my first two years in Albany, I was introduced to a ministry called MOPS (Mothers of Pre-Schoolers) and was offered the coordination role. I consider this ministry a valuable resource for the church and the community as it primarily focuses on mothers. While the mothers engage in positive programs for their mental, physical, and spiritual well-being, the children enjoy on-site care and activities run by a competent group of supervisors.

Deep down, leading this ministry was not my heart's desire. Instead, I longed to be the one invited to speak at events and share my life experiences. Although I found fulfillment in being needed, I knew that my true calling was not in childcare or setting up a women's ministry. My dream was to become a Bible teacher, preacher, or speaker at women's conferences. Despite expressing my doubts to my new friends, their response remained the same: "We think you would be perfect for this role, and we really need someone to set it up!"

I silenced my inner voice and thought it was better to listen to what others thought was best for me. Maybe others saw something in me that I didn't. Possibly, others heard from God more than I did at this time in my life. Underlying my reasoning was that I came from a background that did not encourage women to be in the limelight or to do public speaking, especially in a church setting. So, I accepted the coordinator's role, thinking that I was doing something positive for others and that I should not be picky about what God might want me to do.

I attended the MOPS coordination seminars and enjoyed the trips away from home, talking to other women who were successfully running the program elsewhere in Western Australia. I came home feeling a little more motivated, with more tools and resources to start setting up this ministry in our local church.

Getting all the staff required to start up a MOPS branch proved to be a problem. We needed a group of volunteers to run the children's program that operates parallel to the mothers' activities, but

The Slippery Slope

no one came forward in that first year. I found enough women willing to get involved in the mothers' programs, but we could not run it without volunteers to run the kids' activities. I had to wait for the right people to come forward.

Inside, turmoil kept mounting, and I felt lost and insecure. I dragged myself through the days and became an exceptionally clean housewife. I divided the house into parts, and each day, I scrubbed and cleaned. At any free moment, I was on my knees cleaning the skirting around the floor or wiping the windows. I found a program called *FlyLady* and soon reveled in having the house totally under control. Controlling everything around me seemed soothing, but it was a substitute for the control I lacked in my inner self.

My parents visited, and they became worried. Gently, they asked if I was okay because I seemed over-controlling in my housework. I also felt hungry all day and hated the urge to fill my stomach. It was the deep dissatisfaction within that I wanted to have filled.

I wrote in my journal: "I feel I'm constantly scheming and wearing a mask, not being true to myself all the while not even knowing who I am anymore. Always alert and aware of myself. Watching myself. Observing myself from afar, afraid to make a mistake in my friendships, in my family life, as a mother and wife. So, I adjust like a chameleon to what I think others need me to be, and it is so tiresome; I am sick of myself."

I would learn that these were symptoms of unresolved issues from past trauma and the onset of depression.

The Christmas festive season started early in December, with people shopping for Christmas trees and decorations. The children came home with stories of how the weather would soon become warm and we started to plan where we would go camping during the holidays

At school the children grew excited during the last few days before the school closed for the year. Children were exchanging self-made Christmas cards with each other and their teachers. I listened to the chatter in the classrooms, and instead of feeling happy and full of anticipation for the coming Christmas season, I felt overwhelmed and inadequate. I blamed myself for not being intentional enough in my mothering, for not guiding my kids toward proper social behavior or modeling generosity. I thought maybe I could make up for it by spending more time with other mothers and teaching my kids the principles of giving, sharing, and belonging.

So, I went home and started shopping. I bought Christmas packages that cost over a hundred dollars each, far beyond our budget. I even started making unique gift baskets for the kids to give to their teachers, as if I needed to prove something. And then I thought of extending my generosity to the friends who had helped us settle in. The baskets kept getting nicer and fancier, as if I had to pack all my thankfulness into a payback package. I performed, gave, shared, and tried to nurture my friendships through gifts. But deep down, I was driven by anxiety and a sense of inadequacy, always comparing myself to others and fearing that I would never measure up.

How was I to be the mum I was expected to be in this Australian Western society? I looked at how others did life. I copied their inspiration, then felt guilty that I lacked creativity and fresh input. There was just emptiness in my spirit.

We did go on camping trips. School was finished for the year, and it was the day before Christmas. There were a few campers on the grounds. Most people would arrive after Christmas—after visiting family members and performing their duties, enjoying Aussie BBQs, swimming in the pool, and going for four-by-four drives through the bush. At least, that was how I had gathered "the Australians" did Christmas.

The weather was lovely, and we soaked in the cool water of the endless blue sea. We walked around the edges of the escarpment and found little rock pools teeming with tiny crabs and fish left behind after the waves had crashed over them. Then, when we became too cold, we warmed our bodies on the rocks and gained a tan. I read books and ate too many biscuits and felt guilty.

On Christmas Eve, we suddenly heard the melancholic sound of bagpipes. A lonesome camper stood in the full moon's reflection on the shore of a calm sea. I climbed the rocky outcrop next to the beach and listened to the rolling waves and the sad tones rippling over the water. The music soothed my soul, and I breathed the salty air.

The next day we watched a sturdy local man catch a shark. He needed his four-by-four Ute to drag the enormous shark out of the water. It was slowly reeled in with great care and patience until it lay on the bare flat rocks. The children flocked around, and with interest, they watched how the man cut the shark into pieces. He then went about to all the campers and distributed meat for their BBQs.

It was a wonderful, brief time of catching our breath and enjoying nature at its best. All around, I saw the beauty and ruggedness of one of the most beautiful parts of Australia. Early in the morning, kangaroos with their joeys visited the campsite, picked crumbs from around the table, and nibbled on the fragrant eucalyptus leaves. Large crickets sang in the warming sun. We had found our favorite activity for the holidays, and this first camping trip set the pace for us to spend most of the following holidays camping and exploring the Great Southern parts of the state. Wonderful memories were made on many camping trips. It was a lull in the storms within my mind, a spark of light in the darkness of the soul.

At eighteen months, I weaned Deron from breastfeeding, as I had not slept through the night since his birth and was totally exhausted. It freed me up to attend conferences or meetings in Perth for MOPS. I was craving time away from my daily duties. I was still trying to get the required staff to run the children's part of the MOPS program. I found it all tedious and unfulfilling.

Increasingly, I felt like the odd one out. I hosted the planning meetings and looked at the close-knit group of women in my sitting room. They all knew each other, and they discussed the next step in setting up this ministry. They knew where to get resources for the craft program and where to find the legislation regarding running a children's program. They knew the right websites, knew where to find speakers or health practitioners to give valuable talks to the ladies. They had the network needed to keep programs fresh and relevant. I still felt like a stranger in this land and culture. I had no idea of the legislative rules when setting up a ministry or finding out where to look for information on the childcare ratio, and I wondered why I was even asked to be a coordinator.

One sunny morning, I entered the kitchen to prepare morning tea while the ladies discussed themes, craft options, and possible guest speakers. I reflected on the days in Uganda when my cook and nanny did either the baking or the childcaring as Deron trailed behind me while I did my business in the kitchen. How I missed these helpful ladies in my life. I walked back into my sitting room with a tray full of steaming coffee mugs and to my astonishment, I found the whole team crying! Someone had passed away whom most of the ladies knew, and all of them were unified in their grieving. I had never heard of the person who died and could not be part of their grief which also bound them together. I slowly and quietly put the mugs in front of the women, distributed a box of tissues, and felt lonely.

By now, I started to write down just words in my journal because I could not even find the strength to make whole sentences: Guilt–indecisiveness–shaking jaws and hands–gasping like hiccups–endless yawning–rejection–selfish–sick in the stomach–no relief, no release–lonely in crowds–feeling lost–confused–extremely uncomfortable–surreal feeling–no reality–want to remove myself from others–release from this inner tension–escape in a world of sleep.

I kept asking myself: "Am I a leader? Why should I be the coordinator for MOPS? I have never done this before in Western society. I am a follower, an implementer, not a starter. It looks like I am good, but the expectations are too high. I do not know if I have what it takes." Then the comparison started, I had done this when starting out in Uganda years ago and fell for this trap again.

Maybe, as a reader, you also recognize this as the killer of joy and the feeder of dissatisfaction. It looked like this and consumed my mind as I wrote in my diary:

> Look around you. Other women seem to have time, money, and energy to work on their future career; they have a part-time job or study. They do a little business on the side, work as volunteers in ministries, get an online blog going and do a live stream about their daily life experiences which seem to be worth making public. They enjoy playing with their kids, happily digging in mud and sandpits. They read good books and talk about them at their book clubs, and they do not feel guilty when they go shopping and spend their husband's salaries or have a snooze in the afternoon…

Comparison with others was a tool of the deceiver. It stemmed the flow of creativity and squeezed the life out of me.

I share these personal thoughts and vulnerable moments of my life because I know many others are going through similar experienc-

The Slippery Slope

es. My purpose is to let the reader know that whatever you are going through, someone understands, has experienced it, and has climbed out of this slimy pit of despair. There is a moment in life when we must reach out for help, open up, and share our life stories. Unfortunately, we seem to wait until we hit rock bottom. Much later, I understood that all these were also symptoms of depression. After finally acknowledging that something had gone awry inside of me, I visited a psychiatrist and was given the proper treatment. How this worked out is for later in the book

Broken

The depression became severe. One Saturday morning, as Bart and I sat at the table, mounting pressure radiated through my head, and my heart began to pound wildly. We were discussing our finances and whether we could afford for me to attend another training seminar. This would require Bart to stay home with the kids, and Deron, our active toddler, still required a lot of primary care and attention. It would mean a sacrifice for Bart since he would not be able to relax and enjoy his day off while I was away. He struggled with the permanency of his 9-5 job.

The discussion around finances brought about memories of my childhood in which my parents struggled with financial shortages. I had flashbacks of how Dad would raise his voice, explaining why he needed certain things for his ministry and my mother softly countering by telling him what she needed for the household.

As our voices rose, I became aware that the kids had become unusually quiet. We were doing the exact thing my parents did when I was young—the thing I hated. I could never stand loud voices and harsh words. We should not be discussing things like finances in front of the kids! It was a grown-up discussion that should have been conducted maturely. Instead, we were offloading our frustrations onto each other. Immediately I condemned myself, worried the kids would be left with impressions of a loaded atmosphere around finances, leaving them with negative memories.

Suddenly, something burst in my head. My hands started shaking, and I quickly gathered the dishes from the table. I carried them to the kitchen bench, and there, I lost it. I threw the dishes into the sink, and they shattered into many pieces, scattering spoons, forks, and knives on the floor. Then, I found myself kneading the shards. My hands began to bleed, and I vaguely heard Bart being angry with me. Although I knew it was his deep concern for me, he didn't know how to deal with this explosion. The children started to cry, and I realized I was seriously falling apart. I ran into our bathroom to soothe

the cuts on my hands under the cold tap, while tears streamed down my face.

I struggled with purpose and identity. I had so much love for others from an early age, but I had so little regard for myself. I felt no loyalty to a country, and I did not experience being a citizen with feelings of patriotism. I kept asking myself: What is home? What does it mean to be home, to feel secure and at peace? To me, a home existed only in memories. It meant the smell, color schemes, atmosphere, and the sounds of a clock in a gift shop. The sound of a loud ticking clock reminded me of waiting for the relief of pain in stark white hospital rooms. I did not know who I was. How could I teach my children morals or guide them through life if I didn't have the strength or vision for life to give them direction?

I picked up a book called *Captivating: Unveiling the Mystery of a Woman's Soul* by John and Stasi Eldredge. I appreciated how Stasi addressed the way we try to soothe inner heartaches in chapter three, where she talked about indulging:

"Take a moment and consider yours. Where do you go instead of to God when your heartache begins to make itself known?"[9]

She gives an all too familiar list of how we fill the void in our hearts to make us feel better. It touched on what was going on in my heart. I was not the only one going through a tough time as she wrote about other women going through similar inner conflicts, and I concluded: "My indulgence is at this moment controlling the housework, so I feel in control. And then I follow this up by trying to be significant *for* others, so I *feel* significant."

The pain didn't go away after all the reading and searching for a reason for feeling so at a loss. I needed help. My friend introduced the idea that I might need psychological help, and we looked for a psychiatrist in town. I wanted to discuss my medical history with someone who could prescribe medication if needed. I made an appointment and went to my first meeting with trepidation in my heart.

The psychiatrist listened for two solid hours to my story, and the first thing he did was advise me to take one day during the week to care for myself. Just one day, which would become a moment to look forward to. It was like being permitted to have time off, a moment to read a book, have a coffee, go for a long walk, or just *BE*.

I put Deron in daycare. Although I looked forward to this one day off with no responsibility, it was challenging to leave Deron behind. He always cried when I left. His pitiful begging would start the night before when I tucked him into his little cot. With his big blue eyes filling up with tears and his head lopsided in a begging position, he repeatedly asked, "No school, Mum? Peace! (please)"

The day started with a pain in my heart as I left him behind. Afterward, I went for a swim and visited my psychiatrist. Sharing my piled up self-reflections from the past week dragged me out of the muddy pit of self-destructive thought patterns. While I explained my inner confusion, I unpicked the knots in my thinking, which set me on a solid rock from where I started the healing process.

He asked me, "Are you allowing yourself to be where you are now and leaving all the 'I-shoulds,' 'I-coulds,' and 'I-woulds' alone for a while?" He explained that this meant letting life come as it presents itself and not trying to control everything. He suggested having a conversation with myself as if I were a consultant, distancing myself for a moment from self and only observing and noticing. I thought I was good at that. I did analytical thinking about myself most days; it was just that everything was in such shambles.

He offered valuable suggestions like being in nature, listening to music, reading a book, swimming in the sea, or walking on the beach. He also suggested finding a place where I could relax, and if that wasn't at home, going somewhere else. Several years later, I would give this advice to other women as I found that many others went through similar times of despair.

Permission was given to prioritize self-care, being out of the house, and finding out what would give me pleasure. I took his advice to heart and started the day by exploring the cafés in and around Albany.

One day, as I sat in a café overlooking the harbor inlet of Albany, I leisurely stretched my legs toward the warm sun. I watched seagulls fight over leftover chips and sipped my coffee. I put in my earphones, closed my eyes, and listened to Pachelbel's *Canon in D*. I let myself drift away to the gentle tones of the violins and shut out my busy mind. I remembered how I had heard this piece of music for the first time.

It was during a break from our work in Uganda back in 2003. We were offered a small chalet in Switzerland to relax and catch our breath from the constant work demands back home. Jodie was not yet a year, and I often carried her on my stomach in a baby wrap. I gazed through the large window of the cabin that stood high on a steep hillside. It looked out over white-capped mountaintops. Thin slivers of mist covered the valley below us. We felt like we were floating over the world, as if we were taken up for a moment, leaving behind life as we knew it. Suddenly a ray of sunshine tumbled down from between the mountains. The thin layer of clouds below lit up, changing the scenery before me into a glistering silver world.

Bart had figured out an advanced stereo system in the living room and had put on *Canon and Gigue in D major* composed by Johann Pachelbel. I had never heard this harmonious and serene classical piece before, and the music entered the deepest places of my soul. As violins and cellos were added to each subsequent movement of the canon, my heart began to soar. Slowly it rose to my throat, and I cried. Tears of deep longing dripped down my face onto Jodie's blonde hair while I rocked her gently. It was one of those moments where I could let everything go and rest.

A few years had passed since the last time I heard this beautiful piece of music, and as I listened to it again, peace entered my mind. The brokenness we witnessed in the world during our years overseas now merged with the brokenness of my inner world. Although I felt ravaged by internal conflict and run aground by depression, I knew that just like wars and conflicts ceased, there would also be hope for me.

The Story of the *Doulos*

October 2008 was yet another spring for us as an immigrant family. The ship, the MV *Doulos*, was due to moor in Albany. Operation Mobilisation (OM) International was the organization behind two ships traveling worldwide over the oceans at that moment in time. They were an international floating ministry that shared knowledge, help, and hope through literature, cultural understanding, relief work, and much more.

Churches met together as their forward team organized its arrival and planned the programs for the volunteers on the ground. We were ground volunteers years ago in the Caribbean when its sister ship MV *Logos II* visited Curaçao, and that had been a blessed time. We put our hands up to open our home and host volunteers from the ship and offer these sailors an onshore meal and fellowship. We experienced so many blessings from their ministry in the ports they visited while we were traveling. We often partnered with them when our ministries collided in the countries where they docked.

A great expectation arose among all Christians as the *Doulos*'s arrival day drew near. An overwhelming welcome was planned for this ship as it would dock in Albany for one last time functioning as a floating library and vessel to spread the Gospel. Something else simmered deep inside me, and God was preparing a message for me, a message that would plunge me into the unknown of embracing brokenness and healing.

We drove over Marine Drive, the scenic route that hugged the edge of Mount Clarence. This road wound itself around the outline of the coast with several sharp bends. A string of cars moved slowly before us in the last rays of the setting sun. All were headed toward the harbor. Suddenly the outline of a large ship emerged from the horizon, and it was met by the awaiting pilots who guided the ship smoothly through the Ataturk Channel of the King George Sound. Michaelmas Island and Breaksea Island disappeared into the background as the ship grew larger, while high on the hill above the channel, hundreds of cars lined up, watching its approach.

Suddenly the ship's foghorn resonated through the Sound. Immediately hundreds of car horns answered the call. Every time the ship's horn blasted, the cars responded by pressing their horns. En masse, the vehicles started to follow the ship as if now guided by sea and land pilots to its docking site. Other visitors to the ship who had gathered on the dock shouted out their welcome to the crew who had gathered at the ship's railing as it gently touched the wharf. Flags of all nations fluttered from the sides, representing the international staff of the ship.

A rising emotion within my chest bubbled up, surprising me. And I began to cry. This cry further broke the dam of piled-up emotions that had been dormant for many years. As we approached the ship, I could not stem the tears. Bart grew anxious; he was not used to seeing me cry so much. In the past, he would often beg me to let my emotions go, ask me to cry and be vulnerable so he could care for and nurture me. I would always shut down the desire to cry; crying gave me headaches, and often, days after, I would feel out of balance, insecure, out of control, and miserable.

The tears would not stop flowing. Suddenly, a voice spoke in my head, which shook me to the core. A gentle yet firm voice started to talk and said, "Maria, this is the place where you will go on dry dock and be completely dismantled and cleaned." In my heart, I kept repeating my answer, "No, Lord, no, not a total dismantling. Please, Lord, it will hurt so much." I sobbed and sobbed as we slowly joined the long moving line of cars toward the pier where the ship was docking.

The first visit on board was to the restroom to restore my makeup. I dabbed my face and removed the smudged mascara, as if I were removing a lifelong mask for the last time.

This tour of the *Doulos* would minister significantly to the most southern parts of Australia's mainland. All port volunteers were invited to attend the captain's dinner that night, together with the city's dignitaries. After the speeches of the mayor of Albany, Captain Ashley McDonald stood up and opened his speech, "This will be the last time Albany will welcome this ship in its harbor…" and then he continued to talk about the ship's rich history.

Doulos had visited the port of Albany several times during its years of voyaging. This time, it would be different. It would be a farewell. The ship would go to Fremantle and then to its final resting place. With pain, Operation Mobilisation would say a final goodbye to a faithful vessel that served to spread the Gospel worldwide. (It went on dry dock in 2009, where it was revealed that the cost of necessary repairs was prohibitive, and only then was a decision made to sell the ship.)

My heart stopped momentarily when the captain continued his speech and said, "This ship will be dry-docked. It will be repaired, cleaned, and barnacles removed…" These profound words were spoken to me on our way to the ship. My chest heaved as I let the words sink in. Despair rose as I identified these prophetic words spoken over a ship and my personal life. I was going on dry dock to be cleaned up, scrubbed clean from old rust and the growth of barnacles that hindered the hull from sliding through the waters. *"But what will be left?"* I asked in my spirit. I felt a deep, dark hole opening and cried to God, *"Is there any hope in this process?"*

Then the captain continued, "Enough support has already been raised to start preparing a new ship. Over time, another ship will serve the nations, sailing the seas." After a pause, he said, "A new ship has been purchased, refitted, and made ready to sail, and will be launched in February 2009. This ship has the name: *Logos Hope*!"

The message of hope was delivered simultaneously as I became aware of a massive personal cleanup. Overwhelmed by emotions, I left the table, stumbled again to the small washroom on board, and cried. The time ahead would be painful, but not without hope! Something else lay in store for me. Another time of serving others would come with a new perspective. The old would have gone, and a new hopeful future lay ahead. One day I would sail the seas and see nations again. One day, I will bring the Gospel filled with Good News and a message of hope to the people who are in despair. I had entered that time of dismantling, and the cleansing would come, but I was afraid.

Seeking Support and Building Relationships

The psychiatrist prescribed medication that would relieve the deep depression he diagnosed me with, officially called post-traumatic stress disorder. The medication would help me think more clearly and give me room in my head to work on the issues that arose during our initial talks. We would work on childhood traumas and raising awareness of how to define my identity. This lack of self-knowledge affected my thinking, belief system, perceptions, and behaviors.

I hated the initial side effects of the medicines but decided to continue and work slowly toward the initial goal of just feeling a little better, so life would not seem so bleak. I had disturbing dreams, and they revealed significant inner conflicts; they allowed me to dig deeper into the subconscious. I got in touch with some emotional aspects that I had never acknowledged. I allowed myself to feel grief, sit and embrace loneliness, recognize the pain of rejection, the despair of feeling powerless, and admit I was plagued by anxiety. It brought into focus the moments of hopelessness that I felt during childhood. I could look upon my early experiences and store these away with the appropriate feeling attached to them.

I looked at myself in the mirror and realized how I lived like a chameleon, able to change and wear a mask and hide who I was. I had learned to adjust to various situations and fit into all sorts of people groups without having discovered my own identity. I had thought it a special gift to step into people's shoes and look through their perspectives to be seen as someone who understood them. However, in identifying with others, I could not discover who I was. I was also gullible about opinions and would adjust my ideas to theirs to please them. I was losing myself in the process of adapting.

Fear of rejection is one of the most significant wounds that must be addressed. Often, it threw its ugly head out of the mud of the past the moment I thought I was criticized or corrected. I could not handle or embrace it as constructive feedback; I took it as a personal rejection. I had to learn to sift through comments and glean advice that would build me up, not take it as if people were trying to tear me down.

By discussing these disturbing self-reflections with my psychiatrist, I started consolidating these various aspects of myself and seeing an emerging "me." And the person I encountered was a rich personality worth living with. I indeed had the gift of listening to others and did have the remarkable ability to empathize with them and step into their shoes. I learned not to take on a burden that I was not able or appointed to carry. Listening to others became a privilege without the need to solve problems or find a solution. Just being there, like I now enjoyed being listened to.

I began an exciting yet tricky journey as I experienced the closing and healing of the gaping inner wound. I was in the right place and time to properly and thoroughly address my past and its effects. Opening up to others was challenging; more was to be explored and learned. I still had to learn how to develop safe relationships without going through the filter of distrust and fear of rejection.

Coming to Albany and planning to live there for years while the children grew up, I needed to get a handle on how to "do" long-term relationships. This time, I could not just walk away from people when I did not like them much, or think that after having been hurt, it would not be so important since I would be leaving soon enough. By moving around, I avoided potentially challenging relationships. How do you learn to have healthy relationships? It was a road full of pitfalls. I was bound to make mistakes as I made feeble steps toward trusting others.

I had reasoned away the need for acceptance, acknowledgment, and affirmation, thinking I could do life alone and in my strength. However, we are made for relationships, and I longed for friendships that would fill the void. As a little girl, I had believed a lie that was now stuck in my adult mind: "Your pain is not worth acknowledging. You are not worthy of being heard." All the while, my soul was screaming for attention. There was this insatiable need for someone to recognize my needs. Someone who listened to what I wanted or didn't want and the permission to choose and know that these choices would be respected.

In my brokenness and search for understanding and acceptance, I didn't see the dangers of setting others up to become the "wound stopper." This would end in yet another rejection, as no one can fulfill this high expectation of healing the deep wound of rejection.

As I stepped onto the road of discovery and learned more about myself, I tried to work on healthy relationships. In my eagerness, I did make the mistake of becoming increasingly dependent on a friend who had reached out to me and given me much of her precious time. We had coffee, and she would listen to my stories. I was feasting on attention and lost sight of healthy boundaries in my need to be heard.

The relationship changed from a potentially good friendship to an unhealthy dependence. Before I knew it, I had moved back into a space of becoming what others suggested I should do and be. I did not stick to the emerging path of discovering who I was or what my identity looked like in God's eyes. I did not yet have the tools for conflict resolution or the insight to redirect this rapidly declining relationship. I had not yet discovered and celebrated who I was by accepting my personality and gifts and had not yet learned that God's Holy Spirit would renew my mind and that my core beliefs would change according to whom God said I am. In this friendship, I also overstepped the boundary of which Proverbs speaks: "Seldom set foot in your neighbor's house—too much of you, and they will hate you" (Proverbs 25:17 NIV).

This proved a wise saying, and I did experience a breakdown in this relationship. Emotionally I could not yet deal with it, and I was overwhelmed by the embarrassment of having made a mistake by oversharing my issues with someone who was not a professional counselor.

Looking back, I was learning some profound lessons regarding relationships. I understand better now why God is a jealous God and does not want any human taking His place. He needed to be given the privilege of fulfilling my deepest needs. God had more healing in mind for me.

Hurts by Those in Authority

The next experience I want to share is related to the authorities in our lives. They shape our thinking about physical, emotional, relational, and spiritual care during our formative years. Negative experiences with authority figures can lead to negative connotations toward them.

I want to tell you about an encounter in my life that shows how vulnerable I was because of past negative experiences with people in authority. I also want to point out the importance of having a support group during a healing journey. Once we become victims of any misuse of power or authority, we need good examples and models to readjust our image of healthy authority. There must be a foundation of trust. We need to be able to embrace and trust God, knowing that He is a loving Father who is in authority over our lives; only then can we learn to surrender to any other authority.

In the past, I had been subjected to medical experts who took charge of my body in the hospital without my consent. This resulted in a distrust of authorities in the medical field and made me doubt many practitioners' intentions. I also had been bullied by peers in school and during my hospitalization, and I didn't know how to build healthy relationships with my peers. Caretakers and teachers didn't step up to deal with bullying, resulting in an inability to trust teachers. Early in my life, I concluded that adults were of no help in a crisis; they would not stand up for you. I had other painful experiences with spiritual leaders within the Church that left me with a wrong and warped idea of what Godly authority looked like.

When I was six years old, my family joined a conservative and evangelical denomination where a group of elders oversaw the spiritual well-being of the congregation. These elders made decisions on theological issues and the application of biblical interpretations. There was not just one preacher or pastor in charge, and there was no official board that appointed elders.

The interpretation of Scripture by the unofficial elders dictated our behavior, and I seldom dared to step out of the mold. If sins were exposed, the men in the denomination had a biblical explanation of how to confront sin in the congregation and would discipline accordingly.

Unfortunately, some prominent leaders exercised their position in the Church unhealthily and manipulatively. Emotional and spiritual manipulation was imposed and enforced by a social control system through which accountability was demanded. Unfortunately, I had friends who confided in me and told me of sexual misconduct by leaders of the Church which further consolidated my distrust toward authorities.

In part four, *A New Start*, I wrote about a period during my late teens when I spent significant time with a family who took in youth who needed time to recover from traumatic experiences. Unbeknownst to me, while I was there, the pastoral caregiver sexually abused some girls under his care. Although I suspected things were not as they were supposed to be, he never abused me.

During my years in Curaçao, finally, one of the victims of this well-respected spiritual leader exposed him, and he was put under investigation. I, too, was called to speak up if I had been a victim of this man's misconduct. After a lengthy investigation, the church had to discipline him through excommunication by the church and within the denomination. It severely damaged my trust in spiritual leaders and Christian counselors.

I had not learned what wholesome authority looked like or identified who could be trusted in genuine pastoral care within the Christian community. I wanted to trust elders and spiritual leaders but didn't know how. I searched for mentors and coaches who could guide me toward healing my emotional pain. As I dealt with so much from the past, I fell into the trap of trusting the wrong people.

The extended school break came around, and I decided to take the children on holiday deep inside the Australian outback on a working farm, a cheap and effective way of occupying busy children. I wanted to do arduous physical labor in the dust and heat of the blazing sun. I thought that way, I would stop thinking so much. I envisioned myself walking over outstretched fields with a vast expanse above me. I wanted to find rest for my mind. I looked forward to reading a book and maybe concentrating on my Bible reading.

With my clogged-up mind, it was so difficult to be in a meaningful relationship with God.

Bart had to stay behind for work and would only come up during the weekends to enjoy the peace of the countryside.

A particularly good friend from my weekly women's group warned me this was not a suitable time to be alone, away from caring friends or the church. She recognized that I was vulnerable and might not discern what a safe haven would look like. I should have heeded that wise counsel, but I wanted to flee. I wanted a break from the inner pain and feelings of not being able to live up to what I thought was expected from me.

It was a secluded farm, and many hours' drive from the nearest town. There was no coverage for mobile phones, which I perceived as good and peaceful. Temperatures during the day soared over forty degrees which I didn't mind; I felt I needed this scorching.

The first few days were wonderful as I worked in the field and camped with my children under the few trees on this vast property. We got water from the rainwater tank and cooked in a large shed as the sun stood low in the copper-colored sky.

At night, I would be on my own on an army stretcher in a tent after I put the children to bed. I expected good friendships with the farmers, well-respected Christians, and elders in their church community. I thought I would find relief by sharing life stories while we worked. Initially, it triggered an empathetic response from one farmer, and he would seek me out in the field or the shed. He asked questions, and his interest felt warm and good. And in my brokenness, I desperately wanted to trust him to do some mending. I was too vulnerable to be discerning. I should have known nobody could smooth the pain from inner wounds or bind up a broken heart. Only God can do that. The farmer overstepped personal boundaries, and much later, I understood that I was being groomed to become involved with a married man.

During the hottest time of the day, I was offered a Donga (small cabin), where an air conditioner cooled the air while Deron slept. I often took a nap with him while the other children played games in the room next door. Suddenly the door opened, and the farmer came in. He commented that I had slept enough and suggested keeping me company while Deron still slept. He noticed my hands were tightly clasped together and recommended a relaxing massage.

I froze and kept checking to see if Deron was awake. I was extremely uncomfortable and could not think of an excuse except that I asked him if he would do this to his daughter. His answer was curt, "You aren't my daughter, and I am not your father." Then he got up and left the cabin. I felt terrible and thought I had hurt his feelings as he was so caring... Instead of the peace I craved, I felt totally bewildered.

The rest of my stay became a confusing blur as conversations were laced with inappropriate suggestions and sexually loaded intentions as the farmer visited me while I worked in the field. Was all this supposed to be part of being in the dry dock and having barnacles removed? It did not feel like a safe dry dock or sheltered haven. It felt more like a ship running aground on a rocky coast. I was beaten by the waves and broken into pieces instead of being repaired. And I got a rotten worker on the repair team! It destroyed the tiny bit of hope that I could trust people, especially those who were in spiritual leadership positions.

In the days following the incident, I felt powerless and unable to remove myself from the situation. Overwhelmed, I realized I had no control over myself and believed I had no choice but to stay. This feeling transported me back to my childhood when I often lacked the strength to protest or say "no." During those times, I coped by dissociating and feeling as if it was happening to someone else. This coping mechanism was developed during traumatic experiences and became my default response to trouble.

I found myself silently crying for help on my stretcher at night. To no one in particular, just toward the stars moving in the dark above my tent. The children were sound asleep, and I knew nobody would come to interfere if anything more serious happened.

I left the farm in a terrible mess. The farmer had made me promise not to talk about the loaded conversations, innuendos, and inappropriate touches. It was a burden I could not carry. I nearly collapsed in the days after we returned home, and I knew I had to tell Bart about it. I had no idea how to explain what happened as it felt so covert and shameful. It kept churning inside, and in my journal, I wrote:

> I feel like a piercing sword goes through me, leaving me bleeding at the side, while I should have been given a healing balm. Inside I am consumed

by a raging fire while I try to be a fine morning mist to others. I feel like an erupting volcano, but on the outside, I am just a ripple on the sandy ocean floor. The old lie clouds my mind and becomes louder and louder, coming to a crescendo: 'I am not to BE,' 'I should not be....' 'I am destructive to myself and others.' It is a large looming black hole. I need to confide in someone, but I cannot, and of course, I had promised not to speak to others about what had happened.

I now know that secrecy is never helpful and is always manipulative. I found great solace in the verses in which Jesus speaks of what happened in the dark and it will be exposed to the light. God is a God of justice; He will deal with injustice.

I asked my mom to come to Australia to help me work through the situation. My dad was on a mission trip to India, and my mom could visit while he was away. Eventually, I confided in both my mom and Bart. I knew I needed to confront the farmer, stand up for myself, and gain some respect. This would help me put things into perspective, heal, and learn from the experience. The entire ordeal taught me valuable lessons in discernment and self-defense. I needed to lift the shame I felt and bring the violation to justice. My mom and I traveled back to the farm and spoke with the farmer, which allowed me to find closure. Through this experience, I emerged as a more mature adult.

Part 12

The Healing Journey

God as Father

I write about these experiences to show others that there is hope for healing from the hurt caused by those in authority over us, who may distort our understanding of God as a true Father. God is able to deal with even the most complicated situations if we allow Him to enter our lives. He may permit us to revisit past situations so that we can confront the pain of betrayal and be healed. The purpose of this is to draw us closer to God, to surrender to His restorative power, and to learn to trust Him as the ultimate authority in our lives.

We all need mature and wise counsel, and although life might have proven that it was not available in the past, when we reach out and look around, there are mature and caring people who can speak words of life into our lives.

I needed to embrace the journey of getting to know myself and how self-destructive thinking patterns were formed in the past. Then, these patterns needed to be dismantled and replaced by a new way of thinking. Negative thinking fueled my inner confusion, leading me to an ever-increasing slippery slope of self-rejection and self-absorption. I was so tired of it.

Initially, this journey of self-discovery felt wrong. As a Christian, I should not be self-absorbed or so egocentric. I shared my thoughts and struggles with a visiting friend, and his input was very hopeful: "Being on this self-exploring journey will have good outcomes and the pain will end, and healing will take place. We need to go to places where it went wrong, where some of our deepest unmet needs will confront us. We need to engage with these moments in the past to acknowledge them and put them into the right perspective. Otherwise, it will dictate that we constantly search to find how to fill this unsated need and the hole in our soul. Being a Christian will add another dimension to the journey. We are not doing this alone, and God is on your side."

He continued, "We are born 100% *selfish* and dependent on receiving love. And we will become 100% *selfless* and more Christ-like in giving love. You need to get the first bit first to be able to give the latter."

As days passed, I often cried inside. I screamed to God for help, and when the tension became too much, I fled into my bedroom. I would cuddle a pillow against my chest and roll it into a small ball. Like a baby, I wailed and cried for my mother, smothering the sobs that racked my body. I bit and slobbered into the cushion because I could not stop the sound from escaping my mouth. I heard Danny ask his sister if she also heard something from the room, and I tried to stop shaking and crying, but could not find the stop button. I inhaled air, and my headache increased as I coughed and spluttered. I started feeling sick and vomited. My stomach was upset as my body didn't know how to deal with these violent emotions that came from deep within.

I picked up the phone and called around for someone to take the children out for a moment so I could collect myself and somehow crawl out of this black pit. Nobody was available, and so I sank back into my bed, confirming within myself that when I needed people, they would not be there for me. My faith was not strong enough to expect an answer to my prayers. I resorted to suffering through this moment of despair and just let it wash over me.

As I cried out to God to hear me, another voice interfered, *"Whomever you try to ask for help, they cannot help you. You know from earlier experiences that nobody will be there for you; it has always been the case."* This was another lie of the enemy out to destroy God's beloved. I believed the lie and agreed with it at that time. And this would stand until I broke these inner vows during the Elijah House course. Elijah House is a prayer ministry that offers powerful tools for dealing with the hurts of the past. I will write more about it in later chapters.

Meetings with my first psychiatrist had ceased, as his sessions were unhelpful.. Although he initially listened for hours to my life's story in consecutive sessions, he would delve into too many details about his own life. He indulged in sharing his dying relationship with his wife and subsequent affair with his colleague. He wanted an interactive discussion about our different religious backgrounds and his painful experiences within his denomination. I had to cancel my appointments, as this was not what I needed from a psychiatrist. I learned that seeking help might take some time and involve searching for the right therapist.

I still needed help. I was on medication and needed monitoring. There was still work to be done. Two things happened simultaneously: I received the right psychiatric help and went to a prayer ministry course conducted in our church. The theme that now overarched my journey was that God was working in my situation, and I started to embrace His desire to heal me.

One of the first principles I could grasp was that God was not interested in just *restoration*. He was in the business of *renewal*. He did not just fill in the cracks in my foundations or give a set of tools and crutches to hobble through life. He brought it back to its original design. He had the answer to the meaning of life, a purpose for my life, and my destiny.

During these initial stages of getting Godly counsel and professional psychological help, I was still questioning God. It was sometimes easier to give in to a religious mindset, just trying to obey rigid rules that felt safe, but had nothing to do with trusting God. In my confusion and self-absorption, I resorted to "doing" Christianity. It also had to be addressed as it hindered my understanding of God's character. Not knowing how to allow the Spirit to be in charge and experience freedom, I returned to a default that looked safe but blocked my personal and intimate relationship with God.

Religion is often viewed as adhering to a set of rules to appease a god, resulting in a very judgmental attitude toward oneself and others. However, Christianity should never be like that. Yet in our brokenness, we often resort to obeying rules and regulations to earn God's goodness and favor. But just following rules is never a good substitute for an intimate relationship with God. Sometimes, it seems easier to adhere to rules than to risk being vulnerable in a relationship. I approached God theoretically, with my mind, but I didn't let Him come in as a caring Father or experience Him as the "Lover of my soul." God was out to renew my mind and become a Father and an eternal Friend to me.

I could not comprehend it all yet, as these were heart matters, not mind issues. The walls around my heart needed to come down through God's healing power. Then He could redirect my thinking and shine His light upon my confusion. As I struggled, one thing became clear: I did not want to lose my faith, and although I didn't feel or experience God, I wanted to acknowledge Him as *my* God and Savior through Jesus.

One morning I woke up and a strong impression was imprinted into my spirit. It was as if a voice told me, "Leave your struggle for a moment; God will sort it all out. Instead, confess whom you believe." Straight away, the Apostles' Creed came to mind, which I learned by heart when I was still at the reformed primary school:

> I believe in God, the Father almighty, creator of heaven and earth.
>
> I believe in Jesus Christ, God's only Son, our Lord, who was conceived by the Holy Spirit, born of the virgin Mary, suffered under Pontius Pilate, was crucified, died and was buried; he descended to the dead. On the third day he rose from the dead; he ascended into heaven, and is seated at the right hand of the Father; from there he will come to judge the living and the dead. I believe in the Holy Spirit, The holy catholic Church, the communion of saints, the forgiveness of sins, the resurrection of the body, and the life everlasting. Amen. (https://anglican.org.au/about-us/what-we-believe/)

From that day onward, whenever I had moments of doubt and fundamental questions about God's dealings and sovereignty, I would say the creed out loud. It counteracted my doubts and acknowledged that God is in charge.

I likened God's work in me to the work of a carpenter. He worked on me for decades, and although the shape was positively visible, He had to go over it repeatedly. Sometimes with a chisel, plane, sandpaper, and polisher. Some places in my life needed special attention as there were still slivers of unevenness or imperfections that He wanted to straighten out. He keeps sculpturing me until I will be presented perfectly to His Father one day. It is the work of a lifetime.

At about this time, we heard that our house, which we rented, would go up for sale, and we needed to find another place to live.

Although it threw uncertainty into the mix of my emotions, this development was good, as it opened another chapter, and a new start in my life.

At Home in the Global Village

We bought a house, our first house ever! In 2009 the government offered a "first-homeowners-grant," and we scraped some money together. I still had some funds available in the Netherlands that I could use for the required deposit. It was an adventure, and we were scared. We had never owned or bought something this large; the money we discussed had too many zeros. Soon we found ourselves living in a beautiful, unique home on a hill on the edge of Albany, overlooking an open public space and a paddock.

During the winter, it filled up with rainwater, and many water birds would come and entertain us as they paddled across the green lawn on the shallow puddles. Sometimes the kids ran around in these pools, splashing, and stomping, bringing up mud. In the summer, kangaroos came to feed on the lush grass. The paddocks beyond had either cows or horses roaming around. They brought lots of blowflies in the warmer weather. Beyond the grassy field was a dark, low scrub strip that hid a meandering creek, a place of rest for wildlife. Green surrounded us, birds singing in the high eucalyptus trees that had grown out of proportion on our property. I was invigorated by it all, and I intended to make it a piece of heaven for our kids. We had little bonfires in the warmer seasons, drank wine on the veranda, and Bart built a treehouse. Indeed, we could settle and be at rest. This place would be a home for years to come. For the first time, we were "home" somewhere.

Danny reacted strongly to settling in as a family and staying in one place. He was becoming aware of his identity as a young Australian. During the Australian and New Zealand Army Corps (ANZAC) celebrations, we stood on the foreshore where, in 1914, the last fleet left Australia to join forces in Egypt for the assault on Gallipoli. Reverence settled over us when the last post was played at the Dawn Service. As a family, we cried when people took off their hats and clasped their hands together or held a hand over their hearts.

Even the toughest-looking Aussie fathers with their children on their shoulders sang the national anthem with reverence.

Over the horizon, specks appeared and soon, a formation of planes roared over the crowd. Danny cried that night as he expressed his wish to be an Aussie. With Aussie roots, Aussie parents, and an Australian birth certificate. We'd arrived at the right place in our lives—the right time to give our kids their Australian citizenship. They received this in 2017. We would give them roots to grow so they could have wings to fly when the time was right to leave the nest.

I felt the pages turn toward a new chapter in my life. The healing journey took shape. My new psychiatrist suggested that both my mother and I write down the history of my first eighteen years. This is the account written in part three of this book.

My mother visited me several times over these first years in Albany until she passed the age to fly such long distances. Together we sat at the table in our new house as the sun poured in from the wide windows overlooking the beauty of God's creation. It was a journey for my mother and for me to go through together. Mum also had to revisit these moments in her life, and as far as I am aware, she privately worked through the effects of these events, storing these in her mother's heart.

The outcome and the effect that these writings had on me were transforming. I gained new insights into what trauma was and what it did to a person, and how it influenced my entire life. My life came into perspective, and I felt validated and heard. In this safe environment, I could now face the emotions I should have allowed to be part of my life many years earlier. I was free to tell my story and acknowledge its significance; it made me who I am today. Without guilt, shame, or condemnation, I could embrace my reality. I had begun a journey that touched all levels: spiritually, physically, mentally, and emotionally.

According to my psychiatrist, the abuse in the hospital scaled very high on a scale he used to screen the severity of abuse and neglect, and other trauma by measuring the effects in my life. He explained that abandonment and neglect by primary carers and rejection during the formative years have severe consequences and will influence life as an adult. I suddenly stood in a broader space and could acknowledge the girl in physical and emotional pain. I learned not to minimize any of the events. I stopped telling myself that it was not too bad, that it was not important, and that I could ignore the consequences.

In the following years, I gained valuable insights and learned great truths which I applied to myself. Later, I would be able to use these as a tool for others. My heart became alive again, walls of false protection tumbled down, and love filtered through into my soul. Although light and darkness come and go, I testify that healing is possible. With God's help, we "can advance against a troop," and "with my God I can scale a wall" (Psalm 18:29 NIV).

In my book, I have referred several times to the healing I received through the teachings of Elijah House Ministries. I want to introduce you to these simple yet effective principles and tools. The teachings were delivered with a two-fold perspective: personal healing of past hurts and training participants as prayer ministers themselves.

The course had sprung out of the need to minister to the many "wounded warriors" and "burden bearers." It was especially developed for those who were called and worked in leading ministry positions in the Church and were so often burned out. Often, the ministries ceased because of the brokenness of the ministers.

Our local church offered this course to those who were ready and wanted to deal with their pasts as it influenced their lives and ministries. It took place in a safe environment with trained course leaders and prayer ministers. When I saw the curriculum and content, I knew it was my chance to work through the issues which I experienced as a barrier to going forward.

The Cert III course was over two years and covered topics such as How We See God, Foundational Lies, Unmet Needs and Trauma, Restoring Childhood Foundations, Expressing Healthy Emotions, and many more. I absorbed the taught truths deeply into my soul, and I refer to these principles daily as I continue to change more into the image of our Savior, Jesus Christ. And the ongoing goal is to be transformed in our thinking, the source from which we act.

And we all, who with unveiled faces contemplate the Lord's glory, are being transformed into his image with

> *ever-increasing glory, which comes from the Lord, who is the Spirit (2 Corinthians 3:18 NIV).*
>
> *Do not conform to the pattern of this world, but be transformed by the renewing of your mind. Then you will be able to test and approve what God's will is—his good, pleasing and perfect will (Romans 12:2 NIV).*

Elijah House Ministries are not the only ministry that deals with restoring the soul. Several ministries operate throughout Australia and the world, offering biblical-based teachings that address deep healing and training for the renewal of the mind.[10]

I received a Certificate III in Prayer Ministry and became an active prayer minister. Later, I continued my studies and attained my diploma in Christian Counseling in 2018, opening my private practice in 2023.

Four Universal Laws

After twelve years of living in WA, we moved to Darwin in the Northern Territory in 2018. I wrote this part of the book while sitting in an alfresco café in the botanical gardens in the tropical north of Australia, where the tinkling of dishes, the murmuring of voices, and soft background music filled the air as I sipped my coffee. I often visited this café as huge fans, fastened on adjacent tall palm trees, cooled the humid tropical air. The wind rustled through the variety of trees around me, all planted by a visionary years ago. I seemed to formulate my thoughts into sentences better when life goes on around me while I traveled back over the years past.

The first teachings of the Elijah House course were overwhelming, and all the principles presented landed solidly in my heart. The truths were relentless and cut deep into my soul. I tried to criticize and then wiggle my way out of the applications of some of these teachings as they became uncomfortable and touched on my deepest issues. The training played a vital role in my healing journey as I allowed God "to continue to work out my salvation with fear and trembling" (Philippians 2:12 NIV). I surrendered to the healing power of the Holy Spirit by obeying the Word of God.

The initial teachings explain the truth of the unchanging, universal law of cause and effect, which applies to the spiritual realm as well. When four basic biblical laws are overstepped, it sets in motion forces that we cannot control. We reap in our adult years what was sown in our childhood. It all comes down to the moment we experience pain and react from an unredeemed state or sinful nature. These laws have no regard for who was a perpetrator or a victim; they just set in motion an impersonal principle: each action has a reaction.

The first primary law taught was: "Honor your father and your mother…that it may go well with you" (Deuteronomy 5:16 NIV). We require nourishment, care, safety, and love from primary caregivers to flourish. Ideally, we would have been accepted, acknowledged, and affirmed in growing up in our families. These innate needs are the building blocks of our identity. In the brokenness of this world, after the fall of man, most parents can't fulfill these requirements. We experienced pain from early life circumstances, and we reacted to this pain.

Looking back, I acknowledged that I had deep wounds in my soul from my early childhood experiences. The feeling of abandonment felt like the pain of betrayal. Neglectful nurses, doctors, and teachers established a deep distrust of authority. As a child, I would not have consciously judged my parents, and it was not their choice not to be there. But I was hurting and felt justified in being angry with those who had hurt me. I had many unspoken or unconscious judgments toward those who were supposed to stand up for me and protect me. At some stage in life, I had to stop seeking to blame others for the pain I experienced. It meant to forgive and let them off the hook.

It was hard to admit that I might have trespassed on this first spiritual law. I had to come to grips with the fact that I had developed a generally judgmental attitude.

Let me clarify that it is not our duty to analyze the person who has hurt us, whether they were in the wrong or could not be there due to circumstances, as in my parents' case. We do need to acknowledge the hurt that occurred and its consequences for the rest of our lives. The crux of the matter is that we need to recognize our *reactions* toward the person who caused the pain.

Shortly after thinking through that first universal biblical law, I learned about the second law: "A man reaps what he sows" (Galatians 6:7 NIV).

All of us are born in an unredeemed state, and we will reap destruction in those areas of our lives where our sinful nature rules. The opposite takes place when we sow in our born-again nature. With our spirit alive through God's Spirit, we will reap eternal life and the fruits of the Spirit. In our new nature, the Holy Spirit wants to strengthen the good seeds that have been sown and starve the bad seed.

Whatever was sown, both the good and the bad in my childhood, gained strength in adulthood. I soon realized how I had sown many negative and poisonous thoughts into my mind, resulting in distrust, rebellion, independence, and judgment. Every judgment I made, consciously or unconsciously, had an effect and would bear fruit. I most likely judged everyone who had ever hurt me. I wanted to confess these judgments and eliminate the poisonous fruits in my life. And through God's work in me, I forgave those who had hurt me and became free from resentment, anger, and bitterness toward others.

The third law states, "You, therefore, have no excuse, you who pass judgment on someone else, for at whatever point you judge another, you are condemning yourself, because you who pass judgment do the same things" (Romans 2:1 NIV). After making a judgment in my heart, I continued by consolidating these negative thoughts with an inner vow or self-condemnation. These inner vows became the building blocks for my protection wall, behind which I hid my strongholds (these could be your coping mechanisms, negative thinking patterns and self-destructive behaviors). The judgmental attitude became a filter through which I saw the world around me. I developed a bitter expectancy toward people and circumstances.

The Bible points out that when we have a bitter root, it defiles us and others as it rubs off and invites others to step into a trap to prove our perceived unworthiness. Here lies the foundation of self-sabotage and explains the self-fulfilling prophecies we speak over ourselves. These rotten fruits often find a way into the other person's areas of unhealed pain, and the cycle is set in motion: "Hurt people, hurt people… Healed people, heal people." In the next chapter, I will give some examples of how this works in our minds.

I understood that I had transgressed these first three biblical principles. The fourth law nailed it home: What we sow will return to us multiplied—good and evil. "They sow the wind and reap the whirlwind" (Hosea 8:7 NIV).

John Sandford explained it this way:

> The fundamental laws of God are written into the universe and affect our lives as surely as gravity. We are all subject to these laws, whether we believe them or not. When we transgress them, we set in motion forces that must be reaped by simple, impersonal laws that are absolute and eternal. In our sinful responses to wounding, we begin early to develop patterns of behavior that cause us to

reap in adulthood the very thing we hate. We sow and reap in kindness. We judge and do more of the same. We honor or we dishonor, and in life in which we dishonor, life will not go well with us. The pain we reap often seems disproportionate to the harm we have done, but Scripture clearly states the principle of increase.[11]

I still struggled with the idea that so much work needed to be done in me. I thought Jesus's work on the cross redeemed the past once you became a Christian. I thought that the renewing of my mind would be an automatic happening by the indwelling of the Holy Spirit.

I learned that indeed Christ's work is complete. The moment I accepted Jesus Christ and acknowledged Him to be my Savior, I was born again. This meant I am a new creation in Christ, redeemed and justified, and have salvation and eternal life. That is my eternal position in Christ.

But there was work to be done; a sanctification work of cleansing from resentment and unforgiveness—a transformation work so that I could be transformed into the image of the Son of God. The strongholds I had erected in the past needed to be dismantled, and the renewal of my mind needed to happen. God not only stepped into my life when I asked Him to come in and dwell in me, but I also entered Jesus's life, and being one with Him makes it possible to become like Him.

> *Being confident of this, that he who began a good work in you will carry it on to completion until the day of Christ Jesus (Philippians 1:6 NIV).*

> *Continue to work out your salvation with fear and trembling, for it is God who works in you to will and to act in order to fulfill his good purpose (Philippians 2:12-13 NIV).*

Living Out the Healing

After that first weekend of the course, when the church lights faded and people returned to their homes, I roamed the streets of Albany and finally ended up at the silent graveyard near our church. The teachings exposed my deepest pain and reaction to that pain. It showed a different way of dealing with my past instead of living in victimhood and living from negative thinking patterns. Slowly I acknowledged that I also played a role in it; I had to take responsibility for my sinful response to my pain. I had yet to hear about the healing part of this course, which would be given over the following weekend.

I sat under the foliage of the swaying willows planted above the stretched-out rows with cold headstones on either side. I felt I belonged here, dead and dying inside. I cried and cried. I could not go home to my husband and children. I was in such inner turmoil that I searched my purse for our credit card and booked a room in a chalet in one of the many holiday parks right on the beach.

As the night grew darker, so did my soul. I needed to confide and be comforted and given hope that I would get through this. I defied the old default of not trying to reach out for help, so I phoned a course leader and friend who had gone through the course herself. She testified earlier how God had healed her from the many wounds that others had inflicted. Immediately she came to the chalet and sat with me through the night as I cried and talked. It was one of the most painful moments in my life as I took stock of what had happened in my past and how much I realized I needed God to come and heal me. I also learned for the first time what true friendship means. To this very day, we have stayed close prayer partners and friends, bonded with a spiritual connection as we walk the road of victory and healing over past hurtful experiences.

Between the two weekends, I had time to explore the moments of past hurt and search my heart where my own responsibility lay in my reactions and behaviors. I saw the connections between the past and present, the reaping and sowing, sinful responses to pain, the spoken and unspoken inner vows that imprisoned me. I identified the fruits that resulted from bitter root judgments and expectations as these were the filters through which I observed the world. These were the beginnings of my strongholds and unconscious core beliefs. Here is an example of how it worked in my mind:

- My first reaction to inner pain was self-protection. I took control of my life.
- I covered my inner wound and soothed my pain with my own efforts, often pushing away those who tried to console me.
- I focused on the pain's cause and extended the blame to something or someone and attached a bitter expectancy to the judgments: "That thing or person hurts, so I cannot trust it. You will hurt me. You only demand from me. You will control me. You will not be there when I need you." Here laid the foundation of a stronghold.
- I became angry, I wanted to hurt others, so they experienced what I had to go through. I became bitter and used stabbing words. I sulked, manipulated, ultimately seeking justice. I got stuck in my pain and couldn't get out of the constant loop of relived trauma. I did not mature in these areas; even in adulthood, I reacted childlike when I was confronted with similar circumstances or met people who triggered memories of the past.
- I built protection walls around my heart, entertaining negative thought patterns. These became mindsets and the filters through which I observed the world. Rapidly it accumulated into the next layer, which was consolidating the false build-up refuge by a vow and promise to myself: "I will not trust anyone...."
- I stepped into an agreement with foundational lies: "No one cares for me. No one loves me. Others will always use me. I don't deserve love. I am unworthy. I will never amount to anything...." These were the unconscious core beliefs to which I reacted and were the filter I observed the world around me.
- People started to comply to these bitter expectations,

and they kept their distance from "that over-sensitive, needy person."

- The self-destructive pattern was in motion; what I predicted came to pass. I separated myself from the ones who offered love to me, so I wouldn't get hurt again. I became a law unto myself and thus lonely. Maybe I was perceived as a strong individual, but in reality, I just kept my distance from others. Love could not come out, or into my heart.

The Tool of Prayer Ministry

The course leaders guided and coached me through the healing steps. Elijah House Ministries use the letter "R" for each part of the steps to healing. It can be used as a tool while ministering to others:

RECOGNIZE: Give time to tell and acknowledge the story. Recognize where we must take ownership and responsibility for our reaction to hurt (Matthew 7:20).

During the course's ministry time, I could tell my story for the first time. The non-judgmental listening helped me to identify and acknowledge the traumas I went through and the impact they had on my life. I felt accepted and affirmed as they spoke words of life into my heart.

REPENT: This means acknowledging that you want to change your thinking pattern. Repentance can only happen when we know what we want to turn away from. It is a work of the Holy Spirit as He gently reveals our sinful reactions (1 John 1:9).

I did this in detail for each person I remembered who hurt me and whom I judged by holding them accountable for my pain, holding on to my right to justify myself and condemn the other. I wanted to change my thinking patterns that brought death to my soul.

Even when their hurt wasn't done with intent to hurt, I interpreted it as such and as defense, I would point my finger (judge) them as the one being in error by causing me such pain.

Of course, there are trespasses that need to be brought to justice as it WAS wrong. I do need to acknowledge the pain it caused. And they will be held accountable.

But I can't repay evil with evil, which I do by becoming bitter and resentful (even to ourselves, by rejecting ourselves. These are the self-destructive thoughts and behaviours).

I need to acknowledge that I dishonor people by my immediate judgment, unforgiving attitude and not extending any grace. I need to leave them to God to deal with their wrongdoings. This gave me freedom to find forgiveness in my heart.

RECEIVE AND RELEASE Forgiveness: Ask for forgiveness for the judgments made and receive forgiveness, and release forgiveness to those who hurt you (Matthew 6:14-15).

After sharing many memories and recounting my reactions and judgments, someone expressed forgiveness to me. The practice of giving absolution had never been part of my life, but it has a powerful way of releasing the person from the burden of guilt.

I released forgiveness toward the persons who had hurt me, which was a lengthy process like peeling an onion. Forgiving others would be a lifelong commitment. Jesus put it like this, "I tell you, not seven times, but seventy-seven times" (Matthew 18:22 NIV).

RENOUNCE: Renounce any vows you have spoken over yourself, any agreement you made with a foundational lie you believed in and break off any curse that was spoken over you (Proverbs 18:21).

I became aware of the power of words spoken over us by others or what we say to ourselves. Words can bring death or life. Words are recognized and honored by God and others. Just see how God's Word made heaven and earth. There is power in words.

I broke free from believing a lie like: "I am ugly." And I replaced it with the truth from God's Word: "I praise you because I am fearfully and wonderfully made" (Psalm 139:14 NIV).

I had experienced the devastating effects of hearing how ugly I was and what horrible cat eyes I had. Later at school, they called me a witch because I have pointy ears. Each of these words spoken over me made me feel I was not good enough, not appreciated, not accepted, and not affirmed in who I am. As a result, I began to fix my hair over my ears and was extremely happy to get glasses, as though my eyes would be more hidden.

On the other hand, I also experienced the opposite of hearing words that brought life. God knew how these words had damaged my soul and that I needed to be healed of it. And God did it in such an unexpected way.

While living in New Zealand, I drove to work daily. One day I had to get petrol at a station where I usually would not stop. It was a small petrol station where the patron came to assist in filling up cars instead of self-service. As the man approached me, I waited just outside the car door. He stopped abruptly and kept looking at me.

The Tool of Prayer Ministry

After a moment of uncomfortable silence, he said in the drawling accent of New Zealand, "Ma'am, you have the most beautiful eyes I have ever seen in my life."

After I paid and got into my car, I drove off, stunned, as the words repeatedly tumbled in my mind. Suddenly a flood of grief came over me, and I had to stop the car. Tears flowed down my cheeks as these healing words sunk into my spirit. And from that moment onward, I never had a negative feeling or thought about my physical appearance again. It never influenced my choice of hairdo, and I gladly would have stopped wearing glasses. This man would never know how this one sentence changed my life. Yes, you can speak words of life into other people's lives.

Reckon as dead: Count the deeds of the flesh as dead. Habits and negative thinking patterns have no power or control over you other than what you give them (Romans 6:11).

This means choosing thoughts and actions that bring life, rather than those that bring death. Think of the verses in Colossians 3:1-15 where Paul points out to set our minds on things above and gives a list of what to get rid of. And of the powerful passage in Philippians: "Finally, brothers and sisters, whatever is true, whatever is noble, whatever is right, whatever is pure, whatever is lovely, whatever is admirable—if anything is excellent or praiseworthy—think about such things" (Philippians 4:8 NIV).

I brought any structures or strongholds, harmful habits, and negative thinking patterns that I became aware of to death on the cross of Jesus. He bled and died for these practices. To practice this, I would start my day with a prayer in which I asked the Holy Spirit to be in charge of my mind; giving Him permission to make me aware whenever I resorted to my old way of dealing with triggers that tempted me to take matters into my own hands. This meant that whenever I became aware of a destructive thought, I gave the thought to Jesus in prayer, asking Him to justify me if I was offended, or to forgive me when I judged others.

Resurrect into life: We have died with Christ; we will also live (Romans 6:4).

After putting poisonous root structures to death, we also permit Jesus to prune any branches that do not bear fruit. This is another way of saying that we are learning to live in a new way of life. It also means that we become accountable to others and place ourselves under the authority of Godly, anointed, and appointed spiritual leadership.

At this point, we ask the Holy Spirit to refill us so that we can bring forth the fruits of the Spirit. This is the "putting on" explained in Romans, where Paul says, "Rather, clothe yourselves with the Lord Jesus Christ, and do not think about how to gratify the desires of the flesh" (Romans 13:14 NIV). We give the Holy Spirit permission to activate His spiritual gifts and manifestations so that we can become effective in our lives as we walk out of our healing.

In addition to these first 5 "R"s, we could add two more:

RECONCILIATION: If possible and safe, reconcile with those we have fallen out with (Romans 12:18).

RESTITUTION: If possible and appropriate, make restitution to those you have wronged (Leviticus 6:2-5).

After each session, once we have worked through the 5 "R"s, we offer prayers of healing, comfort, strength, and the renewed infilling of the Holy Spirit. We also pray prayers of "hiding," meaning that while the restoration process is taking place, no other influence will come and hinder the progress. We are made aware that we are engaged in a spiritual battle, not of this world. Paul describes this in Ephesians:

> *For our struggle is not against flesh and blood, but against the rulers, against the authorities, against the powers of this dark world and against the spiritual forces of evil in the heavenly realms (Ephesians 6:12 NIV).*

Throughout the years, I have started to recognize the outworking of the above principles and have applied the healing processes in each area of my life as the Holy Spirit has revealed them to me.

In the past, I blamed others or circumstances for my lack of education or hindrance in stepping into my destiny. But now, I step out and embrace personal development and, at the same time, acknowledge my limits.

I held others responsible for taking away the power to make choices. I am now learning to take responsibility for my choices and maintain appropriate boundaries.

I used to blame others for damaging my trust and depriving

me of the ability to build wholesome friendships. But now, I have a much more open and receptive heart, and I can receive and give love.

I renounced vows and lies and explored God's truth and how He sees me in Christ. As a result, I am more aware and step back from destructive default thinking patterns and the deadly cycle of negative, self-fulfilling prophecies.

I also asked the Holy Spirit to convict me of jealous thoughts and bitter expectations that could block my relationship with Him and with others around me.

The healing journey had a profound effect on our marriage. Bart also attended the course and saw where his wounding affected his actions in life. As we healed, we became more convinced of God's unconditional love for us individually and His grace that He extends every day toward us. We were able to let others off the hook and forgive. I stopped demanding that Bart fix my insecurities and allowed him to grow and develop without asking for continuous acknowledgment and affirmation.

When dealing with my children while they were still living at home, I quickly identified hurts that might result in bitterness. I taught them to forgive and ask for forgiveness while acknowledging their emotions and feelings when they experienced difficulties in relationships.

Trusting authorities is still a challenge for me. I want to be open to receiving guidance and be accountable without having the bitter expectation that others will use me for their ends or wield their power to control me. I pray for discernment on whom to trust and to whom I need to be accountable. I pray for wisdom when asking for feedback, and I pray for God's truth so that I do not perceive constructive feedback as personal criticism and possible rejection.

A last thought:

These improvements do not mean I do not need to keep close accounts with God. Any thoughts that do not honor Him have to be recognized and confessed before it becomes a pattern. So, I ask for daily infilling of the Holy Spirit. He is my Protector, my Rock, my Deliverer, my stronghold. The psalmist writes: "With your help, I can advance against a troop; with my God I can scale a wall" (Psalm 18:29 NIV). A surrendered life is a secure life. I am learning to listen to the prompting of the Holy Spirit and quickly deal with destructive thoughts, identifying which thoughts bring death and which bring life.

Through God's healing power, I slowly became convinced that I am significant not only in His eyes but also in His calling for me to show His healing power to others. I feel secure in my identity in Him, and through His Word, I hear His assurance that I am a person of worth in this world while working in His Kingdom. I pray daily for His revelation and thoughts about me; otherwise, I might get carried away by my mood swings, become overwhelmed by feelings, or be distracted by the opinions of others. I keep short accounts when an encounter triggers judgmental thinking and feeds negative thinking patterns. Assumptions can quickly become an excuse to judge someone and keep others at a safe distance. It means I need to be continually transparent toward God and others, honest and genuine. No masks are allowed to hide my sensitive self or protect myself. Instead, I use God as my Shield. He is my security and my resource.

Each of us longs for a fresh revelation of God in our spirit. We need His life-giving breath to restore our souls so we can renew our thinking, restore healthy expressions of our emotions, and realign our will with God's will. It is important to let God do the healing work and for the Holy Spirit to confirm and establish the work that was done. That means we walk out our healing toward the destiny God has in mind.

He promises freedom and life. He is the Victor of the enemy that works to destroy you. Jesus says, "The thief comes only to steal and kill and destroy; I have come that they may have life, and have it to the full" (John 10:10 NIV). His promise to you is this: "'For I know the plans I have for you,' declares the LORD, 'plans to prosper you and not to harm you, plans to give you hope and a future'" (Jeremiah 29:11 NIV). You can respond to God; he loves for you to be totally restored!

> *"Call to me and I will answer you and tell you great and unsearchable things you do not know" (Jeremiah 33:3).*

I pray that my story, journey, and testimony will encourage you to seek God's healing and restoration of the heart, the mind, and the soul while He enlivens your spirit with His Holy Spirit.

About the Author

Born in 1967 in the Netherlands, Maria Wassink has led an adventurous life that has taken her across the globe. Over the years, she has lived in many countries, experiencing diverse cultures and meeting people from all walks of life. She married her husband Bart on the island of Curaçao in 1994.

Maria is the proud mother of three children, each of whom was born on a different continent. As a result, she has a unique perspective on the world and the challenges that families face in different parts of the globe.

Maria is a registered counselor and a certified prayer minister, with years of experience helping individuals and families navigate difficult times. Her compassion and empathy shine through in her writing, which is always grounded in a deep understanding of human nature.

Currently based in Australia, Maria has worn many hats over the years, including missionary, international aid worker, and dedicated mother. She is passionate about good coffee and loves to share a cup with friends and family.

Throughout her life, Maria has been a dedicated Christian, and her faith is an integral part of her identity. She is a keen learner of the Bible, and her insights into the teachings of Jesus are sure to inspire and uplift readers of all backgrounds. Whether she is writing about her own experiences or delving into the deeper meaning of Scripture, Maria brings a unique and thoughtful perspective to every topic she explores.

Learn more about Maria at:
Heart, Soul, & Mind Counseling Services
https://hsm-counseling.com/

Contact Maria:
mariawassink5@gmail.com

Endnotes

1. Charles Stanley, https://www.youtube.com/watch?v=9bLgDoFkdqo Taking Control of Our Thoughts–Dr. Charles Stanley, accessed July 7, 2023.
2. https://web.archive.org/web/20060619002749/http://www.cyberhymnal.org/htm/s/a/f/safearms.htm, accessed July 7, 2023. This is a translation of the original song written by Fanny Crosby (1820-1915) it was translated into Dutch by Meier Salomon Bromet.
3. Translated from the German hymn Ich bete an die Macht der Liebe by Dimitri Bortniansky (1751-1825).
4. https://www.britannica.com/event/Kosovo-conflict#Article-History
5. https://www.britannica.com/place/Kosovo/Cultural-life, accessed July 7, 2023.
6. Ibid.
7. Ibid.
8. Ibid.
9. Taken from Captivating: Unveiling the Mystery of a Woman's Soul by John and Stasi Eldredge. Copyright © 2005 by HarperCollins Christian Publishing.
10. Some other Ministries available are VMTC (Victorious Ministries Through Christ) https://www.vmtc.org.au/; FIC (Freedom in Christ) https://www.ficm.org.uk/ and Bethel Sozo Australia https://www.bethelsozoaustralia.com/
11. Keys to Transformation, unit 1– "Restoring the Foundations." Biblical basis of EH Ministries. Copyright 1989 to 2017 by Elijah House, Inc. Coeur d'Alene, Idaho USA.
12. Elijah House, https://elijahhouse.com.au/keys-to-transformation/, accessed July 7, 2023.

www.ingramcontent.com/pod-product-compliance
Lightning Source LLC
Chambersburg PA
CBHW012221090526
44585CB00022BA/2486